best church plays

best church plays

A Bibliography of Religious Drama

Albert Johnson

PILGRIM PRESS / Philadelphia / Boston

Library of Congress Catalog Card Number 68-22572

foreword

The current exploding demand for suitable church plays is understandable when we remember that drama began as a religious expression, and that for fully five hundred years the churches of Christendom were virtually the sole patrons of drama throughout the Western world. Now, in this time of religious reevaluation, drama is again a medium of enlightenment. Drama at its best has always been such a medium. The quest, therefore, is for the best.

To assemble a bibliography that purports to be the best of church plays would be a presumptuous undertaking were it not for the semantics of that word best. Plays that are best for the First Church of Suburbia may not be best for Midtown Second Church, and vice versa. The value of any collection of titles lies in its relevancy. Considering the proliferation of productions of a religious nature, the widely diverse need for plays can best be served by a bibliography that is as comprehensive as possible. Furthermore, the contemporary use of drama in churches and in organizations that are religiously oriented is highly diversified. Therefore this directory contains titles that may or may not be suitable for presentation in the chancel. Some may be right for some chancels and wrong for others. The performance of plays having religious significance is not limited to the chancel. On the contrary, dramatic activity nowadays extends to recreation halls, parish houses, patios, gardens, classrooms, lecture halls, school auditoriums, little theatres, hospitals, prisons, juvenile halls, social centers, and even private homes. Plays suitable for all these areas and many others are included in this collection of titles. (Essential publication information has been given whenever possible. Prices are, of course, subject to change.)

The importance of making a wide range of titles available is accented by the present rush of most of our churches into the teeming life of the community. The contemporary church is not only opening its physical facilities to a needy public, but it is finding new ways to take the "good news" into new areas. One of the most exciting and most effective of the new ways is the performance of plays. Hence there is an ever-increasing demand for plays that are pertinent, provocative, and producible.

The terms "church plays" and "religious drama" are terms to ponder. Indeed, they have been pondered, and there is far from unanimous agreement on definitions. There are those who argue that virtually all drama is religious, and there are those who, having been conditioned by inane, inept, irreverent performances of outmoded church-school pageants, consider the term "religious drama" the kiss of death on any play that is so identified. Likewise there is altercation over the term "church plays." What is a church play?

Answers, or at least a quest for answers, may be helpful to many who make use of this bibliography. Therefore the author exercises the prerogative of quoting from himself in offering the following paragraphs from *Church Plays and How to Stage Them,* a recent publication of the United Church Press.

> Any dramatic work that gives the spectator a feeling that the winds of the universe blow against him—rather than with him—is not religious. Whether man goes along with the prevailing Oriental viewpoint that little can be done about improving the earthly journey, or sides with the prevailing Judeo-Christian-Muslim belief that man can improve his earthly existence, he must feel that somewhere a creator, or a supreme being of some kind is concerned about him, if he is to have an experience that is religious.
>
> If the play inspires idolatry—be that idol wealth, power, self, sex, beauty, truth, the church, or the Bible—the play is not religious. Is the dignity of man debased, the brotherhood of man downgraded, the significance of all life deprecated? The play is not religious.
>
> Some recognition of an ultimate reality related to the creation of all that is, an acknowledgment of man's first, final, and highest loyalty to that reality, and some evidence of reverence for life seem necessary requisites to any play that is religious.
>
> Ethics, mores, and morals—be they the kind that change with period, place, or social pressure or present a conflict between good and evil—are all elements of the larger, basic concept. They are the foothills against the three-peaked range, the lightning against the storm clouds, the stars against the infinite sky.
>
> Acknowledgment of a creator, preeminent loyalty to that creator, and reverence for all his creatures, compose the trinity of religious drama. Does this then rule out those plays to pagan gods? No, because the pagan prays and plays to the only God or gods he knows and makes his religious expression, albeit sometimes more akin to superstition than to religion.
>
> If we jump to the conclusion that the so-called trinity (acknowledgment of a creator, preeminent loyalty to that creator, and reverence for all his creatures) must be broadly explicit, we miss the point. Indeed, the trinity may sometimes be so concealed that we must dig to find it. If it is too deeply buried, the play may reach only the esoteric few. If it is too obvious, the play may provoke disgust rather than approval.
>
> These paragraphs about the nature of the drama and the kind of drama which might be called religious suggest that there are many so-called secular plays that can be included in the quest for the inevitable play. Indeed the line of demarcation between the religious play and the secular play is sometimes hard to find. Certainly all secular plays are no more nonreligious than are all religious plays honestly religious.

A further quote from *Church Plays and How to Stage Them* may serve as something of a criterion for the selection of the "best" church plays.

1. *Policy.* Policy determines the kind of plays that are produced under any auspices. Policy may be precisely stated or taken for granted. It may be clearly articulated in a written agreement or merely a general understanding. The policies that govern the selection of plays at the local high school or the community theatre will obviously differ from the policy that determines the choice of plays at the church. A play sponsored by the church should be at least somewhat in line with the tenets of that church. It would be pointless indeed for a church to sponsor a play whose philosophy is in direct opposition to the principles preached from its pulpit. This does not mean that principles and tenets cannot be challenged. They can be and often are so challenged by sermons as well as plays.

2. *Purpose.* The immediate purpose prompts these questions: Are we looking for a play that will contribute to the educational program of the church? Or are we looking for something that will fit the recreational schedule? Are we looking for a play that will speak to the congregation as a whole, or for a play that is specifically for young people or some other age-group? Next, are we looking for a play that will soothe or one that will shock; one that will make everybody feel snug and cozy or one that will challenge? Are we doing a play primarily for the benefit of the participants in the play or are we primarily concerned with whatever benefits may be reaped by the people coming to see it? Are we looking for an Easter play, a Christmas play, or a play suitable to some other holy day? Do we want to present something that will be suitable at any time? Is the purpose of the play something specific, such as the opening of a study of missions? Should the play tie in with a series of sermons or a series of evening meetings, or should it be related to some definite theme such as evangelism? Certainly one purpose of church drama should always be to reach the unchurched. Is this presentation to be connected with some expansion program in the church, or is the purpose to make or keep your church an important center for religious drama? In answering all these questions, the problem of purpose should be clarified and solved.

3. *Place.* Where are you planning to present the play? Your choice of place has great bearing on your choice of a play. Where you do the play will, to a large extent, dictate your choice of content, form, and manner of staging. If the place is the chancel, the play should be suitable as a service of worship or part of a service. The content should be worthy of the dignity of the setting, and the manner of staging will need to be the very essence of simplicity. It would be helpful if someone at this

point could place in your hand a list of ideal plays for the chancel. The truth is that it would be difficult, if not impossible, to prepare such a list. In the first place, what is ideal for the chancel of one church might be all wrong for the chancel of another. In a sophisticated suburban church where a lot of young intellectuals are in attendance, for instance, it is conceivable that Albee's *The Sandbox* might be presented in the chancel and used as a part of a worship service. Such a play performed in the chancels of certain other churches would undoubtedly be considered sacrilege. Unfortunately, there is no handy set of rules to guide a person in the selection of a chancel play. A knowledge of the policy, the congregation, the community, coupled with sound judgment and good taste should be considered. There is no harm in shocking your congregation now and then. In fact, it might be a healthy thing to do, but shock for the sake of shock is foolhardy and if the voltage of the shock is too severe or if the shock occurs too frequently, the effect of the play is lost and you have achieved nothing, except perhaps the ill will of the parishioners. If the place for your presentation is other than the chancel, then your choice is not so restricted. Still adhering to policy, of course, your problems will be more of a physical nature, such as whether or not the play of your choice can be produced in the allotted space. . . .

4. *Production.* You will probably have a headful of production problems even before you start your search for the inevitable play. Shall it be one with a big cast or a small cast? How many men, how many women? Must you do a play with one set or can you handle one with multiple sets? Can you manage something that calls for elaborate staging or must you do something that can be done in utter simplicity? How many man and woman work hours can you count on for such things as rustling up props and costumes, rigging lights and scenery? How much time will the players have for rehearsal? Will they be able to rehearse virtually every night or only two or three nights a week? Or are you obliged to do something that can be prepared in four or five Sunday night rehearsals? How about your own time as director? Can you give yourself freely to this venture or are you obliged to be chary with your time? If your job is merely to select the play and turn it over to someone else for producing, then be sure you have a clear picture of that person's time schedule. Time is of the essence in the preparation of a play. There is no substitute for time and the director who naïvely imagines he can pull a substantial play together in a few short rehearsals will only end up adding disgracefully to the stigma that he and his ilk have given religious drama.

Acknowledgment

For assistance in the preparation of this bibliography I am indebted to my wife, Bertha Johnson, and my secretary, Sue Goodrich, for their generous and competent assistance; to the publishers for their cooperation; and most especially to my student assistant, Jon Parmenter, for his prodigious yeoman service. To them, and to all who have had a share in the collection of these titles, I express my growing gratitude.

Albert Johnson

contents

Foreword	v
Acknowledgment	ix
Listing of Plays	1
Addresses	150
Publishers	150
Authors and Agents	156
Subject Index	159
Biblical Plays	159
Christmas Plays	160
Collections	166
Easter Plays	169
Historical Plays	171
Jewish Plays	172
Missionary Plays	173
Thanksgiving Plays	173
World-Friendship Plays	173
Miscellaneous Plays	173

listing of plays

ABINGDON CHILDREN'S DAY PROGRAMS, by various authors. Collection of church-school exercises, recitations, playlets, etc., ranging from beginning children to adults. Baker's Plays, 35¢.

ABINGDON CHRISTMAS PROGRAMS, compiled by Olaf Hanson. Two full-length plays and a pageant, plus tableaux, pantomimes, etc. Abingdon Press, 35¢. Package, 25.

ABINGDON EASTER PROGRAMS, compiled by Leila T. Ammerman. Full-length Easter play, for nine men and four women; pageant for Holy Week; evening service; two services for sunrise, etc. Abingdon Press, 40¢. Package, 25.

ABRAHAM AND ISAAC. 4 men and angel. Simple set. Short medieval mystery play concerning God's command that Abraham sacrifice his son. Archaic language may pose a production problem. In *Medieval Mysteries, Moralities, and Interludes.* Barron's Educational Series, $1.25. Royalty: none.

ABRAHAM AND ISAAC, by Laurence Housman. 2 men, 1 woman. Based on the biblical narrative, this interesting play explores moral meanings through family relationships. Baker's Plays. Royalty: apply to publisher.

ABRAHAM, FRIEND OF GOD, by Edward Longstreth. Plays 30 minutes. A biblical drama for the chancel, suitable for either reading or staging. $1.25. Royalty: inquire of the author.

ACCORDING TO THE SCRIPTURES and AND YE ARE WITNESSES, by Elizabeth Howard. Chorus of 3 men, 4 women. Chorus reviews events leading to the crucifixion and resurrection as a group, and as individual characters. They realize the fulfillment of the prophecies in the resurrection. Baker's Plays, 75¢. Royalty: $10.

ACTING OUT THE TRUTH, by Sarah Walton Miller. Twenty-three dramatic presentations for programs of worship. Broadman Press, $2.50.

THE ACTS OF ST. PETER, by Gordon Bottomley. Large cast, with chorus. Plays 1 hour. Space set, with several levels. Formalized chronicle of the life of Peter, in verse and one continual act. A difficult presentation, originally given in Exeter Cathedral. Religious Drama Society of Great Britain. Royalty: apply to publisher.

ADAM, anonymous (French or Anglo-Norman), translated by Edward Noble Stone. 18 men plus devils and ministers, 1 woman, chorus. Exterior set. The earliest existing medieval play of great dramatic values, telling of the fall of Adam in the garden, the story of Cain and Abel, and the prophecy of the coming of the Savior. In *World Drama,* Vol. II. Dover Press. Royalty: apply to publisher.

ADAM AND EVE MEET THE ATOM, by Albert Johnson. 2 men, 1 woman. A Drama Trio play which issues a challenge to conscience in the atomic age, based on the Genesis story of creation. One act. Available from the author, $1. Royalty: $10.

ADAM THE CREATOR, by Karel and Josef Capek, translated by Dora Round. 22 men (doubling possible), 3 women, 6 children. Plays full evening. Adam, not approving of the world God has created, destroys it, and is commanded to make another. Theme of the necessity of man facing his problems squarely. In *Dramas of Modernism.* Allen and Unwin. Royalty: apply to publisher.

ADESTE FIDELES, by Louise A. Garnett, music arranged by Mack Ellis. 15 men, 7 women, 5 children, reader, choir (more if desired). Events related to the birth of Christ told in pantomime and pageant. Baker's Plays, 60¢. Royalty: $5.

ADMIRAL PENN AND SON WILLIAM, by Rosalie Regen. Biographical drama of the Society of Friends. Friends Book and Supply House, 15¢.

THE ADORATION, by Frederick A. Wilmot. Large cast for both men and women, with several nonspeaking parts. Groupings and musical background to tell the story of the first Christmas with reverence. Baker's Plays, 60¢.

THE ADORATION OF THE KINGS AND SHEPHERDS, by Mildred E. Cook. Variable cast. Full instructions for production with reader, choir, and tableaux. Pilgrim Press, 75¢.

AFTER THE FOG LIFTS, by Walter Hackett. 3 men, 3 women, 2 men bits. Plays 30 minutes. Interior set. Three couples, fogbound in a small boat and believing that they are about to die, reveal their true selves; but they must once again live with one another as though nothing had happened. Baker's Plays, 60¢. Royalty: $5.

AJAX, by Sophocles, translated by John Moore. 6 men, 2 women, chorus of men. Tragedy of the madness, dishonor, and death of Ajax. Explores the questions of loyalty and honor. In *Sophocles II: Four Tragedies.* University of Chicago Press, $1.95.

THE ALABASTER BOX, by A. J. Harnwell and I. J. Meaker. 4 men, 2 women, 1 boy. Beautiful re-creation, in three short acts, of what happened in the house of the sisters of Bethany from the crucifixion to the resurrection, with a new presentation of the characters of Mary and Martha. McKay's Plays, 85¢. Royalty: $10 if admission is charged; $5 if not.

ALIAS SANTA CLAUS, by Percival Wilde. 14 parts, largely boys. Plays 40 minutes. Interior set. Wealthy father realizes his neglect of his son when the boy is almost kidnapped by two young desperados. Christmas season. Baker's Plays, 60¢. Royalty: $10.

ALICE IN CHANUKOLAND, by Beatrice G. Haniford. 10 men, 3 women. Alice meets a Chanuko Menorah down the rabbit hole. Parody on Lewis Carroll includes a latke minuet danced by potatoes. Age level, 5–12. Union of American Hebrew Congregations, 25¢.

ALL ABOARD FOR CHRISTMAS. 4 men, 4 women, extras. Plays 30 minutes. Interior set. Junior and Senior High play, centering in the family and containing both modern humor and old-fashioned sentiment. The family living room provides the single set. Plays, Inc., 50¢.

ALL HAIL THE RISEN LORD, by Ellen J. Lorenz. A hymn program for Easter with tableaux. Has alternate plan for use of filmstrip of the old masters. Takes those who came to hail their risen Lord as subjects. Eldridge, 50¢.

ALL MY SONS, by Arthur Miller. 5 men, 4 women, 1 boy. Three-act play about a father who unscrupulously builds a business for his son to inherit, then discovers that the son will accept no part of it. Examines guilt, honor, and family ties; called by many a tragedy. In *Six Great Modern Plays*. Dell, 75¢.

ALL THAT FALL, by Samuel Beckett. 7 men, 3 women. Plays full evening. Difficult play concerning an old Irishwoman who awaits her blind husband at a railway junction. She finds frustration rather than happiness in life. Originally presented by the BBC in 1957. Grove Press, $2.50.

ALLELUIA, by Katharine Kester. 10 men, 5 women, singers, extras. Exterior set. The story of a witness to the crucifixion and the resurrection. Samuel French, Inc., 60¢. Royalty: $5.

ALTAR-PIECE, by E. Levy. 4 men, 2 women. Interior set. One-act drama dealing with the fifteenth-century Florentines' hatred of the Jews. Baker's Plays, 50¢. Royalty: $5.

AN AMERICAN CHRISTMAS, by Roma Greth. 2 boys, 4 girls. Plays 25 minutes. Two American girls in Greece forget their Christmas homesickness by coming to know three poor Greek children. Written especially for teen-agers. Eldridge, 60¢ (purchase of 6 copies required).

THE AMERICAN DREAM, by Edward Albee. 2 men, 3 women. The age-old problem of the aging is freshly treated in this play that deals with the problem of communication. In volume with two other Albee plays. Dramatists Play Service, $1.50. Royalty: apply to publisher.

AMERICAN PORTRAIT, by Emmet Lavery, music by Robert E. Moonan. Large cast. Bare stage. The story of Father Hecker, this play covers one hundred years of American history in two acts and choruses. Designed for "reading" without props. Baker's Plays, $1.25. Royalty: $25.

AMERICAN SAINT OF DEMOCRACY, by Fred Eastman. 3 men, 4 women. Plays 30 minutes. An incident in the life of John Woolman, presenting his involvement in the struggle to free slaves. Baker's Plays, 60¢. Royalty: $5.

THE AMERICAN WAY, by George F. Kaufman and Moss Hart. 27 men, 7 boys, 17 women, 3 girls, extras. Plays full evening. Two generations in an American immigrant's family. Dramatists Play Service. May be obtained in manuscript form: $10 deposit, returnable; $2 reading fee. Royalty: $25.

AMONG THIEVES, by Helen M. Clark. 6 men. Plays 1 hour. Exterior set. The preacher from Nazareth teaches a small band of patriots that a higher courage is required not to strike back. Baker's Plays, 60¢.

AMONG THOSE PRESENTS, by Peggy Fernway. 7 women. Plays 30 minutes. Interior set. The Christmas spirit prevails just when a family's Christmas outlook seems darkest. Samuel French, Inc., 60¢. No royalty for amateurs.

THE ANCHOR, by Elizabeth George Speare. 4 women. Plays 30 minutes. Interior set. Family gathers at home of an envied sister; but with understanding and admiration, envy turns to pity. Baker's Plays, 60¢. Royalty: $5.

AND A SONG WAS BORN, by John Marston. 6 men, 4 women. Plays 40 minutes. The part played by a peasant boy in the composition of "Silent Night." Samuel French, Inc., 60¢. Royalty: $5.

AND HE CAME TO HIS FATHER, by Erna Kruckmeyer. 4 men, 2 women, extras. Plays 40 minutes. Exterior set. Story of the prodigal son in highly dramatic presentation. Baker's Plays, 60¢.

AND LO, THE STAR, by Helen M. Roberts. 4 men, 6 women, extras. Plays about 40 minutes. Imaginary scene set in the home of Elizabeth and the infant John, who await the arrival of Mary and Joseph; concludes with a manger scene in a happy key. Banner Play Bureau, 50¢ (purchase of 8 copies required).

AND LOSE HIS OWN SOUL, by Robert St. Clair. 5 men, 5 women. Father Donovan sets wandering members of his parish on the right track again. The three-act comedy drama is set in a garden, easily established. Religious atmosphere, excellent for Roman Catholic churches. Beautiful situations. T. S. Denison & Co., $1. Royalty: $10.

AND MYRRH, by Dorothy Clarke Wilson. 6 men, 5 women, 1 child, offstage voice. Plays 45 minutes. Old and lovely early Christian legend that the wise men came one from Europe, one from Africa, one from Asia. Baker's Plays, 60¢.

AND SO HE DOTH REDEEM US, by Hazel F. Bailey. Variable cast. Interior set. Easter message shown relevant to time of world crisis. Worship service included. Baker's Plays, 60¢.

AND SO THEY CAME TO BETHLEHEM, by Dorothy M. Merrill. Variable cast. Plays 40 minutes. Story of the Christchild from the prophecy of Isaiah to the birth in Bethlehem told in five tableaux and readings. Baker's Plays, 60¢.

AND SUCH A KING, by James Brock. Large cast. Narration and dramatization tell the story of the visit of the magi, symbolizing the coming of the Lord as Savior to all men. In *Modern Chancel Dramas*. Eldridge, $1.25.

AND THE FULLNESS THEREOF, by Annabelle Irwin. 4 women. Plays about 25 minutes. Unable to tithe, as is her practice, a mother gives the Lord a note for the money due, at interest; this causes considerable problems for the Department of Internal Revenue. Pioneer Drama Service, 85¢ (noncommercial acting rights with purchase of 4 copies).

AND THERE THEY FOUND CHRIST, by Rega K. McCarty. 6 adults, 5 young people. Plays about 1 hour. A family finds Christmas by spending it in the country, and they decide in favor of country life. Eldridge, 50¢ (purchase of 8 copies required).

AND THERE WERE SHEPHERDS, by O. G. Herbrecht. Large cast. Plays about 45 minutes. Shows the effects of Christ's birth on youth. Abingdon Press, 25¢.

AND USHER IN THE MORNING, by Joyce V. Drake. 3 men, 3 women, 1 boy, 1 girl, carolers. Worship service containing a play showing the possible damages caused by selfishness in a church organization. In *The Easy Christmas Grab Bag*. Baker's Plays, $1.25.

AND YOU NEVER KNOW, by Nora Stirling. 1 man, 1 woman, 1 twelve-year-old girl, stage manager. Plays 30 minutes. A play intended for discussion, concerning the jealousy of the twelve-year-old for her sister, and the family's understanding of the problem. Nat'l. Assoc. for Mental Health. Royalty: full purchase payment for cast scripts serves as first night's royalty; $1 each succeeding night.

ANDROCLES AND THE LION, by George Bernard Shaw. 16 men, 2 women, extras. Plays about 2 hours. 3 exterior sets, 1 interior set. Shaw's play of the Christian persecutions in Rome about A.D. 45, centering upon the conflict between living beliefs and dying social structures. Characters on both sides are given humanity and fallibility, and the wit of the play sharpens the philosophical insights. Difficult technically and in content. Samuel French, Inc., 65¢. Royalty: $25 each performance.

ANGEL CHILD. 2 men, 4 women. Plays 30 minutes. Interior set. Discovering that others wishing the role have less than angelic motivations, Angela decides to remain a reluctant angel in the Yuletide pageant. Plays, Inc., 50¢.

ANGEL IN REPAIR, by Goldie P. Sutton. 5 women. Interior set. A Christmas play about the problems of accepting an orphan boy into a family. Baker's Plays, 60¢.

THE ANGEL IN THE CLEARING, by Stuart M. DeLuca. 2 men, 2 women. Plays 30 minutes. An angel is assigned to earth, aids a young man who feels responsible for the death of his sweetheart. The angel is aided in her mission by Peter in disguise. Pioneer Drama Service, $1 (purchase of 4 copies required).

ANGEL IN THE LOOKING GLASS. Plays about 20 minutes. Brief visits by the "Christmas angel" affect the lives of families living in an apartment house. Three apartments are represented in the set. For middle grades. Plays, Inc., 50¢.

ANGEL IN THE WINDOW, by Effa E. Preston. 7 men, 7 women. Plays 25 minutes. Interior set. The inspiration that has been offered by a stained-glass window of "The Angel" is realized when it is suggested that the window be replaced. T. S. Denison & Co., 50¢ (purchase of 8 copies required).

ANGEL ON A STEPLADDER, by Alberta Hawse. 3 men, 2 women, extras. Plays 1 hour. A boy's attempts to inspire faith in his father. A short sacred pageant is included. Eldridge, 60¢ (purchase of 7 copies required).

ANOTHER EASY CHRISTMAS BOOK, by Ruth Putnam Kimball. Pageants, tableaux, playlets, services, pantomimes for all types of organizations. Little rehearsal or preparation required, and in most cases no stage facilities necessary. Baker's Plays, $1.25.

THE ANSWER, by Leonard Freeman. 7 men, 1 woman. Interior set. An unlikely hero in the setting of a neighborhood tavern reveals the secret of his earth-shaking play. The play is purported to hold the answer to eternal world peace. A famous television production has been done. Baker's Plays, 60¢. Royalty: $10.

THE ANSWER, by Willard S. Smith. 3 men, 2 women. Plays 20 minutes. Interior set. A blizzard makes it impossible for the doctor to reach the sick daughter of the Elliots. In the crisis, they remember the promise of Psalm 91. Easy to stage. T. S. Denison & Co., 50¢ (purchase of 4 copies required).

THE ANSWER IS CHRISTMAS, by Lawrence Barker. 13 speaking parts, 9 nonspeaking parts, 2 choirs. Plays 40 minutes. Modern attitudes toward Christmas in a contemporary play. Abingdon Press, 25¢. Package, 25.

ANSWERED PRAYER, by Esther C. Averill. 2 men, 2 women, 1 girl. Plays 30 minutes. Interior set. Truth and faith conquer a man's depression and doubt of God. Baker's Plays, 60¢.

THE ANSWERS, by Darius L. Swann. Choral material for speech choir, dealing with totalitarianism and faith. Friendship Press, $1.25 for set of 10 (purchase of 10 copies required).

ANTE ROOM, by Ernest Kershaw. 4 men, 2 women. Plays 25–30 minutes. A play about the afterlife and its connection with this world. Characters well-varied. H. F. W. Deane and Sons, 1*s*. 9*d*. net.

ANTHOLOGY OF ENGLISH DRAMA BEFORE SHAKESPEARE, edited by Robert B. Heilman. Contains "The N. Towne Betrayal," "The York Crucifixion," "The Wakefield Noah," "The Wakefield Second Shepherd's Play," "Everyman," "Gammer Gurton's Needle," "Honorable History of Friar Bacon and Friar Bungay," "The Spanish Tragedy," and "The Tragical History of Doctor Faustus." Holt, Rinehart & Winston, $1.45.

ANTHOLOGY OF GREEK DRAMA, edited by C. A. Robinson, Jr. First series: "Agamemnon," "Oedipus Rex," "Antigone," "Medea," "Hippolytus," "Lysistrata." 65¢. Second series: "Prometheus Bound," "Choephoroe," "Eumenides," "Philoctetes," "Oedipus at Colonus," "The Trojan Women," "The Bacchae," "The Clouds," "The Frogs." 95¢. Holt, Rinehart & Winston.

ANTIGONE, by Jean Anouilh. A modern version of the classical tragedy, focusing particularly on the spiritual and social responsibilities of power. In *Jean Anouilh: Five Plays,* Vol. I. Hill & Wang: cloth, $3.95; paper, $1.75.

ANTIGONE, by Sophocles. Translated by Elizabeth Wyckoff. 3 men, 3 women, chorus of Theben elders (16). The great tragedy of the conflict of responsibilities to family ties, the will of the state, and the will of the gods. In *The Complete Greek Tragedies,* Vol. I. University of Chicago Press, $1.95. Royalty: apply to publisher.

THE APPLE TREE, by Clegg, Rands, and McArthur. The story of Caedmon. In *Past and Present, Three Short Plays.* Religious Drama Society of Great Britain, 54¢.

APPLES FOR TEACHER, by Nora Stirling. A young fifth-grade teacher grapples with problems of children from contrasting backgrounds. Bank Street College of Education. Purchase of kit of 5 scripts, $10; single perusal script, $2.

APPOINTMENT IN GALILEE, by Lowell Medley. 7 men, 2 women. Plays 1 hour. The events from the angel's announcement to the women at the sepulcher of the resurrection to the departure of the disciples for Galilee. Particular emphasis is given Peter, John, Judas, Pontius Pilate, and Marcus the Centurian. Eldridge, 75¢ (purchase of 10 copies required).

ARIA DA CAPO, by Edna St. Vincent Millay. 4 men, 1 woman. Plays 30 minutes. A poetic fantasy beginning with a harlequinade, interrupted by two shepherds under the prompting of Cothurnus, the muse of tragedy. They kill each other innocently, pointing up the futility of war, and the play closes with the resumed harlequinade. Baker's Plays, 60¢. Royalty: $15.

ARISE, THY LIGHT IS COME, by Robert H. Dewitt. Christmas story presented in the modern language of the Phillip's translation of the Gospels. Broadman Press, 35¢.

ARMOUR OF LIGHT, by John W. Bloch. Boy in rebellion against the security and conformity of the modern church, and the resulting conflicts with those around him. Bethany Press, $1.

ARTABAN, THE STORY OF THE OTHER WISE MAN, by Clive Robbins and Paul Nordoff. 15 men, 2 women, 1 child, speaking chorus of 10 or more. The play, with music, begins with the star of the Nativity, and ends beneath the cross as Artaban finds the being that he has sought so long. For either Christmas or Easter. Simple to stage. Baker's Plays, $1.50.

AS EASTER DAWNS, by Mary Harrison. 5 men, 4 women, choir. Plays 45 minutes. A church and congregation are resurrected through the Easter story and its message of faith. Baker's Plays, 50¢.

ASMODÉE, by Francois Mauriac, translated by Beverly Thurman. 4 men, 3 women. Interior, exterior sets. An exploration of sin and guilt serves as a testimony of free will and human dignity. A man, rejected from the priesthood because of fanaticism, extends his influence into a household. Samuel French, Inc., $1.25. Royalty: $35–$25.

AT THE FEET OF THE MADONNA, by Charlotte I. Lee. 6 women, plus speaking and singing choirs. Plays 30 minutes. A procession of women come in adoration to lay their problems at the feet of the Madonna. A choric pageant. Baker's Plays, 60¢. Royalty: $5.

AT THE INN, by Mary Russell. 7 men, 2 women, 3 shepherds (nonspeaking), chorus may be used. Plays 30 minutes or more, depending on musical background. A reverent retelling of the first Christmas. Baker's Plays, 60¢.

AT THE JUNCTION, by Rachel Field. 2 men, 1 woman, 1 girl. Plays 15 minutes. A girl going to New York for a career meets a child, sees her own childhood, and takes courage. Samuel French, Inc., 50¢. Royalty: $5.

AT THE WELL OF BETHLEHEM, by Mona Swann. A group of women narrators, telling the stories of their race at a well-side, draw together the stories of Ruth, David, and "Mary the Mother." Scenes may be presented separately. Baker's Plays, 60¢. Royalty: $10.

ATHALIAH, by Jean Racine, translated by Kenneth Muir. 7 men, 3 women, 2 boys, chorus (girls, 6 minimum), extras. Plays full evening. Vestibule set. From the scripture story, in praise of the preserving of the house of David. One boy of that lineage is kept safe from slaughter at the hands of Queen Athaliah by being kept in the temple. In *Racine, Five Plays.* Hill & Wang. Royalty: apply to publisher.

AUGUST HEAT, by Stanley Richards. 4 men, 5 women. Plays 45 minutes. Conflict of people trying to eke out an existence at a seacoast resort, and hoping for the future. Banner Play Bureau, 50¢. Royalty: $10.

AUNT SABRINY'S CHRISTMAS, by Elizabeth F. Guptill. 7 girls. Plays 30 minutes. Interior set. A girl changes her companions' intention to play an unkind joke to kindness and understanding. Baker's Plays, 60¢.

THE AUTOMOBILE GRAVEYARD, by Arrabal. 5 men, 2 women. Plays full evening. Considered by some to be a modern passion play. It deals with an aggressive gospel in a forceful if not shocking manner. Grove Press. Royalty: apply to Ninon Tallon-Karlweis.

BA THANE, by Edna A. Baldwin. 4 men, 3 women. Plays 45 minutes. Interior set. Presents a mission station in Burma, whose missionaries are held responsible for the whole white race. In *One Act Plays of Spiritual Power.* Baker's Plays, $3.25.

BACK TO BETHLEHEM, by Clara Hooker Miller. 2 men, 3 women, extras. Plays 30 minutes. Grandmother awakens her daughter's family to the spirit of Christmas. Nativity tableau included. Eldridge, 60¢ (purchase of 5 copies required).

BALLISTA, by Richard Tydeman. 3 men, 4 women. An ironic and serious play, using an analogy of Roman times to the present day, and cleverly examining the devastating effects of a "peace weapon." Evans Plays, 2*s.* net. Royalty: 25*s.* net per performance.

BANG! GOES CHRISTMAS, by J. W. Blakley. 8 men, 7 women. Plays 1 hour. Interior set. Comedy for adults, maintaining the Christmas spirit amid its humorous situations. Baker's Plays, 60¢.

BANNER ANTHOLOGY OF ONE ACT PLAYS BY AMERICAN AUTHORS. Fifteen one-acts of particularly high quality. Banner Play Bureau, $3.

BARABBAS, by Michel de Ghelderode, translated by George Hauger. 15 men, 3 women, extras. 3 exterior sets. The story of a barbaric Barabbas who, without understanding what is happening around him, still feels the injustice the mob has done Christ on the cross. In *Ghelderode, Seven Plays.* Samuel French, Inc., $1.95. Royalty: $35–$25.

BARABBAS, by John H. Hanger. 2 men, 3 women. Plays 30 minutes. Interior set. Barabbas takes Jesus into his heart and discovers that lasting victory comes more readily through love than through might. Baker's Plays, 60¢.

BARABBAS, by S. N. Sedgwick. 17 men, 3 women, extras. Based on the events surrounding Passiontide; although Christ does not appear in the play, his voice is heard offstage. Baker's Plays, 60¢. (Give author's name when ordering.) Royalty: $2.50.

BARTER, by Urban Nagle. 5 men, 6 women. The twenty-four hours preceding the crucifixion. Judas Iscariot, Miriam, daughter of

Jobal, and a Roman soldier, Varius, are the central figures. McKay's Plays, $1.25. Royalty: $15.

BE A GOOD NEIGHBOR, by Esther Averill. 3 men, 2 women, 2 boys. Plays 30 minutes. Feuding neighbors are shown the good neighbor policy. Baker's Plays, 50¢.

BEACON OF STRENGTH, by Marlene Brenner. 3 women, 5 girls, extra children. Plays 15 minutes. The beginning of the Girl Scouts. Baker's Plays, 50¢.

BEAUTIFUL DREAMERS, by James Reach. 12 women. Plays full evening. Girls from every part of the United States try for the movies. Some succeed, others do not. Set in the Hollywood residence for aspiring actresses. Baker's Plays, 75¢. Royalty: $10.

THE BEAUTIFUL PEOPLE, by William Saroyan. 7 men, 2 women. The beautiful people, of many types, live together happily on a basis of love for one another. For advanced players. Samuel French, Inc., $1. Royalty: $25.

THE BEAUTIFUL QUEEN. 8 women. Esther, concealing that she is a Jewess because of the hatred accorded her race, teaches love and friendship; she finds favor with the king through courage and gentleness. In *Easy Church Plays for Women and Girls.* Baker's Plays, $1.25.

BECAUSE WE BELIEVE, by Carol L. King. 10 men, 1 woman, angel, child, chorus. Plays 30 minutes. Exterior set. While many see only the tinsel, some see the Christchild because they believe, states the theme of this play. Characters are figures of the Nativity. Baker's Plays, 60¢.

BECKET, by Jean Anouilh, translated by Lucienne Hill. 15 men, 3 women. Plays full evening. Interior and exterior sets. The tragic relationship between the King of England and the man who became his enemy when the king's intrigue made him Archbishop of Canterbury. Very powerful; difficult to present. Baker's Plays, $1.25. Royalty: $50.

BED OF HAY, by Agnes E. Peterson. 3 men, 13 women, angel, shepherds, and unseen chorus of angels. Plays 20 minutes. When no room is available at the inn, a crippled stable boy offers Mary and Joseph his bed of hay. Baker's Plays, 60¢. Royalty: none if 4 copies purchased.

BEFORE THE FLOOD, by A. A. Milne. 5 men, 5 women. Interior set. Noah and his sons build the Ark while Noah's wife, Hannah, assumes the burden of finding provisions for all who will be on board. Baker's Plays, 60¢. Royalty: $10.

BEFORE THE SUN AROSE, by Charlotte D. Widrig. 1 man, 1 woman, 1 girl, and extras. Entertainment, requiring little rehearsal, and with an opportunity to work a gift exchange into the program. In *The Easy Christmas Grab Bag.* Baker's Plays, $1.25.

BEGGARS' CHARITY, by Frank J. Jones. 6 men, 2 women, messenger. Three beggars, seeking alms outside a cathedral on Christmas Eve, share with an old lady and reunite a mother and son. In *The Easy Christmas Grab Bag.* Baker's Plays, $1.25.

BEGINNING AT JERUSALEM. 3 men, 6 women, 3 boys, 1 girl. Plays 80 minutes. A mother, although interested in foreign missions, brings real happiness in her own city by heeding the words of Jesus to his disciples. Eldridge, 75¢ (purchase of 10 copies required).

BEGINNING OF THE WAY, by Henzie Raeburn. 4 men, 4 women, 2 shepherds. 3 easy interior sets. A three-act play; tells the story of the Nativity and the events leading up to it in language related to that of the King James Version of the Bible, while establishing a deep feeling of humanity. Baker's Plays, 60¢. Royalty: $10.

BEHOLD HIS GLORY, by Joy Larson. An Easter cantata, with narration from the scriptures interwoven with old hymns, to show Christ's supreme purpose in coming and the importance of the resurrection. Eldridge, 75¢ (purchase of 10 copies required).

BEHOLD THE CRUCIFIED, by Byron Carmony. An Easter cantata, combining scripture readings with ten original gospel songs, which tells the Easter story with evangelistic emphasis. Eldridge, 50¢.

BEHOLD YOUR KING, by Thomas Doran. 7 men, 7 women, and nonspeaking parts as desired. The passion, death, and resurrection presented as events on which it is possible to reflect with grateful remembrance. May be played with or without scenery. Baker's Plays, $1. Royalty: $15.

A BELL FOR ADANO, by John Hersey. 22 men, 5 women. Plays full evening. Major Joppolo, who has come to establish democracy in a Sicilian town, struggles to regain a lost symbol of security, a bell. Dramatists Play Service, $1. Royalty: $35–$25.

THE BELL OF ST. HILDEGARDE, by Arthur Hobson Quinn and Kathleen Carberry Quinn. 8 men, 5 women, extras, some with lines. Plays 30 minutes. Exterior set. The triumph of faith over science, both simply and charmingly presented. Baker's Plays, 60¢. Royalty: $5.

BELVEDERE, by Gwen Davenport. 5 men, 4 women, 2 children. Plays full evening. The script from which the film *Sitting Pretty* was made. A comedy of an impeccable gentleman in a disordered modern household. Samuel French, Inc., $1. Royalty: $25.

BENEATH THIS SPIRE, by Ormal B. Trick. 3 men, 6 women, extras. Plays 30 minutes. Interior set. An old church is sold to become an antique shop. The new owner sees in a dream what the church has meant to the people, particularly the old grandmother who would like to buy it back for the town. Baker's Plays, 60¢. Royalty: $5.

BESIDE THE MANGER, by Edward Longstreth. Plays 30 minutes. Suitable for reading or staging. In *At the Foot of the Cross*. Royalty: inquire of the author.

THE BESPOKE OVERCOAT, by Wolf Mankowitz. 4 men. An old Jewish watchman dies while a friend is making him that one good overcoat for which he has been waiting all his life. In *Five One-Act Plays*. Baker's Plays, $1.25 (available singly, 60¢). Royalty: $10.

BEST CHRISTMAS PANTOMIMES, by Marie Irish. Pantomimed carols and Christmas stories, with words, music, and specific instructions for each. Baker's Plays, 85¢. Heuer, 85¢.

THE BEST PART OF CHRISTMAS. 6 men, 8 women, extras. Plays 20 minutes. Bare stage. For middle grades. A reporter polls the townspeople regarding "the best part of Christmas," and finally writes an answer to satisfy everyone. Simple to produce, includes all Christmas customs. Plays, Inc., 50¢.

BEST PLAYS OF THE MODERN AMERICAN THEATER, edited by John Gassner. A fine selection of recent plays, 1952–57. Crown, $5.75.

BEST SELECTIONS FOR CHRISTMAS, compiled by Florence E. Wolcott. Plays, monologues, verse-choir readings, tableaux, recitations, and a candlelighting service, for church school use. Baker's Plays, $1.

BEST SELECTIONS FOR EASTER, compiled by Florence E. Wolcott. Readings, prayers, pantomimes, dramatizations, choral novelties, upper room services, etc. Baker's Plays, $1.

BETHLEHEM, by Laurence Housman. 13 speaking parts, extras. Plays 1 hour. Varied, yet simple, sets. Beautiful Nativity play, combining music and drama. Careful cutting needed. Baker's Plays, 60¢. Music, 75¢. Royalty: $10; with music, $12.50.

THE BETHLEHEM ROAD, by M. A. Hubbard. 31 characters. Plays 2 hours. Miriam convinces Herod not to execute her father, encounters the shepherds and the wise men, and experiences the glory of the Nativity. Baker's Plays, 60¢. Royalty: $10 if admission is charged; $5 if not.

BETHLEHEM'S FIELD, by Leonora Sill Ashton. 2 men, 1 woman, 4 boys, 1 girl. Plays 25–30 minutes. A group of children lead a man from grief at the destruction of his family back to the traditional manger scene in Bethlehem's field. A Christmas play. Eldridge, 60¢.

THE BETRAYAL, by Geoffrey Nevil Dowsett, O.M.I. 20 men, 3 women, extras. A historical drama in three acts, beginning with Judas' betrayal of Christ and continuing through Christ's trial until Pilate, in spite of the pleas of others and his own conscience, condemns Christ to the cross. Baker's Plays, $1.25. Royalty: $25–$20.

BETTER PLAYS FOR TODAY'S CHURCHES, selected by Bachman and Browne. Twelve modern religious plays, combining theological substance and artistic quality with low cost of production and suitability for amateur production. Association Press, $8.95.

THE "BETTER YET" CHRISTMAS BOOK, by Helen Ramsey and others. All grades, from tots up. Monologues, plays, pageants, songs, etc. Baker's Plays, $1.

BETWEEN TWO THIEVES, by Diego Fabbri, adapted by Warner LeRoy. 9 men, 4 women. Bare stage. A group of traveling Jews enter a theatre and draw lots for roles in a drama staged nightly since the crucifixion. Their purpose is to examine why the Jews have been persecuted for two thousand years. Taken from Fabbri's *Processeo A Gesu*. Baker's Plays, $1.25. Royalty: $35.

BEWITCHED, by Rosalie Regen. One of a series of biographical dramas of a peaceful people. Friends Book and Supply House, 15¢.

BEYOND HUMAN POWER, by Bjorn-Stjerne Bjornson, translated by Lee M. Hollander. 10 men (plus optional extras), 4 women. 2 interior sets. A faith healer, following what he believes to be the dictates of God in his power, learns tragically late of the power of love. Difficult. In *Chief Contemporary Dramatists,* Series I. Houghton Mifflin Co. Royalty: apply to publisher.

BIBLE CHARACTER IMPERSONATIONS, by Nelson Sweeney. Fifty characters are represented. Old and New Testament heroes tell their life stories in a manner interesting for both young and old. Each is appropriately costumed. Eldridge, $1.25.

BIBLE CHARACTERS IN ACTION, by J. Edward Lantz and Ruth Cox Lantz. Impersonations, occurring within complete worship services, which include: Matthew collecting taxes, Peter in prison, Martha serving Jesus, Ruth following her mother-in-law, Esther freeing her people. Baker's Plays, 75¢.

THE BIBLE COMES ALIVE, by Norman E. Nygaard. Eleven adaptations of great stories from scripture, with casts ranging from one to fifteen characters. May be presented in either play or pantomime form. Baker's Plays, $1.25.

BIBLE PLAYS, Book I—Christmas, by Charles J. Ax. Eight short plays: "The Reprimand" (Elizabeth), "The New Tax" (innkeeper), "The Chosen" (Mary), "Both High and Low" (shepherds), "What Faith Can Do," "Nothing Is Impossible," "So the Blind May See," and "Never Too Late" (plays of Christ's ministry). Fortress Press, 75¢.

BIBLE PLAYS, Book II—Easter, by Charles J. Ax. Fifteen- to twenty-minute lenten plays: "The Warning," "The Trial," "The Seamless Robe," "The Greatest Surprise," "The Beautiful Gate," "No Man Is Common," "The Lost Is Found," "The Meaning of Mercy." In simple language and of varying quality. The figure of Christ appears. Baker's Plays, 75¢.

BIBLE PLAYS FOR CHILDREN. Collection of eight one-acts, fifteen to twenty minutes each, excellent for church schools: "Joseph and His Brothers," "David and Jonathan," "Children of the Bible," "The Stable Boy," "The Steward's Daughter," "Banks of the Jordan," "The Fisherman's Son," "The Day of Hope." Concordia, 40¢; set of 8, $3.

BIBLE PLAYS FOR JUNIORS, by Claribel M. Spamer. Twenty-nine ten-minute plays from the Old and New Testaments. Particularly good for church schools. Baker's Plays, $1.25.

BIBLE PLAYS FOR SMALL CHILDREN, by Ruth Lyndall Tongue. Contains ten short plays for six- to ten-year-olds. Faith Press, 3*s.*

THE BIBLE SALESMAN, by Jay Thompson. 3 characters. Musical comedy. A Negro boy, who has seen a vision of the Lord, is enlisted as a Bible salesman. In manuscript. Samuel French, Inc. Royalty and music rental: apply to publisher.

BIBLE WOMEN COME ALIVE, by Ruth C. Ikerman. Forty monologues on women of the Bible—short, timely, dramatic, and human. Baker's Plays, $2.

THE BIG BOOK OF CHRISTMAS, by Aileen Fisher. Ranges from gaiety, through pathos, to the reverence of Christmas. Sixty-two plays, skits, songs, etc. Baker's Plays, $1.50.

THE BIG CHRISTMAS BOOK, by Dorothy M. Shipman. Fifteen-minute plays suited for use in church school. Dramatic Publishing Co., 75¢.

THE BIG MIDDLE, by Orlin R. Corey. 4 men, 4 women. A young minister's efforts to combat selfishness and bigotry in his congregation. Broadman Press, 50¢.

BILLY BUDD, by Herman Melville, adapted by Louis Coxe and Robert Chapman. 22 men. Plays full evening. Set in the British Navy of 1798, this adaptation of Melville's short novel concerns the conflict of good and evil, of law and the law's spirit. Princeton University Press: cloth, $3; paper, $1.45. Royalty: $50–$25.

THE BIRDS' CHRISTMAS CAROL, by Kate Douglas Wiggins, adapted by Alden Carlow. 2 women, 4 boys, 4 girls. Plays 30 minutes. Interior set. One-act dramatization of Kate Douglas Wiggins' book. The episode in which Mother Ruggles is getting her brood ready to attend the dinner party to be given at the home of Carol Bird. Baker's Plays, 60¢. Royalty: $3.

THE BIRDS' CHRISTMAS CAROL, by Kate Douglas Wiggins, adapted by Virginia Hagemann. 19 characters, chorus. Plays 1 hour. A three-act operetta for junior high students. Kate Douglas Wiggins' story of Carol, who radiates the spirit of Christmas. Eldridge, $1.50 (purchase of 10 copies required).

THE BIRDS' CHRISTMAS CAROL, by Kate Douglas Wiggins. 8 boys, 10 girls. Kate Douglas Wiggins' story, simply dramatized, for a social evening. Plays, Inc., 50¢.

THE BIRDS' CHRISTMAS CAROL, by Kate Douglas Wiggins. 3 men, 3 women, 4 boys, 4 girls. The author's dramatization (in three acts and a prologue) of her own popular Christmas story. Fine scene of the "Ruggleses in the rear" getting ready for their Christmas dinner at the big house. Baker's Plays, 75¢. Royalty: $5.

BIRTH BY DROWNING, by Norman Nicholson. Exterior set and also before a traverse curtain. Elisha, pictured as a country doctor of Cumberland. The mountains provide the effect of a speaking chorus of three voices. Very lively and potent verse and characterization. Faber & Faber. For all inquiries for performance permission, contact author's agent: Margery Vosper.

THE BIRTH OF THE SONG "SILENT NIGHT," by Florence Felton French. Narrator, 4 men, 3 women. Plays 30 minutes, with musical bridges. A radio play, telling the story of Franz Gruber and his Christmas Eve composition, with a pastor, of "Silent Night." Baker's Plays, 60¢.

THE BIRTHDAY OF A KING, by Constance Camp. 15 characters. Plays 45 minutes. Tableaux and reader. "Annunciation," "End of a Journey," "Christmas Day." Banner Play Bureau, 50¢ (purchase of 5 copies required).

A BIRTHDAY THROUGH THE CENTURIES, words and music by Eloise Lowe. Narrator, male quartet, 2 choirs, adults' and children's. Plays 45 minutes. The story of the perpetuation of Christmas through the ages. Eldridge, 60¢.

THE BISHOP'S MANTLE, by Agnes Sligh Turnbull, adapted by Marion L. Johnson. 5 men, 7 women. Plays full evening. A minister and his frank solutions for the problems of his congregation. Dramatic Publishing Co., 90¢. Royalty: $25.

BITTER BREAD, by Walt Anderson. 8 men, 3 women. A short one-act. Puerto Rican family confronts the problems of integration with the American scene. Seabury Press. Royalty: noncommercial acting rights on application to the publisher; commercial rights on application to the author.

"BLESSED ARE THEY," by Walter E. Butts, Jr. 3 men, 4 women. Plays 30 minutes. Resurrection of faith in the church and home in modern setting. Could become melodramatic if not well directed. Dramatic Publishing Co., 40¢.

BLESSED NATIVITY, by Hazel E. Harrison. 3 men, 2 women, extras including 2 readers, soloists, choir, angels, shepherds, etc. A nonsectarian and simple telling of the story of the Nativity. Baker's Plays, $1.25 (purchase of 15 copies required).

THE BLIND MEN, by Michel de Ghelderode, translated by George Hauger. 4 men. Exterior set. Morality play, based on Peter Breughel's painting. Three blind men, seeking a miracle on their road to Rome, come to destruction when they refuse to heed the warning of a one-eyed man that the road leads to death. In *Ghelderode, Seven Plays*. Samuel French, Inc., $1.95. Royalty: $10.

THE BLUE OVERALLS ANGEL, by Anne Martens. 2 men, 1 woman, 1 little girl, extras. Plays 25 minutes. Christmas season. A little girl goes to a church hoping to hear an angel's song, of which she has read, and opens the way for a lesson in humanity and the Christmas spirit among the people she finds there. Eldridge, 60¢.

BLUE-RIBBON PLAYS FOR GIRLS, edited by Sylvia Kamerman. For ages 6–16, encompassing an unusual range. Plays, Inc., $4.

A BOARDING HOUSE CHRISTMAS, by Charlotte D. Widrig. 15 to 20 couples, narrator (cast may vary). Continuity is maintained by the narrator, and everyone has the opportunity to "get into the act." Valuable during a busy holiday season. Baker's Plays, 60¢.

THE BOOK OF JOB, by Orlin Corey. 5 men, chorus of 5 women. Dramatic treatment of the Old Testament story in emulation of the Greek tragedies. Long one-act. Children's Theatre Press. Royalty: apply to publisher.

THE BOOK OF JOB, by Richard Moulton, adapted by Amy Goodhue Loomis. Taken from *A Modern Reader's Bible* by Moulton. For information contact Amy Goodhue Loomis.

THE BOOK OF JOB AS A GREEK TRAGEDY, by Horace M. Kallen. 8 men, speaking chorus. Plays 80 minutes. Set in the ruins outside Job's house, with the text of the book of Job rearranged in the form of a Greek tragedy, attempting to establish Euripidean counterparts. Very difficult. Suitable for performance in a hall, the author's suggested setting not being necessary. Royalty: apply to Dodd, Mead & Co.

BORAK, by Robert D. Hock. 16 men, bit parts for men and women.

Plays full evening. Conflict between nations and individuals accented in a Civil War incident. Dramatists Play Service, $1.25. Royalty: $35–$25.

BORN IN A MANGER, by Ellen Jane Lorenz. The Christmas story as told by the animals in the stable at Bethlehem, in story and song, with sixteen choral arrangements. Eldridge, 50¢. Optional color filmstrip, $5.

THE BOSTON O'TOOLES, by Francis Michael Casey. 9 men, 5 women. Plays 40 minutes. Interior set. An Irish family, by showing unexpected kindness to a small boy angel, pave their way for eventually reaching heaven after purgatory through their one good deed. Samuel French, Inc., 60¢. Royalty: $5.

BOTH YOUR HOUSES, by Maxwell Anderson. 13 men, 3 women. Plays full evening. Christianity working in society is evident in this clash between new and old Congressional politicians. Advanced production. Samuel French, Inc., $1.25. Royalty: $25–$20.

THE BOY ABE, by Betty Smith. 6 boys, 6 girls, extras. Abe and his stepmother meet in a schoolroom. Set in 1819. For younger players. Baker's Plays, 50¢.

THE BOY DAVID, by J. M. Barrie. 14 men, 2 women, extras. 1 interior set, 4 exterior sets. David's early life, including his anointment by Samuel, his slaying of Goliath, and his relationship to Saul and Jonathan. Three acts. Samuel French, Inc., $1.25. Royalty: $35–$25.

THE BOY WHO CARVED BIRDS, by Ken Etheridge. 4 men, 1 woman. A craftsman and his wife help a Samaritan who has been attacked and robbed. Their older son, unseen in the play, has the gift of carving birds that fly. The clue to his gift lies in his identity, revealed at the close of the play. One act. Evans Plays. Royalty: 25*s*. 2*d*. net.

THE BOY WHO DISCOVERED EASTER, by Elizabeth McFadden. 1 man, 2 women, 1 boy. Plays 40 minutes. Interior set. Profound religious message, based on Raymond McDonald Alden's sentimental story of a man and a slum boy, "The Boy Who Discovered the Spring." Baker's Plays, 75¢. Royalty: $5.

THE BOY WHO KNEW JESUS, by Helen Harrington. 4 men, 2 women, 1 boy, extras. Plays 35 minutes. Exterior set. Alvin, a crippled boy of Nazareth, never succeeds in meeting the boy Jesus. He continues to speculate, even as a grown man, on what might have happened had he known Christ, who could heal with a touch. Baker's Plays, 60¢. Royalty: $5.

THE BOY WITH A CART, by Christopher Fry. 7 men, 6 women, extras. Plays 1 hour. Saint Cuthman of Essex builds his church with miraculous aid, combining humor, humanity, and religion. Requires a mature, skillful cast. Baker's Plays, $1. Royalty: $10.

BOYS AT LARGE, by Nora Stirling. Juvenile delinquency problem with stress on dignity of individual. Brooklyn Bureau of Social Service and Children's Aid Society. Perusal script, $2; kit of 5 acting scripts, $12.

THE BOYS FROM MODIN, by Rabbi Norman and Mrs. Rose Goldburg. 3 boys, 5 girls, 12 extras (boys or girls). Boys and girls prepare a skit on Maccabean times. A group of heroes, tempted to take the easy way by joining the Syrians, decide to join the fight for freedom. Explains the reason for celebrating Chanuko. For ages 7–13. Union of American Hebrew Congregations, 25¢.

BRAND, by Henrik Ibsen, translated by Michael Meyer. 9 men (also villagers, doubling possible), 5 women (also women villagers, doubling possible). Exterior sets, 1 interior set. A man, feeling he has heard the call of God, sacrifices everyone close to him to follow the precepts of absolutism. Very difficult. Doubleday. Royalty: apply to Miriam Howell.

THE BRASS BUTTERFLY, by William Golding. 6 men, 1 woman, attendants. Plays full evening. Social and political forms are affected by science and technology as demonstrated in this romance involving early Christians. Curtis Brown. Royalty: apply to publisher.

THE BRASS RING, edited by Amy Goodhue Loomis. Four informal dramas intended for minimal rehearsal, production, and discussion; first presented on NBC-TV's "Frontiers of Faith." The plays, by Stephen Gethers and Mel Moth, are "Headwaiters Know My Name," "The Moon and I," "Look, Ma, I'm Different!" and "The Rainy Season." Lighting and properties are simple. Bethany Press, $1.50.

BREAD, by Fred Eastman. 2 men, 4 women. Plays 30 minutes. Interior set. The problems of a farm family in their economic, cultural, and personal lives. Baker's Plays, 60¢. Royalty: $5.

BREAK OF NOON, by Paul Claudel, translated by Wallace Fowlie. 3 men, 1 woman. 2 exterior sets, 1 interior set. The struggle between the Creator and his creation, approached from the premise that physical passion may lead to spiritual love. Oriental setting. Henry Regnery Co., $1.10. Royalty: apply to publisher.

BREAKFAST WITH PAUL, by Erva Loomis Merow. 5 men, 2 women (optional). Plays 20 minutes. Short comedy involving a family's activities just before leaving for Sunday morning church services. Eldridge, 60¢ (purchase of 7 copies required).

BREAKTHROUGH, by Nora Stirling. Challenge to youth interested in welfare work. Welfare Administration (write publisher for free scripts, in limited supply).

A BRIDE IN SAMARIA, by David Monger. 3 men, 4 women. Interior set. A woman who loved too much is saved from stoning by Christ. Evans Plays. Royalty: 25*s.* 2*d.* net.

THE BRIDES OF BEGERIN, by Ned Gethings. 12 women. A group of women, awaiting the return of their sailor husbands after a storm, become incited against one girl but are stopped from violence by the church bell. A simple and moving play enriched by poetic dialogue. Evans Plays. Royalty: 25*s.* 2*d.* net.

BRIGHT IDEAS FOR EASTER, MOTHER'S DAY, AND CHILDREN'S DAY, by May Elizabeth Freeman, Lucile Crites Sligh, and others. Songs, recitations, dialogues, etc., for various ages. Includes an Easter pageant. Helpful for church school spring celebrations. Eldridge, $1.

BRIGHTEN EVERY CORNER, by George Herman. 6 men, 8 women. Bare stage. Sister Mary Martha, after her seemingly little noticed passing, is remembered by people all across the United States. Samuel French, Inc., 60¢. Royalty: $5.

THE BROKEN CIRCLE, by Dorothy Clarke Wilson. 4 men, 2 women, 2 boys. Plays 30 minutes. Interior set. A strike is slowly ruining a town in this industrial relations play, filled with homely philosophy. Baker's Plays, 60¢.

THE BROTHER, by Dorothy Clarke Wilson. 4 men, 4 women, extras. Plays 1 hour, 45 minutes. The changes in the feelings of James, Jesus' brother, during Christ's ministry. Baker's Plays, 60¢. Royalty: $10 if admission is charged; $5 if not.

BROTHER ASS AND BROTHER LION, by Barbara Willard. 11 men (2 "animals" played by young players). Respectful but highly humorous treatment of the St. Jerome and the Lion story. Baker's Plays. Royalty: apply to publisher.

BROTHER ORCHID, by Leo Brady. 11 men. 3 interior sets. Little John Sarto, a racketeer, comes to a monastery where newspaper publicity and he are unknown. Baker's Plays, $1.25. Royalty: $25.

BROTHER PETROC'S RETURN, by Emmet Lavery. 25 men, 10 women. Simple sets. A young monk, living in the world of 400 years ago, suddenly awakes in the twentieth century and finds that our time brings confusion to his certainty, and that he must find himself again. Samuel French, Inc., $1.25. Royalty: $25–$20.

THE BROWN BIRD, by Mary R. Neild. 1 man, 9 women. Plays 45 minutes. Rooney Brown's faith in eternal values is restored after the death of her sweetheart on the eve of the death of King George V. The restoration of faith surrounds her singing of "The Brown Bird." Abel Heywood & Son, 1*s.* 6*d.*

BUILDERS, by Joseph W. Clokey. Plays 20 minutes. An Easter play for children, beginning with the message of Easter, continuing with an examination of the children's role as builders of the church. H. W. Gray Co., 50¢.

THE BUILDERS, by Francis Dyer Eckardt. 6 men, 3 women, extras. Interior set. Conflict of a worldly father and a son who wishes to become a preacher in a country church. Baker's Plays, 60¢ (give author's name when ordering). Royalty: $2.50.

THE BUNDLE-O'-CHEER CHRISTMAS BOOK, by Willis N. Bugbee. Sketches, recitations, and dialogues for children from kindergarten to high school. Heuer, $1.

BURNING PEWS, by William Leach. 3 men, 2 women, 2 firemen (extras). Plays 20 minutes. Reactions of members of a community when a fire in the church damages some of the pews. Humor with a lesson. Eldridge, 60¢.

THE BUSINESS OF GOOD GOVERNMENT, by John Arden. 10 men, 4 women, attendants. Short play. Forthright treatment of the Nativity story with relevant implications to modern times. One act. Methuen. Royalty: apply to Theatrework.

BY CHRIST ALONE, by Willard S. Smith. 12 men, 3 women. Plays 35 minutes. Easter play. Judas, despised by all, finds forgiveness in the heart of Christ whom he had betrayed. Easy to stage. T. S. Denison & Co., 50¢ (purchase of 10 copies required).

BY THY CROSS AND PASSION, by Irene Caudwell. 11 men, 12 women. A sacred drama, in the mystery play tradition, in ten scenes with seven settings. Faith Press, 3*s.*

BY THY FAITH, by O. G. Blair. 4 men (3 very small parts), 5 women, 3 boys, 1 girl. Plays 40 minutes. Strongly dramatic presentation, with a reader's prologue introducing each act. Particularly good for Easter. Eldridge, 60¢ (purchase of 6 copies required).

BY THY GLORIOUS RESURRECTION, by Irene Caudwell. 16 characters. A Passion play, in the mystery play tradition, with a prologue, eight scenes, and two interludes. Faith Press, 3*s.*

CAIN, by Howard Nemerov. 1 woman, 1 offstage voice. Plays 35 minutes. In this play God is the source of temptation and Cain the discoverer of unknown boundaries. In *Tulane Drama Review,* Vol. IV, No. 2 (1959). In *The Next Room of the Dream.* University of Chicago Press. Royalty: apply to author c/o the Margot Johnson Agency.

THE CAINE MUTINY COURT MARTIAL, by Herman Wouk. 19 men (6 nonspeaking). Plays full evening. Taken from the novel, the play tackles modern ethical problems. Provocative of discussion. Samuel French, Inc., $1.25. Royalty: $50–$25.

THE CAKE-MAKER, by Lois Bailey Wills. 6 women. Plays 30 minutes. Exterior set. A woman proves in the female community of a modern apartment house that battles are won through love, not hate. Baker's Plays, 60¢. Royalty: $5.

CALL ME MAC, by Theodore St. John Cox. 4 men, 2 women. Plays 30 minutes. "If we break faith with us who die, we shall not sleep, though poppies grow in Flanders Field." A vivid wartime dramatization set in a barn in the north of France. Baker's Plays, 60¢. Royalty: $5.

CALLING ALL CHRISTMASES. 7 men, 5 women, extras. Plays 20 minutes. A mock radio broadcast, interviewing children from around the world, reveals that the same light shines in all legends and customs of Christmas. Set in a radio studio. For middle grades. Plays, Inc., 50¢.

CALVARY, by William Butler Yeats. 6 men, 3 musicians. Short play. Christ is confronted by three soldiers and Lazarus in this poetic treatment of the crucifixion. One act. Samuel French, Inc. Royalty: apply to publisher.

THE CANCELLED DEBT, by Isla P. Richardson. 3 men, 5 women. Plays 30 minutes. Interior set. A debt of gratitude to a stranger is repaid on Christmas Eve. In *The Easy Christmas Grab Bag.* Baker's Plays, $1.25.

THE CANDLE IN THE WINDOW, by Clara Childs. 5 boys, 6 girls. Plays 30 minutes. A play with carols. A group of children, awaiting the coming of the Christchild on Christmas Eve, meet a ragged boy to whom they give their gifts as alms for the poor people. Taken from an old legend. Eldridge, 50¢ (purchase of 10 copies required).

CANDLELIGHT, by Irene and David Gass. A pageant of the months, for a large cast of children of all ages, suited to church school presentations. Baker's Plays, 60¢. Royalty: $5.

A CANDLELIGHTING SERVICE, by Dorothy Clarke Wilson. 8 speaking parts (including a pastor or counselor), nonspeaking participants. Plays 20 minutes. A service of consecration for youth. Excellent conclusion to a devotional meeting, teaches that it is "better to light one candle." Set in any church auditorium. Baker's Plays, 60¢. Royalty: first performance, none; $2.50 each repeat.

A CANDLELIGHTING SERVICE FOR CHRISTMAS AND NEW YEAR SEASON, by Margaret Van Dyke Nevins. 15 men, 6 women. Plays 1 hour. Dramatic worship based on "God's Candles We." Samuel French, Inc., 50¢.

A CANTICLE OF THE NATIVITY, by René-Richard Bechet, translated by Sister Mary Constantia, B.V.M. 17 speaking parts, singing choir, variable number of extras. Scenes from the scriptures, from the prophecies of Isaiah to the adoration of the shepherds. Baker's Plays, 60¢. Royalty: $5.

THE CAPTAINS AND THE KINGS, by Channing Pollock. 9 men, 1 woman, 1 child, guards. A child comes among the rulers, but they fail to learn peace. A very powerful play, particularly good for Palm Sunday, Holy Week. One act. Baker's Plays, 60¢. Royalty: $10 if admission is charged; $5 if not.

CAPTIVITY, by E. Lloyd-Barritt. 3 men, 2 women. Plays 25–30 minutes. Set in Daniel's house at the time of the Jewish captivity in Babylon, the play concerns intrigue and espionage resolved in the restoring of Daniel's wife's faith. Scope for the players, and colorful setting possibilities. H. F. W. Deane & Sons, 1*s.* 9*d.* net. Postage, 2*d.*

CAREER PLAYS FOR YOUNG PEOPLE, by Samuel S. Richmond. Thirty-one realistic vocational guidance plays for junior and senior high school. Plays, Inc., $3.75.

THE CAROL OF THE WORLD, by Robert M. Busfield. 3 men, 1 woman, choir. Plays 30 minutes. The story of the writing of "Silent Night," inspired in a priest by a Christmas Eve birth in a small Alpine town, and sung because of a breakdown in a church organ. Historically authentic. Easy to produce. Eldridge, 60¢ (purchase of 5 copies required).

THE CARPENTER, by Dorothy Clarke Wilson. 3 men, 4 women, 3 boys, 1 girl. Interior set. A comedy in three acts, in which a modern carpenter in a small New England town tries to live in the manner that Jesus lived, thus causing speculation among the townspeople. Baker's Plays, 75¢. Royalty: $10.

THE CASE AGAINST EVE, by Eve McFall. 4 men, 4 women, 2 boys. Plays 35 minutes. Interior set. A comedy in which a washer repairman shows a young housewife the way back to a right relationship with God. Baker's Plays, 60¢. Royalty: $10.

THE CASE OF THE MISSING HANDSHAKE, by Nora Stirling. Good manners for seventh- and eighth-graders. Nat'l. Assoc. for Mental Health, $1. Production packet, $5.

THE CASE OF THE SILENT CAROLER. 4 men, 4 women, mixed extras. Interior set. Set in a modern living room. The girl who refuses to go caroling has the gift of song, not in her voice but in her heart. For junior and senior high school students. Plays, Inc., 50¢.

CASEY, by P. W. Turner. 6 men, 3 women. A dramatic meditation relating the event of the crucifixion to modern life. Baker's Plays, $1.25. Royalty: $15.

THE CASTLE OF PERSEVERANCE, freely adapted by Iwa Langentels. Earliest extant morality play, in which man is granted everlasting life through God's mercy. Taken from the *Marco Play of 1425*. Religious Drama Society of Great Britain, 39¢. Royalty: $1.41.

THE CASTLE OF PERSEVERANCE, adapted by Phillips E. Osgood. Plays 40 minutes. For large cast of experienced players and an appreciative audience. The church's attempt to teach its doctrines of salvation after the Norman conquest. Baker's Plays, 50¢.

THE CASTLE OF PERSEVERANCE, abridged with updated language. In *Medieval Mysteries, Moralities, and Interludes*. Barron's Educational Series, $1.25.

CATCHING UP WITH CHRISTMAS, by Anne Coulter Martens. 9 women or girls. Plays 30 minutes. A comedy. The Christmas spirit finally prevails over a family's confusion before a Christmas Eve church program. Eldridge, 50¢ (purchase of 9 copies required).

THE CATHEDRAL, by George Lowther. 2 men, offstage voices. A vicar restores hope in living to a soldier who has lost a leg by telling him the Easter story. Samuel French, Inc., 60¢. Royalty: $5.

CAUGHT BETWEEN, by Helen Kramer. 8 men, 2 women. Plays 30 minutes. A Navajo Indian boy must choose between living with his family or leaving for the white man's world. Friendship Press, 50¢.

CAUSE FOR GRATITUDE. 6 women, 2 men. Plays 20 minutes. Prudence Carver makes a decision for freedom on the first Thanksgiving. Plays, Inc., 50¢.

CAVALCADE OF HUMAN RIGHTS. 30 men, 8 women. Plays 1 hour. For junior and senior high. A play of human rights, and man's struggle, shown through history, to attain dignity. Plays, Inc., 50¢.

THE CAVE DWELLERS, by William Saroyan. 7 men, 5 women. Plays full evening. The world's outcasts meet in an abandoned theatre. An unusually beautiful play, for skilled players. Samuel French, Inc., $1. Royalty: $50.

CAVES OF THE EARTH. 5 men, 2 women, extras. Plays 25 minutes. Exterior set. For junior and senior high. Safety from the atom bomb is to be had for two of every kind in the cave. The selected children refuse to enter, realizing that the only true security is in international understanding and brotherhood. Plays, Inc., 50¢.

CELEBRATING CHRISTMAS, edited by Edna M. Cahill. Plays, worship services, pantomimes, exercises, games, etc. For adults, children. Serious and festive. Baker's Plays, $1.25.

CELESTIAL ERROR, by Patricia Brooks. 8 women. Five women are judged in the forecourt of heaven, and are sent on to paradise or back to earth on the basis of the lives they have led. One act. H. F. W. Deane & Sons, 1*s*. 9*d*. net. Postage, 2*d*.

THE CELL, by John Kirn. Christians await their deaths in the Roman arena. One act. Broadman Press, 50¢.

THE CENTURION'S SERVANT, by Dorothy Clarke Wilson. 6 men, 3 women. The young centurion of Capernaum seeks a lasting faith, and accepts Christ. In *Twelve Months of Drama for the Average Church*. Baker's Plays, $2.95.

A CERTAIN JUST MAN, by Anne Coulter Martens. 3 men, 4 women. Plays 20 minutes. God judges a "just" man on the basis of his actions during the last hour of his life. Eldridge, 50¢ (purchase of 7 copies required).

A CERTAIN MAN HAD TWO SONS, by Robert Finch. 3 men, 2 women. Plays 30 minutes. A modern retelling of the parable of the prodigal son. Baker's Plays, 50¢.

A CERTAIN STAR, by Frank Cooper. 2 men, 3 women, optional choir. Plays 25 minutes. A group of watchers on a rooftop near Bethlehem pass a strange night. Taken from the idea that nothing evil could happen on the night of Christ's birth. Baker's Plays, 60¢. Royalty: none if 5 copies purchased.

THE CHALK CIRCLE, anonymous, translated by Ethel Van der Veer. 18 men (doubling possible), 6 women, 5 boys. The sufferings of innocence, and the eventual triumph of love, in an old Chinese play of the thirteenth and fourteenth century. Simple to stage, yet difficult to perform. In *World Drama,* Vol. I. Dover Publications. Royalty: apply to publisher.

THE CHALK GARDEN, by Enid Bagnold. 2 men, 7 women. Characters clash when an English gentlewoman gives herself to gardening other people's lives. For advanced players. Samuel French, Inc., $1 (production restricted). Royalty: $50.

THE CHALLENGE OF THE CROSS, by Charles A. Marsh. 7 women, choir. Plays 25 minutes. An evangelistic appeal: there is no salvation save in the cross. For Easter, other religious observances. Baker's Plays, 50¢.

THE CHANCEL LILY, by Harriet Faust and Margaret Miner. 4 boys, 3 girls, 8 extras for tableaux, full choir if desired. An Easter play in two acts with ten shadow tableaux. May be adjusted to fit group. Baker's Plays, 35¢.

THE CHANUKO PARADE, by Lillian S. Freehof. 3 girls, 7 boys. For ages 12–14. Children dream that their toys of historical figures come to life. Union of American Hebrew Congregations, 25¢.

THE CHANUKO PLAY, by Minna L. Stoller. 4 men, 2 women, 1 child. For ages 12–14. School setting; no costumes required. Points up our freedoms, particularly religious freedom. Union of American Hebrew Congregations, 25¢.

THE CHERRY ORCHARD, by Anton Chekhov, English version by Sir John Gielgud. Introduction by Michel Saint-Denis. Stage directions included. Heinemann Educational Books, 6*s.* 6*d.* net.

THE CHERRY ORCHARD, by Anton Chekhov, translated by Stark Young. 10 men, 5 women. 2 interior sets, 1 exterior set. The contrast of old and new social forces in Russia have been caught in the characters of this masterpiece. Varying backgrounds keep the characters from reaching one another as human beings. Very difficult, very beautiful. Samuel French, Inc., $1.25. Royalty: $25–$20.

THE CHESTER MIRACLE PLAYS, by I. and O. Bolton King. SPCK.

THE CHESTER MYSTERY PLAYS, edited by Maurice Hussey. Sixteen medieval mystery plays, including production notes, stage directions, and introduction to medieval drama. Heinemann Educational Books, 8*s.* 6*d.* net.

A CHILD FOR A KING, by Arthur C. Risser. Flexible cast. Plays 45–50 minutes. Choric pageant of the birth of Jesus, the events leading up to it, and the magi, with modern reflections. Baker's Plays, 60¢. Royalty: $5.

A CHILD IS BORN, by Stephen Vincent Benét. 4 men, 2 women. Plays 30 minutes. Interior set. A modern Nativity drama, centering about the story of the innkeeper and his wife. Originally broadcast by NBC with Alfred Lunt and Lynn Fontanne in the leading roles. Baker's Plays, 75¢. Music, 75¢. Royalty: $10.

THE CHILD OF PEACE, by Edith H. Willis and Edith Ellsworth. 1 or 2 narrators, chorus or solo voices. Plays 40 minutes. The birth of Christ told from the viewpoint of the experiences of Mary. Original carols, scripture responses, optional tableaux. Baker's Plays, $1. Royalty: $5.

THE CHILDREN, by Minta Meier. 20 children, speech choir. The children's feelings about Jesus, who "never broke a promise." Requires care in directing. Coach House Press, 90¢. Royalty: $10.

THE CHILDREN ARE LISTENING, by Barbara Kay Davidson. Play about racial prejudice. Nat'l. Conference of Christians and Jews. Perusal script, $2 (purchase of kit of 6 copies required).

THE CHILDREN FROM GALILEE, by Gladys Wiles. For advanced children's groups. Religious Drama Society of Great Britain (apply to publisher for price).

THE CHILDREN HEAR ABOUT EASTER, by Francis H. Underwood. 9 boys, 8 girls. Plays 25 minutes. Interior set. New Testament stories told as children would tell them while playing together. Baker's Plays, 60¢.

CHILDREN OF GOD, by Marshall Stedman. 1 woman, 1 girl, 1 boy. Plays 20 minutes. Tenement children seeking help at the missions learn that God does not forget, while a social worker learns another lesson. Banner Play Bureau, 50¢ (purchase of 3 copies required).

CHILDREN OF OTHER LANDS, by Karin Asbrand. Five plays with settings in Sweden, Norway, Holland, France, and Italy. Baker's Plays, $1.

CHILDREN OF THE BIBLE. Plays 15–20 minutes. A Bible message for children to present. One act, with production suggestions. In *Bible Plays for Children.* Concordia, 40¢. Set, $3.

CHILDREN OF THE GOOD SHEPHERD, by Irene Caudwell. 17 characters in 5 scenes. A Passion play for children in modern language. Simple yet effective dramatization. Faith Press, 2*s.* 6*d.*

THE CHILDREN OF THE INN, by Jewell B. Tull. 12 men, 5 women. Plays 25 minutes. The story of those who refused a place for the Christchild. Dramatic Publishing Co., 40¢.

THE CHILDREN'S PROGRAM BOOK, by Karin S. Asbrand. Playlets, games, verses, exercises, etc., with particular selections for special days, including Christmas, Easter, Mother's Day. Baker's Plays, $1.25.

THE CHILDREN'S VISION, by Esther W. Bates. Girls, 12 women, choir. Plays 30 minutes. Three children in their sorrow see a vision of angels in the garden of Joseph. Pageant. Pageant, 40¢.

CHIMES ON THE HILLTOP, by Charlotte D. Widrig. Flexible cast of 15–50. A Christmas skit with music presenting an old-fashioned Sunday school party. In *Jumbo Christmas Book.* Baker's Plays, $1.25.

THE CHINESE WALL, by Max Frisch, translated by James L. Rosenberg. A spectacular spoof on controversial values involving characters from diverse ages. Hill & Wang. Royalty: apply to Kurt Hellmer.

A CHOICE TO MAKE, by Nora Stirling. Problem of personal responsibility in conflict of change. Family Service Assoc. of America. Perusal script, $2; kit of 6 acting scripts, $12.

CHOIRS OF GOD, by Leota Hulse Black. 1 man, 1 woman, 1 boy, choir. Plays 15 minutes. An old flower woman's Christmas, in carols to be sung or spoken by a choir or reader. Baker's Plays, 75¢.

CHORAL SPEAKING ARRANGEMENTS FOR THE JUNIOR HIGH, by Louise Abney. Expression, $1.75.

CHORAL SPEAKING ARRANGEMENTS FOR THE LOWER GRADES, by Abney and Rowe. Expression, $1.50.

CHORAL SPEAKING ARRANGEMENTS FOR THE UPPER GRADES, by Louise Abney. Expression, $1.50.

CHORAL VERSE SPEAKING, by Elizabeth Keppie. Expression, $3.25.

CHRIST CRUCIFIED, by Margaret Cropper. Scenes centering around the Passion, and commented on by five angels who reveal moments not understood by those on the human stage. Baker's Plays, 60¢. Royalty: $5.

CHRIST IN THE CONCRETE CITY, by Philip Turner. 4 men, 2 women. Plays 1 hour. Written by an Anglican priest in an industrial parish, the play relates the Passion of Christ for an audience typical of the parish. From a stage bare except for a central rostrum, the actors play interchangeable historical personalities and characters from their own lives. Baker's Plays, 85¢. Royalty: $15.

CHRIST IS RISEN, by N. B. Dexter. 3 men, 2 women, mixed extras for mob scene. Plays 30 minutes. A modern dramatic service concerning the problems of young people reveals the real meaning of the risen Christ. Baker's Plays, 60¢.

CHRIST THE LORD IS RISEN TODAY, by Robert Faust Schaeffer. Large cast. The pilgrimage from the home of Salome to the tomb. May be elaborately or simply presented. Baker's Plays, 60¢.

THE CHRIST-CHILD, by Irene Caudwell. 19 characters. Four scenes and an interlude. Faith Press, 1*s.* 6*d.*

CHRISTIAN FAMILY BROWN, by Dorothy Clarke Wilson. 1 man, 2 women, 3 boys, 2 girls. Interior set. The Christian ideal of home life is dramatized by a series of episodes in the life of the Brown family. Baker's Plays, 60¢.

CHRISTMAS AND THE FOUR FREEDOMS, by Otis Carrington. Plays 30 minutes. Fifth to ninth grades. No special scenery. Costuming simple. Combines spiritual and patriotic feelings. Eldridge, $1.25 (purchase of 4 copies required).

THE CHRISTMAS ANGEL, by Mrs. Albert Hodgman. 3 men, 4 women, 3 boys, 3 girls. Plays 30 minutes. A white angel for a manger unites an orphaned child with his aunt. Eldridge, 50¢ (purchase of 10 copies required).

THE CHRISTMAS ANGEL, by Peg Lynch. 7 men, 2 women. Interior set. Based on the Ethel and Albert comedy radio and television series. Albert's guilty conscience traps him into becoming an angel in the parsonage Christmas pageant. Baker's Plays, 60¢. Royalty: $10.

THE CHRISTMAS ANGELS, by Martha Mixer. On Christmas Eve, two angels seek those worthy to see Christ. Suggestion for use with gauze curtain, special lighting for beautiful effect. In *Transparent Curtain Pageants for Christmas.* Baker's Plays, $1.25.

THE CHRISTMAS APPLE, by Ruth Sawyer, adapted by Margaret D. Williams. 6 men, 6 women. Plays 30 minutes. 2 interior sets. Baker's Plays, 60¢.

CHRISTMAS AT CASEY'S, by Jessie M. Ford. 3 men, 3 women. Plays 12 minutes. A short farce that maintains the Christmas spirit. Christmas rush breeds thoughtlessness, and uncoordinated thoughtfulness breeds comic results. Eldridge, 50¢ (purchase of 6 copies required).

CHRISTMAS AT CHECKPOINT CHARLIE, by John W. Felton. 1 man, 1 woman, 1 girl (about 10 years). Plays 30 minutes. Exterior set. Two GI guards risk their lives to reunite a German family. The Christmas story of a child emerges against the cold and tenseness of the modern setting. Baker's Plays, 60¢. Royalty: $5.

CHRISTMAS AT 400 GREEN ST., by Gail White. Plays 30 minutes. Understanding and the spirit of Christmas reunite a family of four sisters, thanks to the efforts of their old aunt. Eldridge, 60¢.

CHRISTMAS AT GRECCIO, by Sister Mary Francis, P.C. 6 men, 2 women, 1 child. Exterior set. Drawn from the life of Francis, who resolves the problems about him while completing the creation of the first Christmas crib. Samuel French, Inc., 60¢. Royalty: $5.

CHRISTMAS AT HOME, by Joseph Hayes. 3 men, 4 women. Interior set. The Burgess family, preparing for Christmas on the day before, realize that this will be the first year that all the family will not be there. A series of scenes affect different family members, and the real Christmas meaning is learned by Janet, twelve years old. Samuel French, Inc., 60¢. Royalty: $5.

CHRISTMAS AT MOTHER'S, by Agnes Curtis. 3 men, 7 women or teen-age children. Plays 20 minutes. Interior set. A mother's collapse at Christmastime frightens her children out of their thoughtless ways. T. S. Denison & Co., 50¢ (purchase of 6 copies required).

CHRISTMAS AT THE CROSSROADS, by Henri Brochet. 3 men, 4 women. A modern Nativity play of three short acts, set in France against the ruins of war. A combination of realism and fancy, humor and a spirit of reverence. In *St. Anne and the Gouty Rector and Other Plays.* McKay's Plays, $2.75. Royalty: $10.

CHRISTMAS AT THE GABLES, by Lidian Moore. 6 women. Plays 20 minutes. Interior set. A "family" of spinsters are upset by a newcomer, but reunited at Christmas. Samuel French, Inc., 60¢. Royalty: $5.

CHRISTMAS AT THE SURPRISE TREE, by Beverly Quint. 2 adults, 5 children. Plays 25 minutes. Interior set. Modern family situation at Christmas, with a theme of brotherly love. Abingdon, 25¢. Package, 25.

A CHRISTMAS AWAKENING, by Katherine A. Cutler. 4 men, 3 women. Plays 25 minutes. Interior set. A little girl and a grandfather retain the spirit of Christmas in a household otherwise devoid of it. Carols included in play. T. S. Denison & Co., 50¢ (purchase of 4 copies required).

CHRISTMAS BARRICADE, by Paul S. McCoy. 4 men, 4 women. Interior set. The magic of the Christmas season helps solve the problems of the passengers of a stranded bus. T. S. Denison & Co., 50¢ (purchase of 8 copies required).

THE CHRISTMAS BAZAAR, by Zoe Hartman and Harold Wansborough. 5 boys, 8 girls, chorus. An operetta of the difficulties of two little waifs and their happy solution. Baker's Plays, $1.25 (purchase of 10 copies required).

CHRISTMAS BELLS, by Bettie Severin and Marian Moser. Variable cast. Plays 30 minutes. A Christmas meditation, particularly good for service clubs. Music and readings. Heuer, $1.

THE CHRISTMAS BOOK. Collection of drama and music, well-suited to an evening entertainment. Nat'l. Recreation Assoc. 75¢.

THE CHRISTMAS BOOK FOR THE GRADES, by various authors. Recitations, monologues, plays, etc. Baker's Plays, $1.

CHRISTMAS CAKE, by Bonnie Belshe. 3 men, 3 women, 1 boy. Plays 25 minutes. A boy is determined that Jesus should have a birthday party and cake, and his parents learn a lesson from carols, the manger scene, and a reading of the story of Christmas. Eldridge, 60¢ (purchase of 6 copies required).

A CHRISTMAS CAROL, by Charles Dickens, adapted by G. M. Baker. 6 men, 3 women. Plays 1 hour. Dramatization of the famous Dickens story. Simple staging, yet maintains the spirit of the original. Baker's Plays, 60¢.

A CHRISTMAS CAROL, by Charles Dickens, adapted by Fred Garrigus.

18 characters (doubling possible). Plays 30 minutes. Radio version of Dickens' story with musical interludes. Baker's Plays, 60¢ (mention radio version).

A CHRISTMAS CAROL, by Charles Dickens, adapted by Cora Wilson Greenwood. 8 men, 6 women. Plays 1 hour. The Dickens story in nine scenes connected by a commentator. Samuel French, Inc., 60¢.

A CHRISTMAS CAROL, by John Wallace, Jr. Large cast, male and female. Four scenes, the second containing a series of tableaux. Abel Heywood & Son.

THE CHRISTMAS CAROL, by Harold G. Sliker. Cast may use as many as 50, few speaking roles, even division of male and female roles. Three short acts, no waits. Baker's Plays, 60¢. Royalty: none if 10 copies purchased.

CHRISTMAS COMES TO OLD GROUCH, by Martha Mixer. The Old Grouch sees visions of Christ in her unexpected meeting with a child. In *Transparent Curtain Pageants for Christmas.* Baker's Plays, $1.25.

A CHRISTMAS CRUSADE, by John Houston. 18 speaking parts, optional extras. Plays 1 hour. A pageant play. A boy's simple plan for world peace wins the prize offered by the Archbishop of London. Baker's Plays, 60¢. Royalty: none if 10 copies purchased.

THE CHRISTMAS DRAMA BOOK, edited by Irene Gass. For ages 9–12. George G. Harrap & Co., 10*s*. 6*d*. net.

CHRISTMAS DRAMATIC PRELUDE, by Isabel Kimball Whiting. Large cast. Story of the birth of Christ against its biblical background. In *Jumbo Christmas Book*. Baker's Plays, $1.25.

CHRISTMAS EVE LETTER. 4 girls, 3 boys, extras. Plays 30 minutes. The *New York Sun*'s famous letter to Virginia dramatized. Plays, Inc., 50¢.

CHRISTMAS EVE NEWS. 18 men, 9 women, extras. Plays 25 minutes. A newsboy learns that he is selling the greatest news in the world when, to bring Christmas to his family, he must sell papers headlining the Christmas story. Plays, Inc., 50¢.

THE CHRISTMAS EVE VISITOR, by Renetta Baden. 30 or more boys and girls. Plays 30 minutes. Interior set. A child in Judean dress reveals the true Christmas gift to two modern children waiting for Santa. Includes a biblical pageant of the events leading to Christ's birth. T. S. Denison & Co., 50¢ (purchase of 10 copies required).

CHRISTMAS EVERYWHERE, by Edna Worrell. A pageant of Christmas, presenting other countries' customs through tableaux and carols. Eldridge, 60¢.

CHRISTMAS FAITH, by Ilva Walker. 4 women, 1 girl. Plays 20 minutes. A group of mothers, their daughters hospitalized, bring faith in the future to the nurses. A different aspect of Christmas faith. Eldridge, 60¢ (purchase of 5 copies required).

THE CHRISTMAS FESTIVAL BOOK, by Lenore Hetrick, Maud C. C. Jackson, Beatrice M. Casey, and others. Plays, dialogues, monologues, pantomimes, etc. For intermediate and upper grammar grades. Baker's Plays, $1.

CHRISTMAS FOR THE MIDDLE GRADES, by Dorothy M. Shipman, Willis N. Bugbee, and others. Varied program materials. Baker's Plays, $1.

CHRISTMAS FROLICS, by Germaine Haney. Collection for grammar grades, including monologues, dialogues, tableaux, etc. Baker's Plays, $1.

CHRISTMAS FUN IN '91, by Barbara Eanes. 14 boys, 6 girls, extras. Grandpa learns that the true spirit of Christmas still exists on a Christmas Eve in the gay '90's. Three acts. Baker's Plays, $1.40 (purchase of 5 copies required).

CHRISTMAS GIFT FOR NANCY, by Dorothy C. Allen. 2 women, 1 boy. Plays 25 minutes. Interior set. Left an invalid by an accident, a woman finds courage in the coming of the Christmas spirit. Baker's Plays, 60¢.

A CHRISTMAS GIFT FROM HEAVEN, by Virginia Mitchell. 6 women. Interior set. The coming of a foundling baby turns a morbid Christmas merry. Modern setting; three acts. Samuel French, Inc., 60¢. Royalty: $5.

THE CHRISTMAS GIFTS, by Dorothy Lehman Sumerau. 3 men, 4 women. Plays 25–30 minutes. The Christmas spirit and "unwanted" gifts come to life, teaching Alice the meaning of giving gifts from the heart. For inspiration. Eldridge, 60¢ (purchase of 7 copies required).

THE CHRISTMAS GUEST, by J. R. Clemens. 5 men, 4 women. Plays 30 minutes. Interior set. A strange "guest" gives a blind girl sight in return for hospitality on Christmas Eve. Baker's Plays, 60¢.

CHRISTMAS HOMECOMING, by Grace Sorenson. 3 boys, 5 girls. Plays 30 minutes. Interior set. A brother and sister, with their children, return to their ancestral home and have an old quarrel settled by the sentiment of Christmas. In *Merry Little Plays for Children.* Baker's Plays, $1.25.

CHRISTMAS IN ART. A program built around posings of famous religious paintings. With musical background, readings. Only single rehearsal required. In *Celebrating Christmas.* Baker's Plays, $1.25.

CHRISTMAS IN COVENTRY, by Franklin P. Cole. 4 men, 3 women, extras. Plays 40 minutes. Includes a service of worship. A typical family is seen on a Christmas Eve a few weeks after the bombing of their city, contrasting the brutality of the modern world with Christianity. Baker's Plays, 60¢. Royalty: first performance, none; $2.50 each repeat.

CHRISTMAS IN REVIEW, by Clarence J. Styza. Flexible time and cast, with passages for glee club. Varied, popular, and different Christmas program. Heuer, 60¢ (acting rights with purchase of 5 copies).

CHRISTMAS IN THE HEART, by Esther Bostrom. A flexible play for primary through sixth grades, or primary and intermediate church school. Sheila learns the true meaning of Christmas. Manger scene, few lines and short speeches, familiar carols. Eldridge, 50¢.

CHRISTMAS IN THE MARKET PLACE, by Henri Gheon, English version by Eric Crozier. 3 men, 2 women, extras. Exterior set. A Nativity play. A family of strolling gypsy players present their own simple version of the Nativity, each player changing roles as demanded by the story. Baker's Plays, $1.25. Royalty: $10.

CHRISTMAS INCORPORATED, by Walter Kerr. 6 women, 1 child. A child shows a department store clerk where the true meaning of Christmas may be found. Baker's Plays, 60¢. Royalty: $5.

CHRISTMAS INSIDE, by Winifred Bell Fletcher. Variable cast. The Littlest Angel makes her journey to earth and teaches the earth children that happiness lies in having Christmas inside. For lower grades. Baker's Plays, 60¢.

CHRISTMAS IS A MIRACLE, by Joyce Vernon Drake. Variable cast (doubling possible in small parts). Plays 40 minutes. A faithful old caretaker shows a crippled boy a miracle of the mystery of the first Christmas in an abandoned church. Baker's Plays, 60¢.

CHRISTMAS IS A RACKET, by Austin Cook. 2 men, 4 women. Plays 30 minutes. Interior set. Comedy of a family who, feeling Christmas commercialized, decide not to celebrate; at the last minute they confess their celebration plans. Baker's Plays, 60¢.

CHRISTMAS IS COMING, by Siegmeister and Wheeler. Plays 25 minutes; may be shortened by omission of verses or whole carols. A festive cantata for mixed chorus, narrator, piano, and (optional) instrumental accompaniment. Combination of customs, traditions, and story of Christmas. Eldridge, $1.25 (give authors' names when ordering).

CHRISTMAS IS NOW, by Jacqueline Soans. Large cast. Plays 30 minutes. Interior set. A beggar girl, taken on a journey by an angel to learn the meaning of Christmas, learns love for the first time from the Christchild. Baker's Plays, 60¢.

CHRISTMAS JEWELS, by Karin Asbrand. Play with music for grade school children. Grandparents, fairies, and the Christmas jewels teach the meaning of Christmas to some children. Eldridge, 50¢.

THE CHRISTMAS JOY BOOK. Includes tableaux, pantomimes, dialogues, pageant, etc. For all ages; includes sacred as well as gift-giving emphasis. Eldridge, $1.

THE CHRISTMAS LAMB, by Agnes Emelie Peterson. 1 man, 3 women, 1 boy, several boy and girl extras. Time flexible. Exterior set. From a tradition followed for centuries in Provence. The finest lamb is presented at the crèche during midnight Mass in memory of the shepherds' gifts at the first Christmas. In two scenes. Baker's Plays, 60¢.

A CHRISTMAS LEGEND, by Christine Turner Curtis. 1 man, 2 women, 2 boys, 1 girl. Plays 30 minutes. Interior set. Two poor children unknowingly entertain the Christchild. Baker's Plays, 60¢.

CHRISTMAS LIVES, by Ruth H. Gefvert. 1 woman, 3 children. Plays 20 minutes. A mother telling the Christmas story to her children gives them a mental picture of Christmas in other lands. In *The Easy Christmas Grab Bag*. Baker's Plays, $1.25.

CHRISTMAS MEMORIES, by Esther E. Olson. 3 main characters, offstage chorus. A program of well-loved Christmas carols, set in a modern home. Playing time varies according to number of carols used. Baker's Plays, 60¢.

CHRISTMAS NOVELTIES, by Arthur L. Kaser and Agnes D. Hays. A collection of light Christmas presentations, many in the Santa Claus mood. Baker's Plays, $1.25.

CHRISTMAS ON CLOUD 25, by Merry Anne Gregory and Lois Gurske. An operetta for the elementary grades. The story of Christmas brought to the heavenly realm, told by pink, white, and blue angels. Easy to stage and costume. With staging instructions. Eldridge, $1.40 (purchase of 7 copies required).

CHRISTMAS ON MAIN STREET, by Walt Draper. 2 men, 2 women, extras. Plays 35 minutes. Interior set. Billy, a cripple, cannot attend church; his mother reads him an old legend, and he sees the first Christmas presented in pantomime. A fantasy. Baker's Plays, 60¢. Royalty: $5.

CHRISTMAS ON THE VILLAGE SQUARE, by Henri Gheon, English version by Sister Marie Thomas, O.P. Large cast. Exterior set. A family of strolling players present their own simple version of the Christmas story, changing roles according to the demands of the story. A three-act Nativity. Baker's Plays, 75¢. Royalty: $10 if admission is charged; $5 if not.

THE CHRISTMAS PARTY, by Dorothy Daily. 3 men, 2 women. Plays 25 minutes. Fellowship results when a Puerto Rican woman brings her neighbors together at a Christmas party. Friendship Press, 50¢.

CHRISTMAS PLAYS, by Agnes Curtis. Ten plays for teen-agers, suitable for a church recreational evening. T. S. Denison & Co., 75¢.

CHRISTMAS PLAYS, edited by Cyril Swinson. Four plays to interest children aged 7–10, three of which center on the Nativity theme. Baker's Plays, 75¢. Royalty: 2 plays free; 2 at $2.50 each performance.

CHRISTMAS PLAYS AND PROGRAMS, by Aileen Fisher. Plays, choral readings, poems, etc., both festive and spiritual, traditional and modern. For lower grades through senior high. Eldridge, $5.

CHRISTMAS PLAYS FOR WOMEN AND GIRLS. Eight plays for all-women casts, one large flexible cast, others two to six players. All comedies (except for religious Christmas play, "One Christmas Eve") with twenty-minute playing time and a cast of five women for each. Baker's Plays, $1.25.

CHRISTMAS PLAYS FOR YOUNG ACTORS, edited by A. S. Burack. Twenty-six plays—serious, fantastic, historic, and comic—including two versions of Dickens' *A Christmas Carol.* For children. Plays, Inc., $4.50.

CHRISTMAS PRESENT, by Molly Raynor. 6 women. A lonely and self-pitying young girl finds friends and herself on Christmas Eve. Christmas atmosphere and humorous moments. Office setting. English Theatre Guild, 2*s.*

CHRISTMAS PROGRAMS FOR THE CHURCH. Four complete Christmas programs. "From the Cradle to the Cross," a tableau in six scenes, including scripture and song; "Christmas and You"; "Christmas in Word and Song"; and "The Spirit of Christmas." Eldridge, $1.

CHRISTMAS RECAPTURED. 4 men, 4 women. Plays 30 minutes. A family's Christmas mishaps and happiness. For junior and senior high. Plays, Inc., 50¢.

CHRISTMAS REVELS, by Ray and Pat Darby. A school production utilizing, in episodes, all grades from first to eighth. Extremely flexible, educational features to tie with curriculum, provides projects for the children. Eldridge, 60¢ (purchase of 5 copies required).

THE CHRISTMAS STAR, by Helen Lowrie. Large cast. The Christmas star once more brings its message to the children of earth in memory of Christ, Prince of Peace. In *Jumbo Christmas Book.* Baker's Plays, $1.25.

A CHRISTMAS STAR FOR OLGA, by Barbara Webb. 7 women. Plays 30 minutes. Interior set. Three girls plan to make a mockery of the Christmas season until Olga, a maid, gives vindication to Christmas by transforming a poor gift into a thing of tender beauty, thus softening their hearts. Baker's Plays, 60¢.

CHRISTMAS STORY, by Lenora Ashton. 3 girls, 4 boys. Characters come to life as a boy reads the Christmas story to his sister. T. S. Denison & Co., 50¢ (purchase of 5 copies required).

THE CHRISTMAS STORY, by Ruth Adkinson and Pearl Booth. Plays 30 minutes. Three-character prologue: small boy, small girl, grandmother; Nativity characters, innkeeper for pageant. Little or no setting needed. With music. Eldridge, 60¢.

THE CHRISTMAS STORY, by Norman Nygaard. 15 characters, choir. A parallel in pageant of the biblical narrative, a narrator extending it to the events preceding and following Christ's birth. In *The Bible Comes Alive*. Baker's Plays, $1.25.

THE CHRISTMAS STRANGER, by Charles Emery. 1 man, 5 women. Plays 30 minutes. Interior set. A stranger brings previously unknown happiness to a small New England family. Baker's Plays, 60¢. Royalty: $5.

THE CHRISTMAS TREE, by Ngaio Marsh. 3 adult voices, children portraying characters in the Nativity scene. A Christmas tree in the chancel is the focal point, as the children decorate it and learn its significance. Carols interspersed. Baker's Plays, 60¢. Royalty: $5.

CHRISTMAS TREE FOREST, by Ramond Alden, adapted by Isabel S. Clark. 11 characters, extras. A morality play in three acts. The children find Santa's gifts in the Christmas tree forest only when they seek them to give one another. From the story "In the Great Walled Country." Samuel French, Inc., 60¢. Royalty: $5.

CHRISTMAS UNUSUAL, by Pearl Nielson. 4 men, 2 women. Interior set. The McIlroy family enriches the lives of lonely guests they have invited to spend Christmas with them. Art Craft, 60¢ (purchase of 5 copies required).

THE CHRISTMAS VISITOR, by F. E. M. Agnew. 7 women. The author of a newspaper advice column resolves a problem with her daughter in spite of the advice of her Christmas guests, and with the aid of the Christmas Visitor, and learns that age is not the only measure of maturity. English Theatre Guild.

THE CHRISTMAS VOICE, by Ruth O. Bailey. 4 boys, 7 girls, extras. Plays 30 minutes. Interior set. Young people receive a Christmas Visitor whom they do not recognize, but who leaves their lives fuller and less selfish. Baker's Plays, 50¢.

CHRISTMAS WINDOWS, by M. Christenson and F. M. Frick. 25 boys and girls. Plays 40 minutes. A poor child looking in windows at Christmas time. Five tableaux joined by narrator. Dramatic Publishing Co., 40¢.

THE CHRISTMASING OF JASPER, by James Blakeley. 3 men, 5 women, carolers, etc. Plays 45 minutes. Jasper Crowley's house staff show him that a change of personality is needed if he is to hold friends. Eldridge, 60¢ (purchase of 6 copies required).

CHRISTUS REX, by H. M. Lloyd. Bible readings in a series designed for dramatization during Holy Week. Baker's Plays, 85¢.

CHURCH BELLS, by Esther C. Averill. 4 men, 3 women. Plays 30 minutes. Interior set. A hectic Sunday morning becomes, with the sounding of the church bells, one of realization and return to the path of happiness for the Morrill family. Baker's Plays, 60¢.

THE CHURCH CLINIC, by E. B. Wilson. 2 men, 10 women. Plays 1 hour. Church weaknesses are diagnosed, then cured, in humorous fashion. Eldridge, 60¢ (purchase of 6 copies required).

CHURCH FOR SALE, by Paul Allen. Large cast of men and women. Plays 40 minutes. Exterior set. The townspeople realize how much their church means to them when it is put up for sale. Baker's Plays, 60¢.

THE CIRCLE BEYOND FEAR, by Darius Swann. 6 men, 6 women. Plays 30 minutes. A choral drama. The great commission to preach the gospel is provocatively treated. Friendship Press. Royalty: none.

CIRCUS, PARABLE, AND CONSTRUCTION, by Ralph W. Stone. Problems of modern women, seen against the fantasy of a circus. These plays were especially written for women's fellowship groups. Bethany Press, $1. Royalty: none if no admission charged.

CLERAMBARD, by Marcel Aymé, translated by Norman Penny. 7 men, 7 women. A miracle of Francis of Assisi transforms an impoverished French nobleman from hardness, pride, and eccentricity to love, humility, and eccentricity. Tone is comic and unrealistic. Multiple sets. Costume: upper class, 1910. Samuel French, Inc., $1.25. Royalty: $50–$25.

THE CLOTH OF SENDONY, by Elizabeth H. Emerson. 6 men, 2 women, 3–5 priests. Plays 1 hour. The crucifixion and resurrection as they affect the lives of a small band of people. Easily staged. Baker's Plays, 60¢.

A CLOUD OF WITNESSES, by Esther Willard Bates. 5 men, 7 women, singers. Three spirits of church members, invisible save to each other and the audience, return to participate in Resurrection Day service and convey their knowledge of immortality. Includes choir music and Bible verses. Baker's Plays, 60¢. Royalty: $5.

THE CLOUDED STAR, by John Purves. 6 women. Plays 30 minutes. Interior set. The innkeeper's wife knows there is something special about the child born in the stable next to her inn; he now must be taken away before dawn, or fall victim to the slaughter of the infants ordered by Herod. Baker's Plays, 60¢. Royalty: $5.

THE COAT OF MANY COLORS, by Effa E. Preston. 22 men, 12 women, 10 girl dancers. Plays 35 minutes. 2 interior sets, 1 exterior set. The story of Joseph, sold into slavery by his brothers. A play-pageant in nine scenes. T. S. Denison & Co., 50¢ (purchase of 9 copies required).

THE COCKTAIL PARTY, by T. S. Eliot. 6 men, 4 women. Plays 2 hours. 2 interior sets. Set in a sophisticated drawing room, the play holds levels of meaning from a comedy of manners to deep metaphysical and spiritual speculation. A strange linkage between a mysterious if eminent psychotherapist and two other characters suggests more than natural influence on the lives of these characters. Very difficult. Samuel French, Inc., $1.25. Royalty: $50.

COKESBURY CHRISTMAS PROGRAMS, compiled by Grace Chapin Auten. Three short, three full-length programs, five special services or programs; for children and young adults. Cokesbury Press, 40¢. Package, 25.

COKESBURY EASTER PROGRAMS, compiled by Grace Chapin Auten. For congregation and church school. Two pageants, suggestions for recitations, readings, etc. Baker's Plays, 45¢.

COLLECTED PLAYS OF YEATS. Includes "Sophocles' King Oedipus," "Sophocles' Odysseus at Colonus," "The Resurrection," and others. Macmillan, $6.

COLUMBINE MADONNA, by Glenn Hughes. 4 men, 1 woman. Set on stage of a theatre. A harlequinade. The characters attempt without success to plan their Christmas night play, until a foundling left at the stage door brings them to a deeper understanding of the meaning of Christmas. Baker's Plays, 60¢. Royalty: $5.

COME AND ADORE HIM. The Christmas story, told by the Voice of Scripture and the Interpreter, with familiar carols and optional tableaux. Eldridge, 50¢. Optional filmstrip, $5.

"COME, SEE THE PLACE . . ." by Mary Dickerson Bangham. 2 men, 4 women, 2 readers, extras (cast may vary). Plays 1 hour. Exterior set. Pageant. Combination of tableaux and hymns for Easter. No lines to memorize, minimal rehearsal requirements. Easy and inexpensive to produce. Baker's Plays, 60¢.

COME TO THE MANGER, by Mary Dickerson Bangham. 3 men, 1 woman, shepherds, wise men, several children, choir, organist, etc. Plays 90 minutes. Christmas music and drama unite in a pageant reliving the Christmas story. Baker's Plays, 60¢.

COME YE TO BETHLEHEM, by Irene Caudwell. 18 characters. Nativity play in nine scenes. For adults. Faith Press, 2*s*.

COME YE TO CALVARY, by Irene Caudwell. 18 characters. A sacred drama in ten scenes in the mystery and morality play tradition. Faith Press, 2*s*. 6*d*.

THE COMEDIAN, by Henri Gheon, translated by Alan Bland. 9 men, 3 women, extras. The Emperor Diocletian, bored with his theatre, commissions a play about Adrian, a Roman captain who became a Christian martyr. Striving to understand the role, the actor

Genesius himself becomes a Christian and a martyr. Sheed & Ward. Royalty: apply to publisher.

THE COMING OF CHRIST, by John Masefield. 13 men, 1 woman, chorus. Narrative, in verse and music, of the coming of Christ. Intended for large church and cathedral presentation. The author asks that the play not be used without the music. Baker's Plays, $1; music, $1.25. Royalty: $15; music, $4.

THE COMING OF THE KING, by the Right Rev. Cornelius J. Holland. 22 men, 1 woman, chorus, extras. Poem-play of the Nativity, including familiar music. With complete production notes, diagrams. For high school, adult groups. St. Anthony Guild Press, 75¢.

THE COMING OF THE PRINCE OF PEACE, by Clarence Dickenson. Plays 35 minutes. Nativity with ancient carols. H. W. Gray Co.: complete text, $1; music alone, 20¢.

THE COMMANDMENTS TODAY, by Mildred Good. Ten playlets, each three to five minutes in length, each an application of one of the Ten Commandments. Baker's Plays, $1.

THE COMMON TREASURE, by Robert H. Clausen. Plays 20 minutes. A Reformation pageant. Board of Parish Education, Lutheran Church—Missouri Synod, 20¢.

THE COMPLAINING ANGEL, book by Natalie E. White, lyrics and music by Miss White; J. D. Tumpane, Sr.; M. Francis, P.C.; A. J. Hope, C.S.C.; D. Birder. 8 women, 1 man, 14-woman chorus. 4 interior sets, 4 exterior sets. In this sequel to "Seven Nuns in Las Vegas," the guardian angel of a deceased Hollywood actress is reassigned to a nun, and finds her work no easier. Samuel French, Inc., $1.25. Royalty: apply to publisher.

CONQUEST IN BURMA, by Albert Johnson. 2 men (one playing various parts), 1 woman. Plays 30 minutes. A Drama Trio play. The struggles, pain, joy, and ideals of a husband and wife, Christian missionaries in Burma. Planned for presentation without stage setting and with few or no properties. Friendship Press, 75¢. Royalty: none for church and community performances.

CONSTRUCTION, by Ralph W. Stone. 6 men, 4 women. A builder of bridges in human relations faces crucifixion. Short one-act. In *Circus, Parable, and Construction.* Bethany Press, $1. Royalty: none if no admission charged.

CONTEMPORARY DRAMA, selected by E. Bradlee Watons and Benfield Pressey. Plays from Bernard Shaw through Christopher Fry, particularly good for church discussions. Charles Scribner's Sons, $2.

THE CONTRITE SPIRIT, by Alberta Hawse. 2 men, 3 women. Retelling of the story of Christ's birth from a new angle. Baker's Plays, 60¢ (purchase of 6 copies required).

COUNTED AS MINE, by Sister Mary Francis, P.C. 10 men, 2 women. 1 interior set, 2 exterior sets. The story of Our Lady of Guadalupe, in tableaux, scenes, and choruses (three acts). Our Lady, in the sixteenth century, appears to a South American peasant, and the miracle of roses blooming in the snow occurs. Samuel French, Inc., 75¢. Royalty: $10.

COVENTRY, by Joe Corrie. 3 men, 3 women. The reactions of the family, and others, when an individualistic workman becomes involved in a strike. One act. Evans Plays. Royalty: 25*s.* 2*d.* net.

COVENTRY NATIVITY PLAY, adapted by I. Lee Warner. 14 men, 9 women. Plays 40 minutes. Biblical costuming. An adaptation from the Coventry Nativity play in the Everyman edition, particularly good for schools and churches. Baker's Plays, 60¢.

COVENTRY PORCH PLAYS. Intended for those indifferent to the church; meant to persuade, shock, or intrigue them into questioning. Includes "This Is the End," "The Site," "Who Is There to Ask?" Baker's Plays, $1.25. Royalty: $10 each play.

THE CRADLE, by Alberta Hawse. 3 men, 4 women. A wealthy man, Eden ben Judah, guards an elaborate cradle for the coming of the Messiah, while he personally becomes selfish, ill-tempered, and begins to lose the friendship and love of those around him. His friends try to convince him that the Messiah might prefer to be born simply among the poor. Eldridge, 60¢ (purchase of 7 copies required).

A CRADLE OF WILLOW, by Dorothy Wright. 7 men, 3 women. A beautiful and timeless play. The basket weavers, living their everyday lives, are witnesses to the Nativity; a blind man is cured and spirits raised. Culminates in a scene of great power. Three acts. Evans Plays, $1.25. Royalty: $50–$25.

THE CRADLE SONG, by G. Martinez-Sierra, English version by John Garrett Underhill. 4 men, 10 women, extras. 2 interior sets. A child, brought to a convent where she grows up, brings tenderness into the lives of the nuns. Very beautiful. Baker's Plays, $1.25. Royalty: $50.

THE CRATCHITS' CHRISTMAS DINNER, by Charles Dickens. 1 man, 1 woman, 3 boys, 3 girls. Plays 25 minutes. Interior set. From *A Christmas Carol.* The Cratchits' Christmas meal culminating in the toast to Mr. Scrooge. For youngsters. Baker's Plays, 60¢.

THE CRIB AT GRECCIO, by Irma A. Clarke. Built around the tradition that Francis of Assisi gave the first manger scene to the people of the little town of Greccio. A Christmas masque. Baker's Plays, 75¢ (purchase of 10 copies required).

THE CRICKET ON THE HEARTH, by Charles Dickens, adapted by John Wallace. 4 men, 5 women. Abel Heywood & Son.

THE CRIER CALLS, by Darius L. Swann. For speech choir. Two students are taken on a tour by the town crier, a symbol of conscience, and see depressed groups struggling in the world. Friendship Press: set of 10, $1.25 (purchase of 10 copies required).

CRIME BY PERSUASION, by Cyril J. Burton. 4 men, 2 women. Plays 40 minutes. Interior set. Explores the question of whether a criminal can be rehabilitated, under a proper prison system, and return to lead a completely honest life. Baker's Plays, 60¢. Royalty: $5.

CRITICS' CHOICE, edited by Jack Gaver. New York Drama Critics Circle prize plays for the years from 1935 to 1955. Hawthorn Books, $6.

THE CROSS OF CHALLENGE, by Ben C. Sweet. Intended as a pre-Easter presentation, the message is applicable to the entire church year, the presentation adaptable to all sanctuary facilities. Two acts. Baker's Plays, 35¢.

THE CROSS ON THE HILL, by Rega Kramer McCarthy. 6 adults, 3 young people, 2 children. Plays 1 hour. The power of Easter in the mind; the story of foreign missions, and of their need. Eldridge, 50¢ (purchase of 10 copies required).

CROSSES ON THE HILL, by Eula A. Lamphere. 15 men, 8 women. Mr. Herod, with the aid of Pontius Pilate, produces a pageant of the crucifixion to disprove Easter in Shadowville. So subtly done that no one is sure of his intent until his curtain falls at the end of the crucifixion scene. Mr. Herod himself is not free of emotional reaction to the re-created scenes. Baker's Plays, $1.25. Royalty: $25.

THE CROWN OF THORNS, by Elliot Field. 3 men, 2 women. Plays 30 minutes. The events of the crucifixion affect the lives of the family of Mordecai, member of the Sanhedrin. Baker's Plays, 60¢.

THE CRUCIBLE, by Arthur Miller. 10 men, 10 women. Plays full evening. Several interior sets. Powerful drama of the bigotry, passions, and personal vengeance involved in the Salem Witch Trials, with strongly implied parallels of modern purges. For advanced groups. Dramatists Play Service, $1. Royalty: $50–$25.

CRUSADER FOR THE DAY, by Helen Ramsey. Thanksgiving was nationalized in the 1850's through Sarah Hale. In *The Two-in-One Halloween-Thanksgiving Book*. Eldridge, 85¢.

CRY DAWN IN DARK BABYLON, by P. W. Turner. 4 men, 4 women. Chancel set. A dramatic meditation, in continuous action, on the Christian attitude toward death and the impact on the modern mind of the fact of death. Baker's Plays, $1.25. Royalty: $15.

CRY HAVOC, by Allen R. Kenward. 13 women. Plays full evening. Nurses of every kind under fire on Bataan. When they are rescued, it is only to face the firing squad. Samuel French, Inc., $1. Royalty: $50.

CRY, THE BELOVED COUNTRY, by Alan Paton, adapted by Felicia Komai. 15 men, 7 women, 2 boys, extras (doubling possible). The land can no longer hold Africa's youth. Powerful story. Three acts. Friendship Press: cloth, $1.50; paper, 75¢. Permission for production required; apply to publisher.

A CUP OF KINDNESS, by W. Gordon Mauermann. 3 men, 3 women. Plays 30 minutes. An antique dealer has a valuable book, sought by collectors both worthy and unworthy. Has much charm. Harper, 50¢. Royalty: $5.

THE CUP OF STRENGTH, by Joyce V. Drake. 6 women, 1 little girl. Plays 30 minutes. Interior set. A group of women airplane passengers, wrecked in a mountainous area, try to keep their optimism for the sake of the injured stewardess and a little girl. Explores faith, strength, selfishness, and their opposites, with focuses on both tragedy and humor. Baker's Plays, 60¢.

THE CUP OF TREMBLING, by Elizabeth Berryhill. 6 men, 2 women. Plays 2 hours. A modern play based on the life of Dietrich Bonhoeffer. Musical score arranged by author. Seabury Press. Royalty: apply to the author.

THE CUP OF TREMBLING, by Vivian Johannes. 11 men, 2 women, 1 boy, extras. Plays 90 minutes. The personal struggle of Pilate, with application to modern times. For advanced players. Two acts. Baker's Plays, 85¢. Royalty: $25.

THE CURATE'S PLAY, by Nathaniel Banks. 4 men, 2 women, 12 children. Short play. Poverty-stricken pregnant woman appears at a rehearsal of a children's Christmas play and gives birth to her child. With tableaux and choral music. One act. Dramatists Play Service, 75¢. Royalty: $25.

THE CURSE AND THE CROWN, by Gleness M. McCourt. 3 men, 2 women. A cynical, bitter Roman soldier, appointed one of those to crucify Christ, makes the crown of thorns; he finds belief in the moment of the crucifixion. Two short acts. Eldridge, 60¢ (purchase of 5 copies required).

CYMBALS IN THE MARKETPLACE, by Lucille J. Little. The story of Christ's birth as observed by two kitchen maids in the inn. Three scenes. Bethany Press, 50¢.

CYPRIAN, by Freda Collins. Large cast. The story, in three acts, of Cyprian's martyrdom during the third century. Religious Drama Society of Great Britain, 35¢. Royalty: approximately $5.92.

THE DANCING DOLL DECIDES, by Joyce Pilgrim. Large cast. A letter from a sick little girl to Santa changes the mind of the dancing doll about going in Santa's pack. In *Jumbo Christmas Book*. Baker's Plays, $1.25.

DANIEL AND THE TEMPTER, by Robert H. Clausen. In modern and biblical settings, the conflict for young people between moral values and conformity is explored. One act. Broadman Press, 75¢.

THE DARK DAYS, by Carl Delozier. 7 men, 6 women. Interior set. The last eight days of Christ's life, from his entry into Jerusalem through the resurrection. Three acts. Baker's Plays, 75¢. Royalty: $10.

DARK EYES, by Joyce Ingalls. 5 women. Plays 30 minutes. Interior set. A friend convinces a girl embittered by blindness to continue with her plans for marriage. Baker's Plays, 60¢.

DARK INTERLUDE, by Charles Emery. 3 men, 3 women. Plays 30 minutes. Interior set. Two lonely people with a common bond in mutual deformity encounter jealousy when love comes to one of them. Baker's Plays, 60¢. Royalty: $5.

THE DARK IS LIGHT ENOUGH, by Christopher Fry. 12 men, 3 women. Plays full evening. Set during the Hungarian rising against Austrian rule in 1848, the play tells the story of the Countess, who gives her life for the cause and brings redemption to a scoundrel. Dramatists Play Service, $1.25.

THE DARK NIGHT, by R. W. Hill. 8 men, 4 women, 1 boy, extras. Plays 1 hour. Interior set. If Christianity is to be punishable by death under totalitarian rule, who in a typical English congregation would remain faithful? Baker's Plays, 85¢. Royalty: $15.

DARKNESS AT NOON, by Sidney Kingsley. 18 men, 3 women. Plays full evening. Interior set. A Soviet commissar who has lost party favor is imprisoned and brainwashed; shows the brutality of a totalitarian state. Samuel French, Inc., $1. Royalty: $50.

DARKNESS BEFORE DAWN, by H. Clayton Moyer, Jr. 5 men, 2 women. Plays 75 minutes. Crucifixion play in two acts. Abingdon Press, 40¢. Package, 25.

A DATE FOR JOANNE, by Don Sigal. 5 women. A girl, selfish and overstudious, learns lessons in sportsmanship from her friends. One act. Banner Play Bureau, 50¢ (purchase of 5 copies required).

DAVID, by D. H. Lawrence. Large cast (doubling possible). Plays full evening. A romantic treatment of the David and Saul relationship. In *Religious Drama 1.* World. Royalty: apply to Curtis Brown.

DAVID, A TRILOGY, by Edward Longstreth. Each plays 30 minutes. Biblical chancel dramas, to be read or staged: "David, Arm of God"; "David, the Outlaw"; "David, the King." Each play, $1.25. Royalty: inquire of the author.

DAVID AND JONATHAN, by Effa E. Preston. 16 men, 1 woman, reader, mixed chorus, dance group. Plays 35 minutes. The early life of David, with particular emphasis on his contest with Saul and his victory over Goliath. A pageant play with eight songs and a group dance. T. S. Denison & Co., 50¢ (purchase of 10 copies required).

DAVID AND JONATHAN. Plays 15–20 minutes. Bible play for children. Concordia, 40¢. In set with 7 other similar plays, $3.

DAVY'S STAR, by Edith Quick and James Fluckey. A Christmas operetta, with music and dialogue, easy to memorize and beautiful in thought. Baker's Plays, $1.40 (purchase of 7 copies required).

THE DAWN, by Corona Cook. 4 men, 4 women. Plays 45 minutes. A Bible and a near tragedy reunite a long-separated family at Easter time. Eldridge, 60¢.

DAWN WILL COME, by David Weinstock. 3 men, extras. Two worshipers of light leave a kind of Platonic cave; they see the wonders of nature and, returning, are seized as heretics. Concludes in an excellent parable. Baker's Plays, 60¢. Royalty: $5.

THE DAWNING, by L. R. Bayard. A harmony of the Gospels in dramatic form; tells the story of the resurrection. A pageant with interpretive music. Baker's Plays, 60¢.

THE DAY OF HOPE. Plays 15–20 minutes. Bible play for children with production notes. Concordia, 40¢. In set with 7 other similar plays, $3.

THE DAY THE SKY WENT TO SCHOOL, by Nora Stirling. Problems of communication between school and parents. Plays for Living.

THE DAY'S BEGINNING, by Willis Hall. An Easter play. William Heinemann, Ltd., 2*s.* 6*d.*

DEAD END, by Sidney Kingsley. 22 men, 6 women, extras. Plays full evening. Hard-boiled youngsters and gangsters in a play of social conscience. In volume with other plays. Dramatists Play Service, $3.95. Royalty: $35–$25.

DEAR WORMWOOD, by C. S. Lewis, adapted by James Forsyth. 9 men,

8 women. Plays full evening. A dramatization of part of *The Screwtape Letters.* Dramatic Publishing Co., $1.25. Royalty: $35.

DEATH OF A SALESMAN, by Arthur Miller. 8 men, 5 women. Plays full evening. A salesman relives his past, discovering the reasons for his failure in life, in a play of tragic vision. Very powerful and very difficult. Dramatists Play Service, $1. Royalty: $50–$25.

DEATH OF A TRAITOR, by Anthony Merryn. 7 men, 2 women, extras. The story of Sir Thomas More, with attention to the socio-political and religious implications. Religious Drama Society of Great Britain, 75¢. Royalty: apply to the publisher.

DEBORAH, by Edward Longstreth. Plays 30 minutes. Biblical chancel drama for reading or staging. Royalty: inquire of the author.

A DEBT TO PAY, by Lyda Nagel. 4 women. Plays 35 minutes. The life of a possessive mother, as well as that of her daughter who wishes to marry, is changed by Bill Norton. Baker's Plays, 50¢. Royalty: $5.

THE DECISION, by Monty Pitner. 5 women, 2 men. Plays 25 minutes. Interior set. Eddy Fleming, lying unconscious after an auto accident, is visited by Life and Death. The play unfolds through the hero's subconscious mind. T. S. Denison & Co., 50¢. Royalty: $5.

DEEP ARE THE ROOTS, by Arnaud d'Usseau and James Gow. 7 men, 4 women. The segregation problem is the subject of this plea for decency and justice. Dramatists Play Service, $1. Royalty: $50–$25.

THE DELINQUENT, THE HIPSTER, AND THE SQUARE, edited by Alva I. Cox, Jr. Six one-act plays probing different aspects of these social and antisocial types. Bethany Press, $1.50.

THE DEMON PREACHER, by Columban Duffy, O.F.M. 18 men, 3 women. Disguised as a friar, Satan tempts a group of Franciscans and is defeated. With detailed lighting directions. Three acts. St. Anthony Guild Press, 50¢.

THE DEPUTY, by Rolf Hochhuth. Large cast (doubling possible). A controversial drama based on Pope Pius XII's failure to come to the aid of the Jews during the Nazi oppression. Samuel French, Inc., $1.25. Royalty: $50–$25 (restricted; apply to publisher).

THE DESERT SHALL REJOICE, by Robert Finch. 7 men, 2 women. Plays 35 minutes. Interior set. The story of Nick, who keeps his place on a Nevada desert highway, and who, although he says he doesn't like Christmas, can't give enough to others. Became the Academy Award picture "Star in the Night." Samuel French, Inc., 60¢. Royalty: $5.

THE DESERT TENT, by Nancy Douglas Bowditch. 5 men, 3 women. Interior set. Depicts the family of a Persian rug merchant at the time of the crucifixion, and the experience of the son when he sees Jesus. Baker's Plays, 60¢.

DESIGN FOR A STAINED GLASS WINDOW, by William Berney and Howard Richardson. 10 men, 3 women, extras. Interior set. A woman returns to the Catholic faith in spite of Queen Elizabeth's anti-Catholic edicts. Portrays the makings of a potential saint. Baker's Plays, $1. Royalty: $25.

THE DEVIL A SAINT WOULD BE, by Louis D'Alton. 7 men, 3 women, male voice offstage. The devil impersonates a saint and influences a lady to give away her money; then the real saint appears. Samuel French, Inc., $1.25. Royalty: $25–$20.

THE DEVIL AND DANIEL WEBSTER, by Stephen Vincent Benét. 6 men, 1 woman. Plays 50 minutes. The Dr. Faustus theme is here revisited as Daniel Webster argues dramatically the defense case against the devil. Dramatists Play Service, 50¢. Royalty: $5.

THE DEVIL AND THE DREAM, by Joseph Julian, music by Anita Leonard. A playlet on human relations. A contest between the devil with a dream of war, and a soldier with a dream of peace. Peace is victorious. Anti-Defamation League of B'nai B'rith, 15¢.

THE DEVIL COMES TO CLAIM HIS OWN, by Warren Kliewer. 3 men, 1 woman. Plays 20 minutes. A satirical play involving dramatic art, Satan, and almighty God. In *Kansas Magazine,* 1963. Royalty: apply to the author, c/o Editor, *Kansas Magazine.*

THE DEVIL TO PAY, by Dorothy L. Sayers. 13 men, 3 women, approximately 20 extras. Plays 1 hour and 40 minutes. Traditional Renaissance stage setting. A retelling of the Faust legend with emphasis on its theological implications; the last scene is an argument between the Divine Judge and Mephistopheles for the soul of Faustus. In four scenes, first three particularly colorful theatrically. Royalty: apply to Ann Watkins.

THE DEVIL'S ADVOCATE, by Morris L. West. 9 men, 2 women, extras. 5 interior sets. A dying priest is sent to discredit a man's claims to sanctity. Three acts. Baker's Plays, $1.25. Royalty: $50.

THE DEVIL'S DISCIPLE, by George Bernard Shaw. 11 men (plus extras), 5 women (plus extras). Interior sets, 1 exterior set. The comedy of a young man, in Puritan, revolutionary America, who has come to consider himself a disciple of the devil; he is about to be hanged in the place of a minister because he feels unable to harm another human being. Handled with the control, freshness, and barb of Shaw's wit. Baker's Plays, 50¢. Royalty: none.

DIALOGUES OF THE CARMELITES, by Georges Bernanos, translated by Gerald Hopkins. (See Legat translation below.) William Collins, Ltd. Royalty: apply to publisher.

DIALOGUES OF THE CARMELITES, by Georges Bernanos, translated by Michael Legat (under title "The Fearless Heart"). 7 men, 16 women, extras. A girl who has joined the Carmelite nuns to escape her fears finds the courage to accompany her sisters to the guillotine during the Reign of Terror. Studies of humanity, heroism, and martyrdom on many levels. The Bodley Head. Royalty: apply to publisher.

A DIFFERENT KIND OF CHRISTMAS, by Grace Sorenson. 2 boys, 3 girls. Plays 30 minutes. Interior set. Children plan to exchange Christmases, but learn that the Christmas you most enjoy is the one that belongs to you. In *Merry Little Plays for Children.* Baker's Plays, $1.25.

DINO, by Reginald Rose. 7 men, 11 women, extras. Plays full evening. A juvenile delinquent is rehabilitated through understanding.

Very powerful. Adapted from the Studio One television drama. Dramatic Publishing Co., 90¢. Royalty: $35.

THE DISCOVERY BIBLE PLAYS, Books 1 and 2, by John Anderson. For backward readers, with line illustrations. A companion series to *The Discovery Readers*. George G. Harrap & Co.: each book, 2*s*. 6*d*.

DISPLACED PERSONS, by Elizabeth Milne. 5 men, 6 women. Plays 30 minutes. Interior set. Salty characters at an old men's home are related to the struggle of a Viennese employee, granddaughter of a Jew, to escape her own country. Baker's Plays, 60¢. Royalty: $5.

DISTANT THUNDER, by Evelyn Neuenburg. 4 women. Interior set. One person is regenerated thanks to another. A girl cured of alcoholism is put to the test when she is told she is responsible for her husband's death. The climax is brought into the audience itself. Baker's Plays, 60¢.

THE DIVINE MIRACLE, by Ormal B. Trick. 2 men, 2 women. Plays 25 minutes. Interior set. A blind man finds faith when he takes shelter from the rain in a church and talks to a woman who has held her faith through suffering. Baker's Plays, 60¢.

DIVORCE GRANTED, by Fred Carmichael. 7 women. Plays 30 minutes. Interior set. Women in a courtroom waiting room reveal that they wish divorce because externalities have obscured the basic principles of a happy marriage. Humorous treatment of a serious subject, with laughter and pathos well balanced. Baker's Plays, 60¢. Royalty: $5.

DO IT YOURSELF CHRISTMAS PROGRAMS, by George Crout. For elementary grades, using students of various grades, the programs play about one hour each and are united by a few main characters. Volume includes: "Merry Christmas Fairy"; Christine, the Christmas Doll"; "The Innkeeper Makes Excuses"; "Little Black Lamb"; "The Christmas Rose." Baker's Plays, $1.

THE DOCTOR DECIDES, by Fred Eastman. 3 men, 2 women. Plays 30 minutes. A medical missionary in the southern mountains finds his financial support has failed. Baker's Plays, 60¢. Royalty: $5.

A DOLL'S HOUSE, by Henrik Ibsen, translated by Eva Le Gallienne. 4 men, 4 women, 3 children. Plays full evening. The story of a woman's search to be something more than a mindless doll within the protection and domination of her husband. Difficult. Needs an outstanding actress. In *Six Plays by Henrik Ibsen*. Random House. Royalty: apply to Brandt & Brandt.

DON PEDRO OF BRAZIL. For junior high. Gives atmosphere and facts of country. Encouragement of world friendship. Plays, Inc., 50¢.

THE DOOR IS OPEN, by Stephen Chodorov. Persons smitten with handicaps can find ways of being useful. Vocational Rehabilitation Administration.

THE DOOR OPENS: EVERYBODY WELCOME! by Marion Wefer. Story of ministry to neglected community groups, in eight episodes. Friendship Press, 35¢.

DOPE! by Maryat Lee. 4 men, 3 women, extras. Short play. An addict, a pusher, and an innocent victim are involved in this Greek-like drama. One act. Samuel French, Inc., 60¢. Royalty: $5.

DOWN OUR STREET, by Susan Richmond. 14 women. Plays 30 minutes. Suggestions of three scene sets. A girl finds her place in life. Play for girls, with production notes. Baker's Plays, 60¢. Royalty: $5.

DRAG RACE, by Anne Coulter Martens. 5 men (two policemen), 4 women. Plays 30 minutes. Interior set. In the presence of their distraught parents, young people are shown by the police the seriousness of drag racing on the highway. Baker's Plays, 60¢.

THE DRAGON AND THE DOVE, by James Bridie. 6 men, 3 women. Plays 85 minutes. The Hermit Abraham and the devil engage in an imbroglio over a girl. Constable.

DRAMA OF PRAYER, by Dorothy D. Corrigan. 7 men, 4 women (or 6 men, 5 women), chorus and extra characters if desired. The cast, scattered in the audience, go to the stage one by one to help the Muse discover "What is prayer?" Different answers are found by different people. Chorus selections and hymns. Ends in recital, with audience, of the Lord's Prayer. Two acts. Baker's Plays, 60¢. Royalty: $5.

DRAMATIC PRELUDES AND SERVICES OF WORSHIP, by Isabel Kimball Whiting. Nine services for each month from October through June, each a prelude dramatizing a spiritual search for "God as companion" in the Bible of Christian history. Baker's Plays, $2.50.

A DREAM OF PURIM, by Lydia Caplan. 5 boys, 3 girls. Plays 20 minutes. For ages 5–10. A mother talks about the Purim story with her two children, and they dream of meeting the Purim characters and exposing Haman. Union of American Hebrew Congregations, 25¢.

A DREAM OF QUEEN ESTHER, by Walter Ben Hare. 3 men, 16 women, 1 extra. 1 exterior set, 1 interior set. Plays 2 hours, 30 minutes. Combination of biblical essentials with dramatic action in the presentation of the book of Esther. Good for amateur actors. Needs careful directorial editing. T. S. Denison & Co., 85¢ (purchase of 10 copies required).

DREAM TOWARD BETHLEHEM, by E. Harriett Donlevy. Large cast. Time flexible. Interior set. The Holy Family travels with others on the road to Bethlehem. A prince, who sleeps along the way, finds his dreams troubled with beauty. Baker's Plays, 60¢.

THE DREAMBOOK, by Henry Woolf. 15 men, 4 women, 1 child (boy or girl). For ages 7–12. The characters of the Chanuko story step from the Dreambook to the plot. Songs interspersed. Union of American Hebrew Congregations, 25¢.

DUST OF THE ROAD, by Kenneth Sawyer Goodman. 3 men, 1 woman. Plays 40 minutes. Interior set. From the legend that Judas is permitted to return to earth once a year on Christmas Eve to plead with some soul tempted to betray friendship. Baker's Plays, 50¢. Royalty: $10 if admission is charged; $5 if not.

DUST ON THE CHRISTMAS STAR, by Alberta Hawse. 3 men, 4 women, 1 girl. Plays 90 minutes. A woman, grieving for the death of her daughter, shuts love and the celebration of Christmas away from her granddaughter. Emphasizes the unselfish love given by Christ in Christmas. Eldridge, 60¢ (purchase of 8 copies required).

THE DUSTMAN, by Frances D. Singler. 5 men, 2 women. Plays 35 minutes. Interior set. Blame for a theft is attached to an express clerk in this play illustrating the theme, "Judge not, that ye be not judged." T. S. Denison & Co., 50¢. Royalty: $5.

THE DYBBUK, by S. Ansky, translated by Henry G. Alsberg and Winifred Katzin. 21 men, 13 women (doubling possible). The most famous modern Jewish drama, a sort of shadowed fairy tale, in which a boy dabbles in magic to win the girl he loves when she is refused him; he returns as a spirit after his death to stop her wedding. Overtones of predestination, religion, and mysticism. Difficult. In *Twenty Best European Plays on the American Stage.* Crown. Royalty: apply to publisher.

EARLIER ENGLISH DRAMA, edited and arranged by F. J. Tickner Nelson. Religious Drama Society of Great Britain.

EASTER, by August Strindberg, translated by Elizabeth Sprigge. 3 men, 3 women. Plays full evening. A haunting, though realistic, modern mystery or morality play that is tender and sensitive. In *Six Plays of Strindberg.* Anchor Book A54.

EASTER, by August Strindberg, translated by Arvid Paulson. 3 men, 3 women. Plays full evening. Interior set. A girl of great innocence returns from an asylum to bring light into her family in this parable of rebirth. Set on Holy Thursday, Good Friday, and Easter Eve. Action is realistic, dialogue almost poetic. In *Seven Plays by August Strindberg.* Bantam Books. Royalty: apply to publisher.

EASTER AND THE SPRING, by Nina B. Lamkin. Collection of European folklore, customs. Samuel French, Inc., 75¢.

EASTER AT GALILEE, by Edith H. Willis and Edith Ellsworth. 3 men, 3 women, soloist, accompanist. Exterior set. A dramatic interpretation of the poem "The Light of the World." Pontius Pilate meets with Mary Magdalene, seeking to learn the "truth" about Jesus. Implications for today. Baker's Plays, 60¢. Royalty: $5.

THE EASTER HOPE, by Martha Mixer. 4 men, 8 women, several children, junior choir. The modern and biblical are blended in a background of Easter music. In *Transparent Curtain Pageants for Easter.* Baker's Plays, $1.25.

EASTER PROGRAMS FOR THE CHURCH. Four programs, each capable of filling a complete Easter service. Include: "The Power and the Glory" and "The Meaning of Easter" (plays); "The Hope of the World" (tableau); "He Lives" (pantomime); and "We Have Seen Him" (sunrise service). Music for the programs included. Eldridge, $1.

EASTER SHOES, by Maude C. Jackson. 3 boys, 5 girls. Plays 20 minutes. A spoiled girl learns something of the Easter spirit when she takes the part of an angel in the Easter service. Eldridge, 60¢ (purchase of 5 copies required).

THE EASTER STORY, by Vahan Tashjian. 10 men, 2 women. Plays 30 minutes. Interior set. The Interpreter, in his homespun and humble way, tells the story of the resurrection in modern idiom while the biblical characters appear on the stage. Baker's Plays, 60¢. Royalty: $5.

AN EASTER STRIKE, by Grace Sorenson. 3 boys, 5 girls. Plays 30 minutes. Interior set. A mixture of the beautiful Easter spirit and the practicality of life. In *Merry Little Plays for Children.* Baker's Plays, $1.25.

EASTER SUGGESTION BOOK. Variety of exercises, dialogues, tableaux, etc. All ages. Eldridge, 50¢.

EASTER TIDINGS, by Willis N. Bugbee. 8 girls, singing chorus. Four girls, representing Christianity, convert the other four girls, representing heathen nations, through the news of the resurrection. In *Easy Sunday School Entertainments.* Baker's Plays, $1.25.

THE EASTER TRAIL, by Marian Morris. Younger children's pageant. Eldridge, 50¢.

EASTER WINGS, by Dorothy C. Allan. 1 man, 2 women, 1 boy. Plays 30 minutes. Interior set. An exploration of the theme, "If a man die, shall he live again?" One boy and a chrysalis open to a woman the possibility of immortality. Baker's Plays, 60¢.

EASTER'S FESTIVAL. A children's pageant for juniors, primaries, beginners, and a junior choir. Eldridge, 50¢.

EASY ARENA PLAYS, by Ethel Rogers. Seventeen recreational sketches. Northwestern, $1.

EASY BIBLE PANTOMIMES, by Esther Burch. Simple pantomimes, based on Bible stories, parables. Directions for costuming and staging. Eldridge, $1.

EASY BIBLE STORY DRAMATIZATIONS FOR CHILDREN, by Karin Asbrand. Collection includes "Good Little Servant" (from the Samuel story), "I Will Give Thanks" (a Thanksgiving play), "The Living Lord" (a pageant for Easter), "Jochabed's Sacrifice" (from Moses' story), "Let Justice Be Done" (from the story of Solomon), "The Hidden Manger" (a Christmas play), "Giant Killer" (based on the story of David), and "The Redeemer's Robe" (keynoting faith). Baker's Plays, $1.25.

THE EASY CHRISTMAS BOOK, edited by Theodore Johnson. Plays, programs, readings, etc. Selections for children and adults. Easily acted. Baker's Plays, $1.25.

THE EASY CHRISTMAS GRAB BAG, edited by Edna M. Cahill. Well-balanced collection of unusual Christmas programs. Particularly useful for teachers, pastors, etc. Baker's Plays, $1.25.

EASY CHURCH PLAYS FOR CHILDREN, by various authors. Short plays for church group children between the ages of four and twelve; all-boy, all-girl, and mixed casts. Half are for any season, the remainder for Christmas and Easter. Baker's Plays, $1.25.

EASY CHURCH PLAYS FOR CHILDREN, by various authors. Short plays for church groups of children from 4–12. Eldridge, $1.25.

EASY CHURCH PLAYS FOR WOMEN AND GIRLS, by Karin Asbrand. Ten plays of religious or moral background, including plays for Christmas, Easter, Mother's Day, and other holidays, all suitable for church production. Baker's Plays, $1.25.

EASY EASTERETTES, by Karin Asbrand. Short programs for all ages, including drills, acrostics, plays, pageants, etc. Both serious and light programs, all in a religious background. Baker's Plays, $1.25.

EASY GRADE SCHOOL PLAYS, by Claribel Spamer. Plays emphasizing days that can be celebrated in the classroom, such as Easter, Christmas, and Thanksgiving. Plays are short, for easy memorization by children. Baker's Plays, $1.25.

EASY GRANGE PROGRAMS, by Ruby L. Moeller. Plays, pantomimes, candlelighting services, etc., with themes arranged for the months and including Christmas, Easter, Thanksgiving; twelve complete programs in all. Baker's Plays, $1.25.

EASY PROGRAMS FOR CHRISTMAS, by various authors. Plays, readings, recitations and other Christmas program materials for primary grades to advanced teens. Baker's Plays, $1.25.

EASY PROGRAMS FOR CHURCH HOLIDAYS, by Karin Asbrand. Includes programs for Easter, Christmas, other special days. Many programs require very little rehearsal. Baker's Plays, $1.25.

EASY PROGRAMS FOR MOTHER'S DAY, edited by Theodore Johnson. Plays, readings, and other program suggestions. High level of both quality and quantity. Baker's Plays, $1.25.

EASY SUNDAY SCHOOL ENTERTAINMENTS, by Karin Asbrand. Programs for Easter, Christmas, Mother's Day, etc. A large collection of plays and programs for children's instruction and expression. Baker's Plays, $1.25.

EASY TO ASSEMBLE, by Virginia Coigney. United Community Funds Crusade play showing the value of family life. United Community Funds and Councils of America.

AN ECHO OF WINGS, by George Herman. 15 men, 7 women. Bare stage. A newspaper editor seeks the truth and divine wisdom in the deaths resulting from a parochial school fire; he searches through the living to the dead themselves, and discovers that tragedy lies only with the living. Baker's Plays, 60¢. Royalty: $5.

EDGE OF GEHENNA, by Alberta Hawse. 2 men, 3 women. Plays 45 minutes. A valley between the potter's field and the walls of the Holy City had been blasted by the promise of God when its lush forest became the site of idol worship. Called Gehenna, its name by the time of Jesus was a synonym for hell. A fictional story with a spiritual truth. Eldridge, 60¢ (purchase of 5 copies required).

EDWARDIAN PLAYS, edited with an introduction by Gerald Weales. Four plays, including "Loaves and Fishes" by Somerset Maugham and "The Prodigal" by Hankin. Mermaid Dramabook 25: cloth, $5.95; paper, $2.45.

THE EFFECT OF CAROLING, by Regnis P. Drawde. 6 men, 3 women. Plays 40 minutes. Carol-singing background. The influence of carol-singing brings a deeper understanding of the practical, true meaning of Christmas in several people. Baker's Plays, 60¢.

EGOR BULYCHOV AND THE OTHERS, by Maxim Gorki, translated by Alexander Bakshy. 13 men, 9 women. Plays full evening. Interior set. A dying member of the Russian bourgeoisie loved only by his illegitimate daughter sees the beginning of the revolution as the end of his kind. In *Lower Depths and Other Plays.* Yale University Press. Royalty: apply to Maxim Lieber.

EH? by William D. Fisher. One-act comedy. For average church budget, stage equipment. Baker's Plays, 50¢ (purchase of 5 copies required).

EL CRISTO, by Margaret Larkin. 4 men, 2 women. Plays 20 minutes. Interior set. Strange customs of a religious sect on the border of Mexico. Samuel French, Inc., 60¢. Royalty: $10.

ELECTRA, by Jean Giraudoux, translated by Winifred Smith. 8 men, 7 women, 6 girls. Plays full evening. Based on the Greek legend, this tragedy of ideas shows Electra driven by hate in her quest for vengeance; destruction comes to the state, encompassing both the guilty and the innocent. In *The Modern Theatre,* Vol. I. Doubleday. Royalty: apply to publisher.

ELECTRA, by Sophocles, translated by David Grene. 7 men, 3 women, chorus, extras. Orestes and Electra revenge their father by killing their mother and her lover Aegisthus. The second in Sophocles' *Orestia* trilogy, exploring the conflict of a morality based upon personal revenge and family loyalty or based upon the law. In *The Complete Greek Tragedies.* University of Chicago Press. Royalty: apply to publisher.

ELIJAH, THE FIREBRAND OF THE ALMIGHTY, by Norman E. Nygaard. Elijah burns the pyre to prove before Ahab the existence of but one God. In *The Bible Comes Alive.* Baker's Plays, $1.25.

ELIZABETH THE QUEEN, by Maxwell Anderson. 17 men, 7 women, extras. Plays full evening. The conflicts of love, power, and responsibility between and within Elizabeth and Essex. Excellent and very powerful historical character portrayals. Samuel French, Inc., $1. Royalty: $25.

EMMANUEL, by James Forsyth. 11 men, 4 women. Plays 1 hour, 40 minutes. A poetic and exciting account of the Christmas story. Requires skillful acting and directing. William Heinemann, Ltd. Royalty: apply to Margery Vosper, Ltd.

EMPTY HANDS, by Helen M. Clark. 5 men, 1 woman, 1 child. A missionary in India continues, despite his ill health, his work of comfort. Friendship Press, 25¢.

THE EMPTY ROOM, by Dorothy Clarke Wilson. 4 men, 3 women. Plays 40 minutes. Interior set. Mary and Joseph are refused room at the inn but the night's occurrences end in the revelation of the Way. Baker's Plays, 60¢.

THE ENCHANTED CHRISTMAS TREE, by Percival Wilde. 2 men, 1 woman, 19 or more children. Plays 45 minutes. Interior set. The tree allows some children to hold a trial of a grouchy couple, but when their little maid begs they be given another chance, the children learn that the couple have kind hearts and have each been grouchy to please the other. Baker's Plays, 60¢. Royalty: $10.

ENDOR, by Howard Nemerov. 3 men, 1 woman. Plays 1 hour. A play in verse concerning the return of faith to King Saul. Abingdon Press. Royalty: amateur groups apply to Abingdon Press; professional groups apply to the author, c/o Margot Johnson Agency.

ENEMIES, by Margaret Parsons. 2 women, 1 boy, 1 girl. Interior set. A mother teaches the futility of war to peasant children whose fathers fought on opposite sides in World War I. In *The Woman's Club Playbook.* Baker's Plays, $1.25.

AN ENEMY OF THE PEOPLE, by Henrik Ibsen, adapted by Arthur Miller. 10 men, 3 women. Plays full evening. Dr. Stockmann's fight for truth against the interests and opinions of his entire town. Very difficult though rewarding. Dramatists Play Service, $6. Royalty: $25.

ENGLISH MIRACLE PLAYS, MORALITIES AND INTERLUDES, compiled by Alfred W. Pollard. Oxford University Press.

ENTERPRISING OSWALD, by Reby Edmond. 2 women. Plays 20 minutes. Oswald's mother and aunt are wrapping his Christmas gifts and discover both have fulfilled his wish by buying him a dog. Then begins the deluge because Oswald, just to be sure, has put an ad in the newspaper. In *Two by Two.* Baker's Plays, $1.25.

ESTHER, by Edward Longstreth. Plays 30 minutes. Biblical chancel drama to be read or played. Royalty: inquire of the author.

THE ETERNAL HILLS, by Elliot Field. 7 men, 4 women, extras. Plays 30 minutes. Interior set. Christmas carols and biblical promises set against a story of courage in an air raid shelter. Baker's Plays, 60¢. Royalty: $5.

THE ETERNAL LIGHT, by Morton Wishengood. Twenty-six Jewish legends adapted from the radio series. Crown, $3.

THE ETERNAL MAGI, by Bessie Reed Walton. Flexible cast. Plays 30 minutes. Missionary emphasis in the Nativity. Wetmore Declamation Bureau, 60¢.

EUREKA CHILDREN'S DAY RECITATIONS, edited by Mattie B. Shannon. Exercises, tableaux, plays, etc., for beginners through intermediates. Baker's Plays, 25¢.

EUREKA EASTER RECITATIONS, edited by Mattie B. Shannon. Pantomimes, plays, etc., for beginners, juniors, and intermediates. Baker's Plays, 25¢.

THE EVE OF CHRISTMAS, by J. Paul Faust. Two readers deliver the story with organ interludes. Ends in congregational singing of the Christmas Gloria. No memorization. In *Two Religious Dialogues.* Baker's Plays, 60¢.

EVEN THE HATER, by Albert Johnson. 2 men, 1 woman. Plays 50 minutes. A timeless treatment of the Cain and Abel theme in which a man, a youth, and a girl involve the audience in the struggles of man against man, woman, race, and nation, pulling the audience itself into the conflict of love and hate at the climax. Rich in poetry, humor, power, and profound in message. May be produced on bare or space stage, without props, special lighting or costumes. A Drama Trio play. Baker's Plays, 60¢. Royalty: $10.

EVER ON CHRISTMAS EVE, by Marguerite Kreger Phillips. 5 women. Plays 45 minutes. Interior set. Three young women in need of money visit their aunts in hope of prying some away. The aunts have their own plan to bring about the spirit of Christmas fellowship. Baker's Plays, 60¢. Royalty: first performance. none if 5 copies purchased; $5 each repeat.

EVER SINCE APRIL, by Nora Stirling. Problem of the aged and constructive use of retirement. American Assoc. of Retired Persons.

THE EVERLASTING DREAM, by Bessie M. Stratton. 3 men, 3 women, extras. Plays 45 minutes. Interior set. Drawn from the words "And his mother kept all these things in her heart." Baker's Plays, 60¢.

THE EVERLASTING LIGHT. 12 speaking parts, mixed choir. Plays 50 minutes. A dramatic cantata for Christmas, combining singing and acting. Eldridge, 75¢ (purchase of 10 or more copies required).

EVERY WOMAN, by Walter Browne. A modern morality of the pilgrimage of Every Woman in quest of love. Acting edition from the Henry W. Savage production. College Book Service, $5.

EVERYBODY LIKES PRETTY THINGS, by Anne Coulter Martens. 6 women. Interior set. Dodie switches Aunt Emily's gifts with the young people's, and Aunt Emily is thrilled with the frivolous things. In *Five Plays for the Junior Miss.* Baker's Plays, $1.25.

EVERYBODY'S CHRISTMAS PROGRAMS, by Dorothy M. Shipman. Children's fifteen-minute plays, readings, and sketches. Dramatic Publishing Co., 75¢.

EVERYBODY'S REHEARSALLESS CHRISTMAS BOOK, by various authors. Skits, pantomimes, services, etc. Eighteen programs of varying tones requiring no rehearsal. Eldridge, $1.

EVERYBODY'S REHEARSALLESS CHRISTMAS BOOK, by various authors. Pantomimes, skits, services, parties, for all ages. Baker's Plays, $1.

EVERYMAN, anonymous. 11 men, 6 women (may be all male or female cast). Plays 90 minutes. The old English religious play with its beauty intact. Fifteenth-century costumes. Samuel French, Inc., 60¢. Royalty: none.

EVERYMAN, anonymous. 17 characters. Plays less than 1 hour. Fifteenth-century English morality play. In *Religious Drama,* Vol. II. Meridian. Royalty: apply to publisher.

EVERYMAN, edited by Esther Willard Bates. Large cast, men or women. Plays 90 minutes. Set may be adjusted to needs. Fifteenth-century costume. The beautiful English medieval morality play. Baker's Plays, 60¢.

EVERYMAN, adapted by Ida Lublenski Ehrlich. The 1908 Carew version, a Protestant version of the great morality play. Everyman's Theatre. Royalty and acting rights by arrangement.

EVERYMAN, by Hugo von Hofmannsthal, translated by John Reich. 18 men (doubling possible), 8 women, extras. A modern treatment of the rich man called by Death. The poetic simplicity of the old morality play with depth and dramatic impact. Goodman Memorial Theatre. Royalty: apply to publisher.

EVERYMAN, edited by Vincent F. Hopper and Gerald B. Lahey. The famous medieval morality play. Death, by God's order, calls Everyman. In searching for companions for his journey, Everyman finds the things of the world melt away and must seek companions on the way to salvation. Allegorical characterizations. In *Medieval Mysteries, Moralities, and Interludes.* Barron's Educational Series, $1.25.

EVERYMAN, by Albert Johnson. Large cast. A new treatment of the medieval morality play which has been extensively produced with both simple and elaborate staging, the latter calling for choirs, symphony orchestra, and organ. In *Church Plays and How to Stage Them.* Available in manuscript from author, $1. Royalty: $25–$15.

EVERYMAN AND MEDIEVAL MIRACLE PLAYS, edited by A. C. Cawley. Everyman's Library, Vol. 381. E. P. Dutton & Co., $2.25.

EVERYTHING IS FOR THE BEST, by Ray M. Cook. 13 boys, 8 girls, extras. For ages 5–8. Choral operetta with its basis in the legend of Rabbi Akiba. In five scenes. Amusing and delightful. Union of American Hebrew Congregations, 75¢.

EVERYWHERE CHRISTMAS, by Alice Very. 25 children. Plays 15 minutes. Children of all nationalities and the way they celebrate Christmas. Plays, Inc., 35¢.

EXCEPT FOR JOHN LELAND, by Albert Johnson. 4 men, 4 women (6 of these take various parts, double as speaking and singing chorus). The story of a little-known American hero who took a stand for individual and religious liberty at the time of the ratification of the Constitution. May be done with elaborate or with bare or space staging. Pioneer Drama Service. Royalty: $10–$5.

EXCEPT FOR JOHN LELAND, by Albert Johnson. 2 men, 1 woman. Adaptation of the author's small-cast play of the same title, concerning a little-known American hero at the time of the adoption of the Constitution. The Drama Trio Play may be performed on a bare or space stage with no props or special costuming. Available in manuscript from author, $1. Royalty: $10–$5.

EXCUSE FOR LIVING, by Beatrice M. Casey. 2 men, 2 women. Plays 15–20 minutes. 1 interior set. A wealthy and self-centered woman is shown the hollowness of her ways by a doctor. Eldridge, 60¢.

THE EXTRA ANGEL, by Edith M. Quick and James O. Fluckey. Versatile Christmas pantomime production for junior high, high school, church groups. Eldridge, $1.25.

EYE OF THE HURRICANE, by Nora Stirling. A social worker confronts a family counseling problem. Plays for Living.

EYES OF FAITH, by Mina Maxfield and Lena Eggleston. 10 women. Plays 35 minutes. On the night of the Passover, with the thought that Jesus may return and heal her, a blind girl joins Magdalene in her search for Christ. Baker's Plays, 60¢.

EYES UPON THE CROSS, by Don A. Mueller. A cycle of playlets for Lent which equate the people of the audience with the people on the hill at the crucifixion to ask "What will I do . . . with this same Christ?" Baker's Plays, 85¢. Royalty: each performance of complete play, $20; $2.50 each separate cycle.

FAITH OF OUR FATHERS. The Mayflower Compact and the first Thanksgiving in a pageant. Nat'l Recreation Assoc., 25¢.

THE FAITHLESS, by John Hayden. 4 men, 2 women. Plays 20 minutes. Exterior set. Nearly two thousand years ago a husband, later identified as Judas, returns to his deserted house and an eventual suicide. Samuel French, Inc., 60¢. Royalty: $5.

THE FAMILY NOBODY WANTED, by Helen Doss. 7 men, 9 women. Plays full evening. A minister's adopted family of many nationalities may make his son's wedding plans difficult. Adapted from the book by Helen Doss. Dramatic Publishing Co., $1. Royalty: $35.

FAMILY PORTRAIT, by Lenore Coffee and William Joyce Cowen. 12 men, 10 women. 1 interior set, 3 exterior sets. The last three years of Christ's life and the reaction of those around him told through the story of an ordinary family. Excellent and difficult. Three acts. Baker's Plays, $1.25. Royalty: $25–$20.

THE FAMILY REUNION, by T. S. Eliot. 6 men, 6 women. Plays full evening. 2 interior sets. Lord Harry Monchensey passes from sin through redemption to holiness. Samuel French, Inc., $1.45. Royalty: $25–$20.

THE FAR COUNTRY, by Dorothy Clarke Wilson. 3 men, 2 women. Plays 30 minutes. The call of Abraham illuminated by new discoveries concerning Ur of the Chaldees. Emphasis on the spirit of the search of a young man for God. In *Twelve Months of Drama for the Average Church.* Baker's Plays, $2.95.

THE FATHER, by Dorothy Clarke Wilson. 4 men, 3 women. Plays 30 minutes. Interior set. The home of Joseph and Mary; the voice of Christ initiates the climax. Appropriate for Father's Day. Baker's Plays, 60¢.

FATHER CHRISTMAS AND THE DUCHESS, by Harold Brooke and Kay Bannerman. 1 man, 5 women. A hospital's private ward on Christmas Eve. An unidentified woman is brought in while the Duke of Billsborough is there dressed as Father Christmas. One act. Evans Plays. Royalty: 25*s.* 2*d.* net.

FAUST, Part I, by Johann Wolfgang von Goethe, translated by C. F. MacIntyre. 22 men, 10 women, doubling possible. Plays full evening. Multiple sets, interior and exterior. Goethe's magnificent tragedy of Faust, his relation to the universe, and his bargain with Mephistopheles. New Directions, $1.30. Royalty: apply to publisher.

FAUST, Part I, by Johann Wolfgang von Goethe, translated by Alice Raphael. Holt, Rinehart & Winston, $1.25. Royalty: apply to publisher.

THE FAVORITE MOTHER'S DAY PROGRAM, by Beatrice Casey. For mothers' and daughters' evenings. Baker's Plays, 75¢.

FEAR IS A MURDERER, by Evelyn Neuenberg. 4 women. Plays 30 minutes. Interior set. A house in East Berlin is politically divided. The play's message lies in a prayer for world awareness of the political menace, a plea to act for freedom before it is too late. Baker's Plays, 60¢. Royalty: $5.

FEAR NOT, by Jeanne Carruthers. 8 men, 1 woman, extras. The father of two college students in India embraces Christianity in the face of communism. Friendship Press, 50¢.

THE FEARLESS HEART, by Georges Bernanos, translated from the French "Dialogues des Carmelites" by Michael Legat. 10 men, 20 women. Plays full evening. Study of how a community of Carmelite nuns in Paris in 1774 face persecution and execution with fear and courage. The Bodley Head.

THE FEAST OF THE STAR, by Harold Friedell. Narrator and choirs. Plays 45 minutes. A fine Epiphany pageant. H. W. Gray Co., $1.

A FELLOW NEEDS A FRIEND, by Kate Crehan and Paul Scott. 12 men, 5 women, 1 girl. Interior set. Father Madden's attempts to stage a play lead to comic results and the eventual resolution of all problems, including his own. Three acts. Baker's Plays, $1. Royalty: $25.

FENCES, by Rose Leiman Schiller. Deals effectively with school integration problem. Plays for Living.

A FESTIVAL OF FREEDOM. Patriotic songs illustrated by stories and tableaux. Nat'l. Recreation Assoc., 15¢.

THE FESTIVAL OF LIGHTS. Ten Hanukkah tableaux. Anti-Defamation League of B'nai B'rith, 5¢.

FESTIVAL OF THE CAROLS, by Ellen Jane Lorenz and Rosemary Hadler. For Christmas. Song and story with filmstrip accompaniment. Eldridge, 50¢. Filmstrip, $5.

FIAT LUX, by Faith Van Valkenburgh Vilas. 3 men, 1 woman, extras. Plays 30 minutes. Interior set. An aged man is given courage and faith by two supernatural visitors. Has Christmas message for all. For adults. Baker's Plays, 60¢.

THE FIDDLER'S PURIM, by Ray M. Cook. 8 boys, 1 girl, 2 narrators, extras, townspeople, chorus. Plays 30 minutes. For ages 8–12. Operetta of a one-tune fiddler, associated with the Purim characters. Staging, costuming notes included. With original melodies. Union of American Hebrew Congregations, 75¢.

52 SHORT DEVOTIONAL PROGRAMS FOR YOUTH AND ADULT. Christmas, Easter, other special-day services, each with scripture, suggestions for hymns, prayers, etc. Eldridge, $2.50.

THE FIGURE ON THE CROSS, by R. H. Ward. 2 men, 1 woman, speaking chorus. Plays 75 minutes. Exterior set. The seven last words from the cross interpreted in the light of modern times. In verse. Baker's Plays, 85¢. Royalty: $15.

THE FINGER OF GOD, by Percival Wilde. 2 men, 1 woman. Plays 30 minutes. Interior set. A girl shows a man to himself as he is, preventing his committing a crime. Baker's Plays, 60¢. Royalty: $10.

FINGER PLAYS AND HOW TO USE THEM, edited by Tessa Colina. For very small children. Includes Bible, missionary finger plays. Kindergarten, preschool. Standard, 60¢.

THE FIRST CHRISTMAS, by E. B. Dykes Beachy. Variable cast. Either simple or elaborate production possible. Christmas pageant with tableaux, readings by the Seer. Based on biblical account, traditions. Eldridge, 60¢ (purchase of 10 copies required).

THE FIRST CHRISTMAS, by Ada Richter. The biblical story for children, with tableaux, pantomime, and narration. Traditional carols may be included. Baker's Plays, $1.25.

FIRST CORINTHIANS, by H. F. Rubenstein. 6 men, 6 women. Plays 35 minutes. Interior set. Troubles in the little Christian community in Corinth lead to the writing of Paul's first epistle. H. F. W. Deane & Sons, 1*s.* 9*d.* Postage, 2*d.* Royalty: apply to publisher.

FIRST FREEDOM. Variable cast. Plays 20 minutes. John Peter Zenger fights for freedom of the press in 1735. Radio technique. Plays, Inc., 50¢.

THE FIRST GOOD JOY, by Isabel Revdell. For junior and intermediate age, advanced children's groups. Worthwhile. The Religious Drama Society of Great Britain (apply to publisher for prices).

THE FIRST LEGION, by Emmet Lavery. 11 men. 3 interior sets. The problems and feelings of a group of Jesuit priests. Three acts. Baker's Plays, $1.25. Royalty: $25.

THE FIRST MIRACLE, by Isabel Burr. 4 men, 3 women, 2 attendants, extras. Plays 20 minutes. The marriage feast at Cana. In *Jericho Road and Other Miracle Plays*. Baker's Plays, 75¢. Royalty: apply to publisher.

THE FIRSTBORN, by Christopher Fry. 10 men, 3 women. Plays full evening. Moses' attempt to free the Jews from bondage in Egypt, his conflicting loyalties to his people and his foster son Rameses, and the killing of the firstborn. Powerful. Dramatists Play Service, $1.25. Royalty: $50–$25.

THE FISHERMAN'S SON. Plays 15–20 minutes. For children. Concordia, 40¢. In set with 7 other similar plays, $3.

FISHERS OF MEN, by Norman E. Nygaard. 5 men, 1 woman. Peter explains Christ's promise to make "fishers of men." In *The Bible Comes Alive*. Baker's Plays, $1.25.

FIVE DAYS, by Henry Zeiger. 8 men, 1 woman. Plays 30 minutes. A regiment in the Yellow Army in a play about war. Apply for information to Margaret Mayoraga.

FIVE MORE CHRISTIAN PLAYS, by Freda Collins. Four plays of an apocryphal nature about the early church, and *The Runaway Slave*, about Onesimus, based on the book of Philemon. Religious Drama Society of Great Britain, 50¢.

FIVE ONE-ACT PLAYS, by Wolf Mankowitz. Includes the well-known "The Bespoke Overcoat," "The Baby," and "The Last of the Cheesecake" (based on Chekhov stories), "It Should Happen to a Dog" (a humorous treatment of the story of Jonah), and "The Mighty Hunter" (biblical theme of a man who forgot he was only a man). Evans Plays, 5*s*. Royalty: "The Bespoke Overcoat," 25*s*.; all others, 15*s*.

FIVE PLAYS, by Kaj Munk. Plays on the free soul of man by one of Denmark's best World War II playwrights. Naturalistic technique; intensity of feeling. Included are "Herod the King" (of man and God), and "He Sits at the Melting Pot" (of strength from the spirit). American-Scandinavian Foundation, $3.50.

THE FIVE VIRGINS, by Guillaume Van der Graft. 1 man, 6 women. Plays 30 minutes. Modern verse morality play on the biblical theme of the foolish virgins. Netherlands Centre of the International Theatre Institute.

THE FLIGHT INTO EGYPT, by Thornton Wilder. 1 man, 1 woman, 1 donkey. Takes place on the road between Egypt and the Holy Land; presents the theme "Bear Your Master On." In *One Act Plays of Spiritual Power*. Baker's Plays, $3.25.

A FLOWER FOR MOTHER'S DAY. 14 children. Plays 10 minutes. Among all the flowers, the unnoticed carnation is chosen. Plays, Inc., 35¢.

THE FLOWERING PEACH, by Clifford Odets. 7 men, 4 women, 4 animals (men or women). Plays full evening. Noah and his family symbolize all people under God, seeking to replenish a peaceful world. Dramatists Play Service. Available in manuscript from the publisher. Royalty: $50–$25; $10 deposit is returnable.

THE FLOWERING STAFF, by Loraine Huntington Miller. 5 men, 4 women. Plays 30 minutes. Exterior set. A miracle befalls Mary's suitors before she marries Joseph. Baker's Plays, 60¢. Royalty: $5.

FLOWERS FOR MOTHER. 10 girls, 6 boys, extras. Plays 10 minutes. The vendor allows Betty to take one flower for Mother, and Violet volunteers. Plays, Inc., 35¢.

FOG, by Evelyn Neuenberg. 3 women. Plays 25 minutes. Interior set. Three women, a mother, a wife, and a young girl, are each waiting for the safe return of the one closest to her heart—and they discover it is one man. Baker's Plays, 60¢. Royalty: $5.

FOLLOW THE STAR, by Dorothy C. Allan. 9 women. Plays 30 minutes. Exterior set. A Roman-Jewish girl of the Vesta leaves her offices to follow the way of the star. Christmas. Baker's Plays, 60¢.

FOLLOW THE STAR, by Karin Asbrand. Large cast. Plays 45 minutes. Good Christmas story pageant. Baker's Plays, 40¢.

FOLLOW THOU ME, by Mary S. Hitchcock. 5 men, 8 women, extras. Plays 2 hours. Interior set. Daniel and his struggles to remain true to his faith. Biblical drama. T. S. Denison & Co., 85¢ (purchase of 10 copies required).

FOOD FOR FREEDOM, by Stanley Kauffman. 7 boys, 4 girls, extras representing nations. Plays 20 minutes. Part of food in peace, war, international relations. United Nations play for elementary-age children. Baker's Plays, 60¢.

THE FOOD OF LOVE, by Christopher Bond. 6 men, 3 women. Plays full evening. The music master of a boy's school realizes the answer to his ambitions and struggles in a broadcast of *The Messiah*. H. F. W. Deane & Sons. Royalty: apply to publisher.

FOOTBALL HERO, by Stanley Kauffman. 3 men, 3 women. Plays 25 minutes. A girl teaches a quarterback the real meaning of thankfulness. Has humor, a sense of the realistic. Plays, Inc., 50¢.

FOR COUNTRY AND MANKIND, by Bernard J. Reines. 6–8 characters in each. Twelve plays about dreams that come true, based on the lives and courage of famous people. Longmans, Green & Co., $2.25.

"FOR FREEDOM'S SAKE!" by Percy Jewett Burrell. 50 or more characters. Plays 45 minutes–1 hour, 45 minutes. Three actions in celebration of victory, peace, and freedom. Adaptable pageant. Baker's Plays, 75¢. Royalty: apply to the publisher.

FOR HE HAD GREAT POSSESSIONS, by Dorothy Clarke Wilson. 5 men, 4 women, 1 child. A young ruler of great wealth and his wife come through sorrow to understanding and a close fellowship with Christ. Baker's Plays, 50¢.

FOR HEAVEN'S SAKE! book and lyrics by Helen Kromer, music by Frederick Silver. 5 men, 5 women. Plays full evening. A revue concerning a little man playing "the almighty King" in sketches, ballads, and connecting material. Baker's Plays, $1.50. Piano score, $5. Record, $5.48 postpaid. Royalty: $5.

FOR THE TIME BEING, by W. H. Auden. 20 speaking parts, verse chorus. Plays 1 hour, 45 minutes. A Christmas oratorio spanning the time from Advent to the flight into Egypt and emphasizing Christ as a gift to the world. Difficult and rewarding if well-handled. In *Religious Drama 1.* Meridian Books. Royalty: $25 if admission is not charged; otherwise, apply to Curtis Brown.

FORGIVE US OUR CHICKEN COOPS, by Jean M. Matson. Variable cast. Some humor and some pertinent questions concerning the current ecclesiastical scene. Baker's Plays, 60¢. Royalty: $5.

THE FORGOTTEN GIFT, by Karin Asbrand. 6 men, 4 women, extras. Plays 45 minutes. A gift from the Christchild brings a miracle to a sick girl. Musical numbers included. For Christmas. Eldridge, 60¢.

THE FORMULA, by Beatrice Haniford. 10 boys, 5 girls. A new feeling for Chanuko develops in a high school student absorbed in science. Union of American Hebrew Congregations, 25¢.

A FOUNTAIN OF PEACE, by Effa E. Preston. 8 boys, 8 girls. Exterior set. A peace play. A poet draws inspiration for the inscription on the fountain of a memorial park from the people who visit the park on Armistice Day. T. S. Denison & Co., 50¢ (purchase of 7 copies required).

FOUR CHRISTMAS PLAYS FROM THE HORN BOOK. Three simple Nativity plays, one play of the Druid festival. Worthwhile if carefully directed. Horn Book, Inc.

FOUR EASY SKITS FOR CHURCH, by Elmer A. Kettner. Includes: "Bring Them In" and "Ken Johnson Bears Witness" (stressing church attendance); "Oh, Doctor" (concerning church organizations); "Christmas Away from Home"; and "The Three Trees" (a dramatized vesper service). Eldridge, $1.

FOUR MODERN PLAYS. Ibsen: "Hedda Gabler"; Shaw: "Pygmalion"; O'Neill: "The Emperor Jones"; Chekhov: "The Cherry Orchard." Holt, Rinehart & Winston, 95¢.

THE FOURTH WISE MAN, by Karin Asbrand. 11 men, 5 women. Plays 1 hour. The fourth wise man on his way to Bethlehem is assaulted, robbed, and wounded, and meets the Holy Family fleeing to Egypt. Baker's Plays, 60¢ (purchase of 10 copies required).

FREEDOM HALL, by Harold Franklin. 10 men, 7 women. Plays 30 minutes. A Hanukkah play in which Freedom Hall statues of Washington, Joan of Arc, Baccaben's Bolivar, and Garibaldi come to life. Dramatic Publishing Co., 40¢ (purchase of 12 copies required).

FRESH VARIABLE WINDS, by Nora Stirling. The problems of a man and his ten-year-old son. An American Wing Play. Nat'l. Assoc. for Mental Health, $1. Production packet, $4.50.

THE FRIENDLY CHURCH, by Frances Eckardt. 3 men, 3 women. Plays 35 minutes. Interior set. A family discovers satisfactions in a church club. Baker's Plays, 50¢ (purchase of 6 copies required).

FRIENDS OF JESUS, by Marsha Bayly Shannon. 5 boys, 5 girls, extra children. Thoughts of Jesus as the perfect friend ends two girls' argument over the nature of friendship. For Children's Day and church school. Baker's Plays, 60¢.

FROM HEAVEN ABOVE. A worthwhile Christmas program outline for children of primary and kindergarten ages. Augsburg, 25¢.

FROM STORY TO STAGE, adapted by Marvin G. Robinson. Eleven short dramatizations, including "Dr. Heidegger's Experiment" and "The Little New Neighbor." Good for church social evenings. Baker's Plays, $1.

FROM THE NURSERY OF HEAVEN, by Phyllis Potter. For junior and intermediate ages of advanced children's groups. Worthwhile. The Religious Drama Society of Great Britain (apply to publisher for price).

FROM THE PALMS TO THE LILIES. Easter song and story cantata, for reader and choir. Eldridge, 50¢ (purchase of 12 copies required).

THE FRONTIER, by Ormal B. Trick. 3 men, 1 woman. Plays 30 minutes. Interior set. An inscription on the wall of a crypt helps three people near a national border decide whether or not to risk crossing the frontier into a new life. Baker's Plays, 60¢. Royalty: $5.

THE FROZEN HEART, by Ivory Brides. 5 women. Plays 30 minutes. Interior set. On Christmas, 1943, three Germans and one Belgian occupy a kitchen in the midst of an icy storm. Their despair gives way to amazement when a nun knocks at the door. Baker's Plays, 60¢. Royalty: $5.

THE FULFILLMENT OF THE LAW, by E. C. W. Rusted. 22 characters and narrator. Nativity play composed of Bible extracts. Faith Press, 1*s.*

FUNNY FIDGETS, by Thelma Segar. 1 boy, 2 girls, extras. Interior set. The night before Christmas and two naughty children have an experience. One act. In *The Easy Christmas Book.* Baker's Plays, $1.25.

GABRIEL'S AVE AND OTHER RELIGIOUS PLAYS, by the Rev. F. H. Drinkwater. Children's religious plays, easy to present. Baker's Plays, $1.25. Royalty: none if 3 copies purchased.

GALLANT QUEEN, by Mina Maxfield. 3 men, 3 women. Plays 30 minutes. Exterior set. Queen Esther brings justice through diplomacy and thwarts Haman's plans to have the Jews killed or driven from Persia. Baker's Plays, 60¢.

GALLOWS GLORIOUS, by Ronald Gow. 18 men, 4 women, extras. Plays full evening. Dramatization of John Brown's life story. Samuel French, Inc. Royalty: apply to publisher.

THE GARDEN, by Wilfrid Grantham. 7 women. Living room-study setting. A woman discusses Christ with women of the Old Testament. The appearance of the virgin Mary climaxes the play. One act. Evans Plays. Royalty: 25*s.* 2*d.*

THE GARDENER WHO WAS AFRAID OF DEATH, by Henri Brochet. 3 men. Plays 20 minutes. An early Christian undergoes trial of soul as he attempts to gather courage to go to death at the hands of two

Roman soldiers. Beautiful if played with sensitivity. In *St. Anne and the Gouty Rector and Other Plays.* McKay's Plays, $2.75. Royalty: $10 if admission is charged; $5 if not.

THE GAY CHRISTMAS BOOK, by Ethel Rogers. Readings, plays, pageants, etc., for first to eighth grades. Baker's Plays, $1.

G'DEE CELEBRATES THE HOLIDAYS, by Mildred Berry. 2 boys, 2 girls (hand puppets may be used). Play for the Tu Bi-Sh'vot, Shovous, Sukos, and the Sabbath. Holiday segments may be performed independently. For primary grades. Union of American Hebrew Congregations, 25¢.

THE GENTLE ONE, by Marlene Brenner. 6 women. Plays 30 minutes. Exterior set. Five women each desire something, only one having faith to believe her desire may be realized. A stranger comes among them, teaching each something. Baker's Plays, 60¢. Royalty: $5.

GERALDINE AND THE WHITE ROBE, by Jon Conde. 6 men, 6 women. Plays 25 minutes. Alternating action between angels and the Rogers' home at Christmas where Geraldine is petulant because she has not received the coat she desired. Baker's Plays, 60¢. Royalty: none if 8 copies purchased.

THE GIANT CHRISTMAS BOOK, No. 1, by Lenore Hetrick. Material for all grades, including junior and senior high. Many plays, pageants, monologues. Baker's Plays, $1.50 (specify No. 1 when ordering).

THE GIANT CHRISTMAS BOOK, No. 2, by Lenore Hetrick. Plays, pageants, other materials, for junior and senior high children and adults. Baker's Plays, $1.50 (specify No. 2 when ordering).

GIANT KILLER, by Karin Asbrand. 2 boys, 4 girls. Plays 18 minutes. The story of David condensed into one short act. In *Easy Bible Story Dramatizations for Children.* Baker's Plays, $1.25.

THE GIFT, by Marie A. Foley. 2 men, 1 woman, 3 children. Plays 40 minutes. Interior set. During our Lord's lifetime, in Judea, a small lame boy and a blind man are cured by their faith in him. Samuel French, Inc., 60¢.

GIFT OF MUSIC, by Edward P. James. 2 men, 3 women. Plays 15 minutes. Interior set. A fantasy. A man refuses to celebrate Christmas (his wife died on that day) until the spirit of his wife appears to him. T. S. Denison & Co., 50¢ (purchase of 5 copies required).

THE GIFT OF TENYIN, by John Tumpane. 2 men, 6 women. Plays 30 minutes. Christmas play in the oriental fashion. Among the emperor's birthday gifts from his daughters is a play at whose climax he sets out with a gift for a baby king. Dramatic Publishing Co., 50¢. Royalty: $5.

GIFT OF THE LAMB, by Nellie McCaslin. 6 men, 5 women. Plays 20 minutes. Interior set. Unusual one-act play of the coming of the Christchild. Baker's Plays, 60¢. Royalty: none if 8 copies purchased.

THE GIFTS, by Dorothy Clarke Wilson. 4 men, 2 women, 1 boy, reader, three wise men. Plays 40 minutes. Interior set. The story of what happened to the gifts given the Christchild. Baker's Plays, 60¢. Royalty: first performance, none; $2.50 each repeat.

GIFTS FOR THE CHRIST-CHILD, by H. V. Lupton. 9 characters and children. A Christmas play in three scenes. Two tableaux. Faith Press, 1*s.* 6*d.*

GIFTS OF MYRRH, by Karin Asbrand. 4 men, 3 women, extras. A lonely little rich girl mistakes a burglar for a wise man. She dreams of the Nativity. Eldridge, 60¢. Royalty: none if 6 copies purchased.

THE GIFTS OF ST. PATRICK, by J. C. McMullen. 2 men, 4 women. Plays 40 minutes. Interior set. Entertaining character sketching and a powerful lesson. Samuel French, Inc., 60¢.

THE GLAD TIME CHRISTMAS BOOK, by Marie Irish. For schools or church schools, all ages. Plays, dialogues, etc.; a large collection. Eldridge, $1.

THE GLAD TIME THANKSGIVING BOOK, by Lenore K. Dolan and Marie Irish. Anthology of plays, recitations, etc., for all ages. Eldridge, $1.

THE GLASS MENAGERIE, by Tennessee Williams. 2 men, 2 women. The illusions of Laura, her mother Amanda, and her brother Tom cross with the world of a gentleman caller. Very difficult. Dramatists Play Service, $1. Royalty: $50–$25.

GLORIA, by Katharine Kester. 11 men, 4 women, extras (singers). 1 interior set, 1 exterior set. Plays 40 minutes. A shepherd boy, a mother fleeing Herod's edict, and a wise man all make active sacrifices; although they miss seeing the Christchild, they are rewarded with a vision of the Nativity. One act and prologue. Baker's Plays, 60¢. Royalty: $5.

GLORIOUS ODYSSEY, by Frederick Wiseman. Large cast. Plays 90 minutes. A Sikh, Sundar Singh, and his efforts among the Indians, Nepalese, and Tibetans. Difficult but rewarding. Religious Drama Society of Great Britain, approximately 21¢.

GO AND TELL, by Samuel H. Cox. A program for Children's Day offering inspiration for missionary work. Combines several elements including poetry, scripture, and sermon. Eldridge, 75¢ (purchase of 10 copies required).

GO DOWN MOSES, by Philip J. Lamb. 3 men, chorus of 4 women, chorus of angels. Plays 2 hours. The calling of Moses, and an artistic examination of his character. Deep theological significance. Difficult but rewarding; particularly good presentation for Advent. Two acts, five scenes. Baker's Plays, 85¢. Royalty: $15.

GO YE TO BETHLEHEM, by Albert Johnson. Plays 30 minutes. A Christmas drama of the cantata type with verse and singing choirs and organist. Spoken with interpolations of music. Harper, 50¢ (purchase of 10 copies required).

GOD CREATED CHRISTMAS, by Shirley Ann Lockhart. 5 speaking parts, 14 nonspeaking parts, carolers, choir. Plays 40 minutes. The birth of Jesus told through the eyes of a contemporary family. Abingdon Press, 25¢. Package, 25.

GOD SO LOVED THE WORLD, by Karin Asbrand. 5 men, 5 women. Plays 45 minutes. The niece of Judas is in need of Christ's healing after the Master has been sold. She is restored by her faith. Eldridge, 60¢.

GOLD, FRANKINCENSE AND MYRRH, by Temple Bailey. An elderly couple give their gold to the poor rather than spend it for luxuries. Baker's Plays, 50¢.

GOLDEN BOOK OF CHURCH PLAYS, compiled by L. M. Brings. Contains many plays worthwhile for church production. T. S. Denison & Co., $4.50.

THE GOLDEN LAND, by Marlene Brenner. 5 women. Plays 30 minutes. Interior set. God, through an unusual turn of events, proves final judge in the dispute over the inheritance of a farm. The conflict concerns two sisters, one jealous and one deserving. Baker's Plays, 60¢. Royalty: $5.

GOLGOTHA, by Irene Caudwell. 20 characters. A Passion play in eight scenes and two interludes. Faith Press, 2*s*. 6*d*.

GOOD FRIDAY, by John Masefield. 7 men, 1 woman, extras. Plays 1 hour. Exterior set. A verse Passion play, powerfully showing Pilate's final yielding before the mob, who acknowledge Caesar as their own king. Baker's Plays, 75¢. Royalty: $15.

GOOD KING WENCESLAS, by Vera Arlett. For junior and intermediate advanced children's groups. Religious Drama Society of Great Britain (apply to publisher for prices).

GOOD LITTLE SERVANT, by Asbrand and Fisher. 1 man, 1 boy, 1 woman, voice. Plays 10 minutes. Little Samuel in the temple. In *Easy Bible Story Dramatizations for Children*. Baker's Plays, $1.25.

GOOD MORNING, PARSON, by Lillian D. George. 3 men, 4 women. Plays 20 minutes. Interior set. Monday morning at the parsonage brings grouchy callers and one appreciative one. Comedy. T. S. Denison & Co., 50¢ (purchase of 6 copies required).

GOOD NEIGHBORS, by Robert Ray. 2 men, 10 women. Plays 2 hours. Two swindlers who come to a town are converted into good citizens. T. S. Denison & Co., 75¢. Royalty: $10.

A GOOD SHEPHERD, by Dorothy Clarke Wilson. 3 men. Plays 30 minutes. A young shepherd of Bethlehem finds God in sacrifice and the darkness of the hills. For either Christmas or Easter. In *Twelve Months of Drama for the Average Church*. Baker's Plays, $2.95.

A GOOD SOLDIER, by Dorothy Clarke Wilson. 4 men, 1 woman, 1 male nonspeaking part. Plays 30 minutes. An imaginary incident during Paul's imprisonment. His guard comes to realize the full meaning of the Christian message, and of faithfulness even to death. In *Twelve Months of Drama for the Average Church*. Baker's Plays, $2.95.

GOOD THINGS FOR MOTHER'S DAY, by Beatrice Casey. Dialogues, plays, readings, etc. T. S. Denison & Co., $2.75.

GOOD TIMES CHRISTMAS BOOK, by Evelyn Hoxie. Recitations, plays, tableaux. Good collection by a popular writer. Baker's Plays, $1.

GOOD WILL TOWARD WOMEN, by Dorothy Sterling. 6 women. Plays 30 minutes. Interior set. The promise of good will toward men settles a Christmas quarrel between two sisters. Baker's Plays, 60¢.

THE GOSPEL WITCH, by Lyon Phelps. 4 women, 9 men, extras. Plays full evening. Witchcraft trials in New England, emphasizing the struggle with the spirit instead of historical fact. In *Religious Drama 3*. World, $1.65. Royalty: apply to Lucy Kroll.

GRAB AND GRACE OR THE SECOND STEP, by Charles Williams. 3 men, 2 women, 1 boy. Plays 30 minutes. Sequel to "The House by the Stable." A verse-play using symbolic characters in the manner of a medieval morality play. A subtle interplay between good and evil. In *Religious Drama 3*. World, $1.65. Royalty: $5. Permission for production required. Apply to Miss R. J. L. Spalding.

GRANDPA HANGS THE HOLLY, by Don Elser. 4 men, 7 women, extras. Interior set. Humor, pathos, and fantasy. Grandpa learns and teaches the Christmas spirit. Three acts. Baker's Plays, 85¢ (purchase of 11 copies required).

THE GREAT CHOICE, by Fred Eastman. 4 men, 4 women. Interior set. The conflict between conscience and loyalty to the state during the war. Powerful. One act. Baker's Plays, 60¢. Royalty: $5.

GREAT CHRISTIAN PLAYS, edited by Theodore M. Switz and Robert A. Johnson. Book I, Medieval Plays: "Abraham and Isaac," "The Resurrection," "Conversion of St. Paul," "Totentanz," "Everyman." Book II, Choral Readings: "Four Apostles," "The Royal Parkway," "The Suffering of Mary" (from Charles Peguy's *God Speaks*), "Christ Our Savior," (from the gospel of John). Excellent. Seabury Press, $7.50.

THE GREAT REFUSAL, by Lillian Weston. 5 men, 2 women, extras. Plays 45 minutes. The wife of a young rich ruler is healed of leprosy by Christ, but convinces her husband not to follow him. Eldridge, 60¢ (purchase of 7 copies required).

THE GREAT THEATRE OF THE WORLD, by Pedro Calderon de la Barca, translated by Mack Hendricks Singleton. 7 men, 3 women, child. God is author, director, and judge of the play of life, in which mortals act. Long poetic drama, drawn from the morality play tradition. Unit setting. In *Masterpieces of the Spanish Golden Age*. Holt, Rinehart & Winston, $1.45. Royalty: apply to publisher.

GREATER THAN ANY MAN, by Albert C. Smith. 6 men, 3 women, several boys. Plays 25 minutes. Interior set. The dialogue of a church school pageant breaks down self-interest and averts a tragedy. T. S. Denison & Co., 50¢ (purchase of 6 copies required).

GREATER THAN GOLD, by Muriel Hemmings. 9 men, 3 women. Plays 1 hour. 1 interior set, 1 exterior set. A wealthy young Pharisee visits a family, part of which believes in Christ, part of which is scheming and money-mad. A missing silver chest and a disaster bring the climax. Four acts. T. S. Denison & Co., 50¢ (purchase of 10 copies required).

THE GREATEST OF THESE, by Carolyn C. Dain. 4 men, 4 women. Plays 1 hour. A group of young college people find the spirit of Christmas love is not confined to one season. Eldridge, 75¢ (purchase of 8 copies required).

THE GREEN BLACKBOARD, by Nora Stirling. Demonstrates the danger of putting children under too much pressure. Plays for Living.

THE GREEN BOUGH, by Tom Taggart. 4 men, 4 women. A spinster

schoolteacher brought to a widower's home to help raise his six children is bound into the family by the "green bough" of love and hope. Samuel French, Inc., $1. Royalty: $25.

THE GREEN PASTURES, by Marc Connelly. 39 men, 15 women, 4 boys, 1 girl, extras (doubling possible). Plays full evening. Negro children in a Louisiana Sunday school ask questions about the Old Testament, calling up the stories as they might be seen by a southern Negro. Simple and very beautiful. The Lord follows the action of men, mingling with them. A spiritual introduces each episode. Dramatists Play Service. Royalty: $25. Music, apply to publisher.

THE GREEN WOOD, by Henzie Raeburn. 3 men, 2 women. Church or chapel set. A liturgy built around a dramatization of the presentation of Christ in the temple. If carefully handled, a thoughtful and impressive service. Baker's Plays, 60¢. Royalty: $5.

A GREENE CHRISTMAS, by Effa Preston. 8 men, 8 women. Plays 40 minutes. Peace on earth is restored when strangers and Grandma Greene clear away family problems. Comedy. T. S. Denison & Co., 50¢ (purchase of 10 copies required).

THE GUARDIAN, by Frances B. O'Brien. 3 men, 4 women, choir. Joseph, betrothed to Mary, portrayed as a man of deep religious scruples. Climax in the birth of Christ and the singing of shepherds. Baker's Plays, 60¢. Royalty: $5.

GUEST HOUSE, VERY EXCLUSIVE, by Reby Edmond. 4 men, 6 women. Plays 30 minutes. Interior set. A woman attempts to build a family from the guests at her boarding house, but finds them joined at Christmastime by something unexpected. Samuel French, Inc., 60¢. Royalty: none for amateurs.

GUIDANCE THROUGH DRAMA, by M. Jerry Weiss. Six plays concerning common family problems. William Morrow & Co., $3.95.

THE GUIDING HAND, by Elmer A. Kettner. On Christian education. Concordia, 20¢.

HALLOWEEN AND THANKSGIVING, by Nina B. Lankin. Variable Cast. Simple Thanksgiving plays. Samuel French, Inc., 75¢.

HAMLET, PRINCE OF DENMARK, by William Shakespeare. 27 men, 2 women. The magnificent tragedy of the Prince of Denmark who, feeling the pulls of Renaissance reason and moral sensitivity, must obey his father's commands for revenge and also be answerable to God for his actions. Pelican Books. Royalty: none.

HAMP, by J. L. Hodson, adapted by John Wilson. 13 men. Plays full evening. Private Hamp, an almost simple-minded nonentity, walks away from a battle during the war and is court-martialed and executed according to military ceremony. A powerful treatment of the pity of war. Taken from the novel *Return to the Wood.* Evans Plays, $1.25. Royalty: $50–$25.

HANDY BOOK FOR CHURCH SPECIAL DAYS, by Louise Novotny. Twenty or more plays and pageants for all special church days; maintain a highly spiritual tone. Baker's Plays, $1.25.

HANDY CHRISTMAS PROGRAM BOOK. Readings, playlets, recitations, etc., adaptable for all grades. Eldridge, $1.

HANNAH, book and lyrics by Helen Kromer, music by Frederick Silver. 6 men, 5 women, 1 boy, 1 girl, chorus of 3 men, 3 women. Plays 2 hours, 15 minutes. A demonstration of reconciliation between peoples in parable form, as a woman and her family accept and are accepted by a community. Points man's mission as glorification of God. In musical comedy style. Baker's Plays, $1.50. Musical score, $7.50. Royalty: $50.

HANNELE, by Gerhart Hauptmann, translated by H. Frenz and M. Waggoner. 11 men, 8 women, 1 girl, extras. Interior set. A girl is dying in the almshouse and dreams that among those around her are her mother and Christ. She dreams of being taken to heaven by angels as she dies. Requires sensitivity in direction. Fantasy sequences might prove a problem. Leaves the question of whether the girl's experience is illusion or truth. In *Gerhart Hauptmann, 3 Plays.* Holt, Rinehart & Winston. Royalty: apply to publisher.

HANS BRINKER OR THE SILVER SKATES, by Mary Mapes Dodge, adapted by Dorothy Albert. 8 men, 5 women. Plays 1 hour. Interior set. In three scenes, most of the original intact, and told with dramatic flair. Baker's Plays, 60¢.

HAPPY CHRISTMAS TO ALL. 3 men, 3 women. Plays 20 minutes. A visit with the family of Dr. Clement Moore as he writes " 'Twas the Night Before Christmas." Plays, Inc., 50¢.

THE HAPPY LIFE, by Robert St. Clair and Dr. M. K. W. Heicher. 4 men, 3 women, extras. Plays 35 minutes. A businessman remains faithful to Christian ideals in spite of a financial disaster. T. S. Denison & Co., 50¢ (purchase of 7 copies required).

HARK, THE HERALD ANGELS SING, by Denise Carlton Dean. 5 soloists, mixed singing chorus. An old vagabond dreams of the wise men and receives assurance that the mission of Christ is to save human lives. Operetta for Christmas. Baker's Plays, $1.25 (purchase of 10 copies required).

HARK, THE LITTLE ANGELS SPEAK, by Karin Asbrand. Play, pageant, variety show, etc.; a Christmas program for young children. Baker's Plays, $1.25.

HARRIET, by Florence Ryerson and Colin Clements. 7 men, 10 women. Plays 2 hours, 30 minutes. Samuel French, Inc., $1. Royalty: $50.

THE HASTY HEART, by John Patrick. 8 men, 1 woman. Plays full evening. The skepticism of a convalescent soldier is changed by the unselfish actions of his nurse and fellow soldiers. Dramatists Play Service, $1. Royalty: $50–$25.

HE, by Albert Savoir. 12 men, 2 women, extras. Plays full evening. Delegates of the Society of Free Thinkers meet for the purpose of abolishing God. Samuel French, Inc., $1. Royalty: $25.

HE CAME SEEING, by Mary P. Hamlin. 3 men, 2 women. Plays 40 minutes. Interior set. A young man comes under Christ's influence and discards his former belief. Baker's Plays, 60¢. Royalty: $5.

HE IS COME! THE MESSIAH! by Natalie Wagner. Large cast. Plays 30–45 minutes. Reader and pantomime pageant of the Nativity.

Play is elastic in form, has beauty of presentation. Eldridge, 60¢ (purchase of 5 copies required).

HE IS NOT HERE! HE IS RISEN! by Paul Nagy, Jr. Minister, choir, congregation, and the traditional Bible characters. An Easter sunrise service containing "The Legend of the Holy Fire." Christ as the Light of the world. Baker's Plays, 60¢.

HE IS RISEN INDEED, by Robert Horspool. 9 men, 3 women. Plays 35 minutes. The legend of the belief in Jesus' innocence of Claudia, wife of Pilate. Abingdon Press, 35¢.

HE KNEW THE MASTER, by Avon Knox. 3 men, 4 women. Exterior set. Two brothers learn to know the Master in very different ways. Three acts. Baker's Plays, 75¢. Royalty: $10.

HE LIVES, by Gertrude R. Goudey. 5 men, 5 women. Plays 30 minutes. A possible sequel to the story of the rich young ruler. Baker's Plays, 60¢.

HE PASSED THIS WAY, by Margaret Ann Hubbard. 6 men, 6 women, extras. Plays 2 hours. Exterior set. A thief to be crucified with Christ finds, with the woman he loves, peace in repentance. Three acts. Baker's Plays, 60¢. Royalty: $5.

HE WHO GETS SLAPPED, by Leonid Andreyev. 20 men, 3 women. A man in a world circus finds his words are met only with misunderstanding laughter, and he finally comes to die for love when he at last faces life. Samuel French, Inc., $1. Royalty: $25.

HE WHO SAYS YES, HE WHO SAYS NO, by Bertolt Brecht. 5 men (or boys), 1 woman, small chorus. Two short plays after the form of the Japanese Noh plays. Designed to cause thinking about custom and when it should determine action, the plays present different answers. In *Accent,* Vol. 7 (Autumn, 1946). Royalty: apply to *Accent.*

HE WHO WALKS IN LOVE, by Elizabeth Hellier. 4 men, 4 women, extras. Plays 40 minutes. A pageant-play for Christmas. A slave girl's relationship to the Holy Family earns her freedom. Eldridge, 60¢ (purchase of 8 copies required).

HEALING IN ITS WINGS, by Clyde Cruse. 6 men, 3 women, 2 children, extras. Plays 35 minutes. Interior set. Lives are changed during rehearsal for a Christmas pageant; a child is believed lost in a storm until the protection of a higher power is recognized. Baker's Plays, 60¢. Royalty: $5.

HEART OF THE HOUSE, by Nora Stirling. A disabled mother faces the challenge of rehabilitation. Vocational Rehabilitation Administration.

HEART-SOUND OF A STRANGER, by Anne West. 2 men, 3 women. Plays 30 minutes. A Mexican woman is welcomed in the hotel in which she seeks lodging after saving the life of an American child. Some cutting may be needed at the end. Friendship Press, 50¢.

HEATHEN PIONEER, by Joel Climenhega. 2 men, 2 women. Plays 30 minutes. A young man believes God has told him to go to South Dakota to convert the heathen there. Comedy. Baker's Plays, 60¢. Royalty: $5.

THE HEAVENLY HOST, by Lyman R. Bayard. 29 men (doubling possible), 9 women, 1 boy, choir, angels. Plays 1 hour. A Nativity with minimum rehearsal and staging problems. Music included. Baker's Plays, 50¢ (purchase of 15 copies required).

THE HEDGE, by Louis F. Haeberle. 11 men. Plays 35 minutes. Exterior set. Judas' collapse as he plots against Christ. Even he, however, is capable of gaining forgiveness. T. S. Denison & Co., 50¢ (purchase of 10 copies required).

HELLO AND GOODBYE, by Elizabeth Blake. Conflict between strict and permissive attitudes toward the young. Division of Health and Welfare, United Presbyterian Church in the U.S.A.

HENRY HEREAFTER, by Hal D. Stewart. 12 men, 6 women. Henry VIII and his six wives are questioned about their lives on earth in the region between heaven and hell. Evans Plays. Royalty: 25*s.* 2*d.*

HERE COME THE CLOWNS, by Philip Barry. 10 men (1 a dwarf), 3 women. Plays full evening. Interior set. A group of vaudeville players representing the world in miniature come under the influence of a demoniac illusionist capable of making men tell the truth; finally one of them sees God in man's free will. Combination of realism and symbolism. Samuel French, Inc., $6.50. Royalty: $50.

HERNANI, by Victor Hugo, translated by Linda Asher. (See Crosland translation below.) Mentor Press. Royalty: apply to publisher.

HERNANI, by Victor Hugo, translated by Mrs. Newton Crosland. 21 men, 3 women, extras (some doubling possible). Plays full evening. Set in the Spain of 1519. Hernani, a noble in revolt against the king, remains faithful to his pledges even when they call for his suicide. Style of bigger-than-life characterizations may be difficult for modern audiences to accept. Little, Brown. Royalty: apply to publisher.

THE HIDDEN GIFT, by Walter Butts. 4 men, 4 women. Plays 1 hour. A family discovers, thanks to the visit of a Stranger and the opening of an old box, the legacy of happiness that comes from within. Eldridge, 60¢.

THE HIDDEN MANGER, by Karin Asbrand. 5 men, 2 women, 1 boy, 1 girl, extras. Two children seek the manger and are led to Bethlehem. In *Easy Bible Story Dramatizations for Children.* Baker's Plays, $1.25.

HIGH GROUND (BONA VENTURE), by Charlotte Hastings. 3 men, 8 women. Interior set. A nun saves the life of a girl and unearths a murderer. Understanding and justice emerge from the serene atmosphere of the convent. Three acts. Baker's Plays, $1.25. Royalty: $50.

HIGH PRESSURE AREA, by Nora Stirling. Problems of junior high girls. Nat'l. Assoc. for Mental Health, $1. Production package, $4.50.

THE HIGH SCHOOL CHRISTMAS BOOK, by Helen Starr. Plays, pageants, skits, etc., for high school. Heuer, $1.

HIGH TOR, by Maxwell Anderson. 16 men, 2 women. Plays full evening. The beauty of nature in conflict with man's attempts to replace it with modern mechanical systems. Dramatists Play Service, $1. Royalty: $35–$25.

THE HIGHWAY AND THE WAY, by M. Creagh-Henry. Chancel drama for mature men and women. Sheldon Press (apply to publisher for price).

HOLIDAY BOOK FOR VERSE CHOIRS, by Gertrude Enfield. Eleven short plays at the junior high school level. Expression, $1.50.

HOLIDAY PLAYS, by Shirley Ruth Cotzin. Four playlets in rhyme, one each for Tu Bi-Sh'vot (done in pantomime, with reader), Purim, Passover, and Chanukah, for primary grade children. May be done independently. Union of American Hebrew Congregations, 50¢.

HOLIDAY PLAYS FOR LITTLE PLAYERS, by Deborah Newman. Thirty-three short plays for holidays. Plays, Inc., $5.

HOLIDAY PLAYS FOR TEENAGERS, by Helen L. Miller. Twenty-one comedy one-acts at the junior high level. Plays, Inc., $5.

HOLIDAY PLAYS FOR YOUNG ACTORS, by Grace Sorenson. T. S. Denison & Co., $1.

HOLIDAY PROGRAMS FOR BOYS AND GIRLS, by Aileen Fisher. Large variety of material from which to choose carefully. Plays, Inc., $5.

THE HOLLOW CROWN, by John Barton. 3 men, 1 woman. Plays full evening. Music, poetry, letters, etc., in the words of the monarchs of England, devised into an entertaining dramatic evening. Samuel French, Inc., $2. Royalty: $35–$25.

THE HOLLY AND THE IVY, by Wynyard Browne. 4 men, 4 women. At Christmastime in an old vicarage the characters of the play come to see one another as they really are for the first time. Evans Plays, $1.25 (plus postage). Royalty: $35–$25.

THE HOLY CITY, by Nancy Douglas Bowditch. 9 characters, chorus. A pilgrimage to Jerusalem in search of the Messiah. Baker's Plays, 60¢.

HOLY FAMILY, by R. H. Ward. 9 men, 3 women. Plays 1 hour. A relation of the story to modern life is established through the use of a "shock tactic." Excellent drama touched with inspiration. Christ's birth, a dramatic comment on his death and resurrection. In verse. Baker's Plays, $1. Royalty: $15.

THE HOLY NATIVITY, by Harvey B. Hatcher. Silhouette presentation of the story of Christmas. Broadman Press, 35¢.

THE HOLY NATIVITY, by Mary Litsinger and Mattie B. Shannon. 1 man, 1 woman, choir, readers, extras. Pageant with music. Abingdon Press, 35¢.

THE HOLY SEARCH, by Robert St. Clair. 9 men, 2 women (may vary). Plays 25 minutes. The three wise men are principal characters in a very human play. Musical background may be employed. Four scenes. T. S. Denison & Co., 50¢ (purchase of 8 copies required).

HOLY SMOKE, by Margaret Williams Stevens. 5 men, 5 women. An embittered widower finally, after a climactic turn of events, agrees to sell land for church building. Three acts. Eldridge, 85¢ (purchase of 10 copies required).

THE HOLY WOOD, by Martinus Nijhoff. Variable cast. Three short verse-plays: Nativity, Easter, and Pentecost. Daamen (apply to publisher for price).

HOME FOR CHRISTMAS, adapted by Anne Martens. 6 men, 10 women, extras. Plays 90 minutes. The Clayton family turns back the clock, coming home for Christmas. Comedy, two acts. Eldridge, 75¢. Royalty: $15.

HOME FOR CHRISTMAS, by James F. Stone. 4 men, 5 women. Pop, a traveling salesman, coming home for Christmas, finds a lack of "peace and good will." Comedy. Baker's Plays, 85¢ (purchase of 9 copies required).

HOME OF THE BRAVE, by Arthur Laurents. 6 men. Plays full evening. The psychological study of a Jewish soldier, obsessed by the idea that his fellows are prejudiced against him, who recovers his confidence. Dramatists Play Service, $1. Royalty: $35–$25.

THE HOME THE STAR SHONE ON, by Esther C. Averill. 8 men (5 bit parts), 4 women. Plays 40 minutes. Exterior set. Young lad gives sanctuary to the Holy Family, and the lives of the members of his family are changed. Baker's Plays, 60¢.

HONORING FRIENDSHIP, by Emilia Ritari. 2 boys, 5 girls, extras. Plays 40 minutes. Pan-American customs for children. Baker's Plays, 35¢.

HONOUR THY MOTHER, by P. Henry Lotz and Grace Chapin Auten. Programs for mother-daughter occasions, Mother's Day. Baker's Plays, 35¢.

THE HOPE OF THE WORLD, by Helen M. Roberts. Speech choir, 3 readers, 14 characters for tableaux. Plays 1 hour. Eight episodes from the Bible story of the Nativity compose the pageant. Banner Play Bureau, 75¢. Royalty: $5.

THE HOPEFUL TRAVELLERS, by G. M. Martens, adapted from "Les Geux au Paradis" by Andre Obey, translated by Iris Capell. 15 men, 5 women, 1 child, 4 singing companions. Plays 2 hours, 30 minutes. A gay and humorous play concerning the attempt of two rascals to bluff their way into heaven. J. Garnet Miller, Ltd.

HOTEL UNIVERSE, by Philip Barry. 5 men, 4 women. Plays full evening. People seeking themselves find very different solutions to similar problems. Unique treatment of complex human problems. Samuel French, Inc., $1. Royalty: $50.

THE HOUR GLASS, by William Butler Yeats. 5 men, 1 woman, 2 children, extras. Plays 50 minutes. Interior set. A wise man who regrets the disbelief he has instilled in others is saved by the fool who has retained belief. Holds a necessary touch of fantasy. Technically easy to produce. Samuel French, Inc. Royalty: $10.

THE HOUR OF FATE, by Helen Clark and Henry Burns, Jr. Plays 25 minutes. A Muslim girl who has learned about Christianity conflicts with her family. Banner Play Bureau, 50¢ (purchase of 6 copies required).

THE HOUR OF TRUTH, by Percival Wilde. 3 men, 3 women. Plays 35 minutes. Interior set. A family's integrity is put to the test. One act. Baker's Plays, 60¢. Royalty: $10.

THE HOUSE BEAUTIFUL, by Channing Pollock. 7 men, 4 women. Various interior and exterior sets. An exploration of the secret of true happiness and where it is to be found. Three acts. Samuel French, Inc.: cloth, $2; paper, $1.25. Royalty: $25–$20.

THE HOUSE BY THE STABLE, by Charles Williams. 4 men, 2 women. Plays 30 minutes. Should be played together with "Grab and Grace," its sequel. The incarnation and the grace granted in it are dealt with in verse. The struggle between good and evil, through the clash of opposites, reveals a new truth. Subtle wit and unusual treatment of angelic characters in a different point of view. In *Religious Drama 3*. World. Royalty: $5.

THE HOUSE OF MARY, by a Religious of C.S.M.V., S. Th. Narrator, choir. Plays 70 minutes. An attempt to give Holy Week and Easter life by showing how forgiveness and new life extend from the historical account in the book of Acts. Baker's Plays, 60¢.

THE HOUSE ON THE SAND, by Elliot Field. 4 men, 5 women. Plays 1 hour. Interior set. The deciding of an important moral issue unifies a family; worship service precedes it. Baker's Plays, 60¢.

THE HOUSE THAT JACK BUILT, by Elizabeth Blake. Demonstrates the relationship of health to faith. Division of Health and Welfare, United Presbyterian Church in the U.S.A.

THE HOUSETOP, by Cecil Tugman. 7 men, 3 women. Plays 90 minutes to 2 hours. Exterior set. Christ's last days, death, and resurrection. No power is capable of withstanding the power of Christ. Baker's Plays, $1.25. Royalty: $15.

HOW FAR IS IT TO BETHLEHEM? by Elizabeth Jones. Reverent treatment of an ageless theme. Horn Book, Inc., $1.50.

HOW JOHN LEARNED ABOUT HANUKKAH, by Elsie-Jean. Uses the technique of the play within a play. Anti-Defamation League of B'nai B'rith, 10¢.

HOW MUCH IS ENOUGH, by Joyce Myers. 4 men, 3 women. A young man who would be a social worker learns something of the Christian spirit in his home. Christian Board of Publication, 25¢; 8 for $1.50.

HOW THE GREAT GUEST CAME, by Lionel Adams. 6 men, 2 women. Plays 25 minutes. Interior set. An old shoemaker's kindness in succoring several people fulfills his dream of a visit by the spirit of Christ. Samuel French, Inc., 60¢. Royalty: $5.

HUMAN, by Zona Gale. 3 men, 8 women, 1 boy. Plays 20 minutes. Interior set. A boy, unable to visit his mother who is ill in a sanatarium, plans to send her a rose for Christmas; he then finds his desire fulfilled. In *The Easy Christmas Book*. Baker's Plays, $1.25.

THE HUMAN CONDITION, by James Brock. Symbolic witnesses represent modern society at a committee hearing on the human condition and man in the anxieties of modern life. In *Modern Chancel Dramas*. Eldridge, $1.25. Royalty: $10.

THE HUMBLEST PLACE. 7 men, 3 women, extras. Plays 30 minutes. The words of the wise men convince the greedy innkeeper. Retains the wonder of the night of Christ's birth. One act. Plays, Inc., 50¢.

THE HUSBAND OF POVERTY, by Henry Neville Maugham. The life of Francis of Assisi. College Book Service, $17.50.

I CREATED SANTA CLAUS, by Valentine Bean. Large cast. Plays 45 minutes. A modern morality in which the true meaning of Christmas is sought through a series of historical and biblical scenes. Baker's Plays, 60¢. Royalty: $5.

I HAVE SPOKEN TO MY CHILDREN, by Darius Swann. 3 men, 4 women, verse choir. A Negro mother helps her daughter cope with violence in a newly integrated high school. Verse choir may be omitted where such skills are limited. Friendship Press: set of 10 acting scripts, $1.25. Royalty: none.

I LAY IN ZION, by William Gibson. 4 men, 4 women. Plays 40 minutes. Interior set. Peter's denial of Christ and his final acceptance of going to Rome and the cross. In verse. Baker's Plays, 60¢. Royalty: $5 (play may be released, by instruction of the author, only to amateur groups with nonsegregated audiences).

I MADE CHRIST'S CROSS, by Esther C. Averill. 3 men, 2 women. Plays 30 minutes. Interior set. The story of the man who made the cross on which Christ was crucified. Baker's Plays, 60¢.

I SAW HIM, by Sarah Walton Miller. An Easter pageant. Personifications of eleven places or things connected with the death of Christ and his resurrection deliver short speeches. Broadman Press, 35¢.

I SAW THE CROSS, by Jean M. Mattson. 17 men, 5 women, extras. Plays 30 minutes. Interior set. The events leading to the cross seen through the eyes of Judas, Simon, Longinus, Pilate, and Peter. Five scenes. A reader establishes the relevance of the story to our world. T. S. Denison & Co., 50¢ (purchase of 10 copies required).

I WILL GIVE THANKS, by Karin Asbrand. 5 boys, 5 girls. Plays 10 minutes. The Christian martyrdom in Rome. In *Easy Bible Story Dramatizations for Children*. Baker's Plays, $1.25.

IF THE LIGHT BE DARKNESS, by Phyllis Benbow Beardsley. 3 men, 1 woman. Interior set. A young veteran, disturbed that the world does not accept Christ of whom he had a vision during the war, changes the life of a pastor with his story. Baker's Plays, 75¢. Royalty: $1.

IF THINE ENEMY, by Frank A. Cooper. 3 men, 2 women, 1 girl. Plays 40 minutes. A little girl and an angel solve the problem of an impossible-to-live-with man in time for Christmas. Eldridge, 60¢ (purchase of 6 copies required).

I'LL BE GLAD WHEN IT'S OVER, by Edrie Drach. 7 men, 6 women, extras. A woman who has lost all touch with the meaning of Christmas has a dream of the Nativity. One act. Eldridge, 50¢ (purchase of 12 copies required).

I'M TALKING ABOUT JERUSALEM, by Arnold Wesker. 6 men, 4 women, extras. Two young people try to escape the modern commercial world, but find they cannot build their paradise in one day. Evans Plays. Royalty: 6–5 *gns.* 6*s.* 6*d.*

THE IMAGE OF CHRISTMAS, by Karin Asbrand. 2 men, 5 women, 3

children, reader and chorus. Nine tableaux show Christmas as seen by each member of the family. Description by reader. No memorization, little rehearsal required. Baker's Plays, 60¢.

IN CHRISTMAS CAROL LAND, by E. B. Dykes Beachy. Large cast of children. Plays 30 minutes. Exterior set. A joyous pageant showing the history of the Christmas carol and its geographic scope. Baker's Plays, 60¢.

IN JOSEPH'S GARDEN, by Winifred Bell Fletcher. 2 men, 2 women, narrator, voice of Christ, choir, soloist. Plays 1 hour. The story of Joseph of Arimathea in an Easter choric drama. Cokesbury Press, 25¢. Package, 25. 12 for $2.50.

IN JOSEPH'S GARDEN, by Martha Mixer. 6 men, 10 women, children, junior choir. A thief taken by the beauty of Joseph's garden is brought by angels to an awareness of Christ's resurrection. In *Transparent Curtain Pageants for Easter.* Baker's Plays, $1.25.

"IN MY FATHER'S HOUSE . . ." by E. Flo Collitt. Plays 1 hour. A modern family learns the importance of Christ in the Christmas celebration. Very human, with a strong message. Eldridge, 75¢ (purchase of 10 copies required).

IN PESACH LAND, by Lillian S. Freehof. 11 boys, 1 girl. Judy is helped by Mr. Matzos, Mr. Wine, Charlie Charoses, Lanny Lambone, and other characters to discover the password from Uncle Haggadah in the City of Deder. Much fun. For ages from nine to fourteen. Union of American Hebrew Congregations, 25¢.

IN THE BEGINNING, by Isabel Barr. Includes "The Coming," 3 men, 1 woman, a Nativity (20 minutes); "The Passing," 12 men, 1 woman, four scenes after the crucifixion (25 minutes); and "The Return," 11 men, 2 women, resurrection of man through Christ and the disciples. Baker's Plays, 75¢. Royalty: each play, $5; all, $10.

IN THE FULLNESS OF TIME, by Gloria Roe. Choir and narrator. A beautiful Christmas cantata, personalizing the message of the coming of the Savior. Eldridge, $1.25 (purchase of 10 copies required).

IN THE PRESENCE OF DEATH, edited by Chalmers Dale. For youth presentations. Four one-act dramas of people faced with death in their personal lives. "Till Death Do Us Part" by William Hamilton, "The End of the Story" by Craig Gilbert, "Journal of Vera Grey" by Stephen Chodorov, "Room for Death" by William Hamilton. Bethany Press, $1.50.

IN THE SAME COUNTRY, by Alice Geer Kelsey. 4 speaking parts, choric speakers, tableaux. Plays 45 minutes. Luke collects materials for his Gospel in Bethlehem fifty years after the Nativity. For Christmas. Cokesbury Press, 35¢. Package, 25.

IN THE SHADOW OF THE CROSS, by Irene H. Fussler. Large mixed cast. Plays 1 hour. Three episodes and six scenes. "Persecution, Crucifixion, and Resurrection" in the life of Christ, each followed by a modern parallel. Baker's Plays, 75¢.

IN THE SHEPHERD'S FIELD, by Alice D. Donovan. 12 men, 4 women. Exterior set. A group of Americans stop in a shepherd's field outside Bethlehem and witness the pageant of the Nativity. Baker's Plays, 60¢.

IN THIS SIGN CONQUER, by Paul Nagy, Jr. Plays 1 hour. Minister, choir, symbolic characters, and congregation characters take part to show the candle of the cross dispelling the darkness of evil. Baker's Plays, 60¢.

IN WHITE AMERICA, by Martin B. Duberman. 3 Negro characters (2 men, 1 woman), 3 white characters (2 men, 1 woman). Plays full evening. History of the Negro in the United States, a dramatization from historical records. Samuel French, Inc., $1.25. Royalty: apply to publisher.

INFANTA, by Oscar Wilde, adapted by Lewy Olfson. 2 men, 3 women. Drama of the Infanta and the hunchbacked dwarf Le Bosan. Harper, 50¢ (purchase of 5 copies required).

INHERIT THE WIND, by Jerome Lawrence and Robert E. Lee. Large cast. Plays full evening. Dramatization based on the Scopes evolution trial, an exploration of man's right to free thought and the social limitations imposed on it. Excellent acting parts, particularly for two men playing characters based on Clarence Darrow and William Jennings Bryan. Powerful and difficult. Dramatists Play Service, $1.25. Royalty: apply to publisher.

THE INN AT BETHLEHEM, by Anna D. Lutz. Small cast. The first act is the Nativity; the second is set forty years later, and shows the influence of Christ on the lives of those present at the Nativity. Cokesbury Press, 35¢.

THE INNKEEPER, by Leonora Sill Ashton. 10 men, 2 women, chorus. Stunned to know he has turned the infant King from the door, the innkeeper comes to understand the meaning of the wise men's words when he saves an infant from Herod's men. Baker's Plays, 60¢.

THE INNOCENT, by Albert Johnson. Small cast. A short Nativity play with a fresh approach. Concerns the Holy Family and the people of the inn. Requires simplicity and delicacy of production. In *Church Plays and How to Stage Them.* Available in manuscript from author, $1. Royalty: $10–$5.

THE INS AND OUTS, by Nora Stirling. 3 boys, 2 girls. Problems of those who do and do not "belong" among high school students. Nat'l. Assoc. for Mental Health, $1.

INTO THY KINGDOM, by Dorothy Clarke Wilson. 5 men, 3 women. Plays 40 minutes. Events in the home of a Jewish high priest after the crucifixion of Christ. Baker's Plays, 60¢.

INVASION FROM THE STRATOSPHERE. 5 boys, 2 girls, extras. Plays 25 minutes. UN achievements dramatized for young people. Plays, Inc., 50¢.

THE INVISIBLE ONE, by Mona Swann. 15 characters, extras. Plays 1 hour. Choral-speaking version of an Indian legend of great beauty. Baker's Plays, 50¢.

THE INVITATION, by Sadie B. Atkins. Drama concerning a Christmas invitation with the power to touch the heart. In *Recitations Chosen for Children.* Baker's Plays, $1.25.

IPHIGENIA AT AULIS, by Euripides, translated by Moses Hadas and John McLean. 6 men, 2 women, chorus of Women of Chalcis (6–18), extras. Agamemnon is told by the Oracle that he must sacrifice his daughter Iphigenia in order to be victorious at Troy. Emphasis on the internal conflicts and pains of the characters, concluding in Iphigenia's resolution to die for Greece. Difficult in style and scope. In *Ten Plays by Euripides.* Bantam Books. Royalty: apply to publisher.

IPHIGENIA AT AULIS, by Euripides, translated by Charles R. Walker. In *The Complete Greek Tragedies.* University of Chicago Press. Royalty: apply to publisher.

IRISH MIRACLE, by Stefanie Fone. 4 men, 3 women, extras. Plays 30 minutes. Interior set. Serious depiction of the reactions of the people of a village when an Irish girl shows the gift of healing. Baker's Plays, 60¢. Royalty: $5.

IS IT I, LORD? by Letitia M. Hollinshead. 4 men, 7 women, offstage voices. Plays 45 minutes. Maundy Thursday and the betrayal, Good Friday and Christ before Pilate, Easter and the watchers at the tomb. Baker's Plays, 60¢.

ISAIAH, THE STATESMAN PROPHET, by Norman E. Nygaard. Monodrama of Isaiah's condemnation of the nobles of Israel. In *The Bible Comes Alive.* Baker's Plays, $1.25.

IT ALL ADDS UP, by Esther Hawley. 2 men, 2 women. The workings of UNESCO dramatized for junior and senior high school ages. American Theatre Wing, 50¢. Royalty: $2.50.

IT CAME TO PASS, by Isabel Barr. 3 men, 4 women. Plays 20 minutes. The story of the daughter of the ruler of the synagogue who is raised from the dead by Christ. In *Jericho Road and Other Miracle Plays.* Baker's Plays, 75¢. Royalty: apply to publisher.

IT IS I, by Ethel G. Rockwell. 3 men, 2 women. Plays 1 hour. Exterior set. The power of Christ's redemption in the lives of Judas and Mary of Magdala. For Easter or any season. Baker's Plays, 60¢. Royalty: $5.

"IT IS MORE BLESSED—" by Albert Carriere. 2 men, 2 women. Plays 30 minutes. Interior set. A story of sacrifice is used by a girl to convince her father to make a contribution to the church and understand the spirit of Christian sacrifice. Baker's Plays, 60¢.

IT IS SO! (IF YOU THINK SO), by Luigi Pirandello, English version by Arthur Livingston. 7 men, 7 women, extras. 2 interior sets. A woman seeks her daughter, but is she a man's deceased first wife or present wife? A parable of the necessity of illusion and the illusiveness of truth. Difficult. In *Naked Masks.* E. P. Dutton & Co. Royalty: apply to publisher.

IT SHOULD HAPPEN TO A DOG, by Wolf Mankowitz. 2 men. A humorous, human, and unsaintly Jonah who simply cannot understand the purpose of the Lord in ordering him to sea. In *Five One-Act Plays.* Baker's Plays, $1.25. Royalty: $10.

IT'S EASTER, DR. JORDAN, by Sherwood Keith. 1 man, 1 woman. Plays 30–45 minutes. Involves the true meaning of resurrection. Baker's Plays, 60¢ (purchase of 2 copies required).

J.B., by Archibald MacLeish. 12 men, 9 women. Interior set. Job's question of how the world may be given justification asked in powerful verse, with great relevance for our times. Baker's Plays, $1.25. Royalty: $50.

JEANNE D'ARC, by Myrtle McCormick Grimes. 1 man. 5 women. Plays 30 minutes. Interior set. A crippled boy has visions of the sainted Jeanne, and through him her destiny is recounted. Strong peace theme. Baker's Plays, 60¢.

JEANNE D'ARC, by Percy MacKaye. 35 men, 5 women. Plays full evening. The tragedy of Joan of Arc, focusing most strongly on her early life and campaigns. The visions are played on stage as visible and audible only to her. Multiple settings. Macmillan (out of print). Royalty: apply to publisher.

JERICHO ROAD, by Isabel Barr. 6 men, 4 women, 2 lepers (men or women), extras. Plays 30 minutes. In three episodes. Story of the blind beggar Bartimeus, whose healing is a message of hope. In *Jericho Road and Other Miracle Plays.* Baker's Plays, 75¢.

JERICHO ROAD AND OTHER MIRACLE PLAYS, by Isabel Barr. Three plays: "Bartimeus, the Blind Beggar"; "The Ruler's Daughter"; "The Marriage Feast of Cana." Baker's Plays, 75¢. Royalty: apply to publisher for each play.

THE JEW OF MALTA, by Christopher Marlowe. Plays full evening. The Jew destroys everyone who stands in the way of his diabolic thirst for possession in a world he conceives of as devoid of charity and love as he is himself. Modified Elizabethan staging. Greater part of play in verse. Some technical difficulties. In *Christopher Marlowe: Five Plays.* Hill & Wang, $1.65. Royalty: none.

THE JEWISH HOLIDAY ON PARADE, by Dorothy F. Zeligs. Flexible cast. For ages 9–14. All the Jewish holidays of the year treated in a pageant play. Union of American Hebrew Congregations, 25¢.

JOAN OF ARC, by Dana Thomas. 10 men, 7 women, extras. A moving and delicate drama of Joan of Arc, carefully following the historical account of her life. Three acts. T. S. Denison & Co., $1. Royalty: $25.

JOAN OF LORRAINE, by Maxwell Anderson. 18 men, 4 women. Plays 2 hours. The life of Joan of Arc is told through the device of rehearsals for a play concerning the saint. The characters struggle with the moral implications and meaning of her story, with particular depth given the question of compromising with evil in order to do the will of God. Dramatists Play Service, $1.25. Royalty: $50–$25.

JOANNA AND THE CANDLES, by Joyce Dennys. 9 women. Plays 25–30 minutes. Interior set. A prioress protects a girl who has just become an heiress to a large fortune from her unprincipled relatives during the reign of Henry VIII. H. F. W. Deane & Sons, 5*s.* net. Postage 4*d.* Royalty: apply to publisher.

JOCHABED'S SACRIFICE, by Karin Asbrand. Plays 10 minutes. A play concerning Moses, for women and girls. In *Easy Bible Dramatizations for Children.* Baker's Plays, $1.25.

JOHN, by Philip Barry. 16 men, 2 women. 3 interior sets. A psychological portrait of John the Baptist and the influence of the figure of Christ during his last days. Samuel French, Inc., $2. Royalty: $50–$25.

JOHN DOE, by Bernard V. Dryer. 6 men, 1 woman. Plays 40 minutes. A mixed group of people who have died either by cruelty or for the sake of conscience wait in limbo for the Gates of Judgment. Baker's Plays, 60¢. Royalty: $5.

JOHN, WHOSE SURNAME WAS MARK, by P. G. Morgan Dennis. 7 characters. A morality play in three acts. Faith Press, 1*s*. 6*d*.

JONAH 3, by James Bridie. 6 men, 3 women. A tale of Jonah and the whale, leaving room for the modern director to apply his imagination wholeheartedly. Constable. Royalty: apply to publisher.

JOSEPH AND HIS BROTHERS. Plays 15–20 minutes. Bible play for children. Includes production notes. Concordia, 40¢. In set with 7 other similar plays, $3.

JOSEPH AND THE NATIVITY, by Ellen Jane Lorenz. The Nativity as viewed by Joseph in song and story. Eldridge, 50¢. Optional filmstrip (35 mm.), $5.

JOSEPH OF ARIMATHEA, by Dorothy Clarke Wilson. 5 men, 4 women, reader. Plays 40 minutes. Interior set. The events of Good Friday and Easter as they affected the lives and spirits of Joseph and Nicodemus. Baker's Plays, 60¢.

JOURNEY OF PROMISE, by William Kozlenko. 7 men (extras), 1 woman. Plays 30 minutes. Interior set. A stowaway discovers a time bomb in the hold of an ocean liner and responds to his feeling of duty. Baker's Plays, 60¢. Royalty: $5.

JOURNEY OF THE STAR, by Edward Murch. 7 women. A Nativity play linking the present-day refugee problem to the Christmas story. The queens of the wise men precede their husbands to the manger. One act. H. F. W. Deane & Sons.

THE JOURNEY OF THE THREE KINGS, by Henri Gheon, translated by C. C. Martindale, S.J. 12 characters and nonspeaking parts. Plays 30 minutes. Children's version of the journey of the wise men, their audience with a wrathful Herod, and their return home. Baker's Plays, 85¢. Royalty: $10.

JOURNEY TO JERUSALEM, by Maxwell Anderson. Flexible cast. The doctors in Jerusalem and the boy Christ. Dramatists Play Service (available in manuscript from publisher). Returnable deposit $10; perusal script, $2.

JOURNEY TO JUDGMENT, by Albert Johnson. Large cast (room for flexibility and some doubling). A full-scale drama celebrating the Protestant Reformation. The narrator is the Witness, one who professes before a chorus of inquiring and challenging youth. Usually produced with choir and organ, but may be more simply produced with great success. Available in manuscript from the author, $1. Royalty: $25–$15.

JOY FILLS MY HEART, by Lucile G. Green. 2 men, 5 women. Plays 45 minutes–1 hour. The death and resurrection of Christ cause reaction in Barabbas and his household. Much quoting of the gospel;

conveys the message that Christ died not only in the stead of Barabbas, but of all men. Two acts. Eldridge, 75¢ (purchase of 8 copies required).

JOY IS BORN, by Shirley Lockhart. Christmas candlelighting service, with a complete order of worship. Abingdon Press. Package, 500.

JOY TO THE WORLD, by Robert St. Clair. 6 men, 4 women or 5 men. Plays 30 minutes. A play with narrator and music, telling the story of the events leading to the birth of Jesus. Baker's Plays, 50¢.

JOYFUL AND TRIUMPHANT, by Mattie B. Shannon. Large cast possible. Plays 30–40 minutes. Grandma and Grandpa read the Christmas story, providing opening for songs and tableaux. Eldridge, 60¢ (purchase of 5 copies required).

JOYFUL MYSTERY, by John L. Bonn, S.J. A dramatic poem of man's searching, since the fall of Adam, for the light found at the crib of Christ. Baker's Plays, 75¢.

JOYOUS PROGRAMS FOR SPRINGTIME CELEBRATIONS. Recitations, dialogues, etc., for Easter, Mother's Day, and others. Eldridge, $1.

THE JOYOUS SEASON, by Philip Barry. 6 men, 6 women. Interior set. A youthful mother superior returns to her temperamental family, thanks to an inheritance, and sets their lives on paths of faith and joy. Strong character comedy. Three acts. Samuel French, Inc.: cloth, $2; paper, $1.25. Royalty: $50–$25.

JUAREZ THE JUST. Junior-high world-friendship play, with atmosphere and facts of Mexico. Plays, Inc., 50¢.

JUDITH, by Jean Giraudoux, translated by John K. Savacool. 20 men (doubling possible), 4 women, 1 boy. Interior set. An unbiblical Judith becomes heroine of Israel through a night of illness and terror, rather than through humility or love. In *The Modern Theatre,* Vol. III. Doubleday. Royalty: apply to publisher.

THE JUGGLER OF OUR LADY, by Anatole France. 9 men, 2 boys, 2 girls, choir. The sincerity of the gift of a humble juggler proves more acceptable than the lavishness of other gifts. In *Jumbo Christmas Book.* Baker's Plays, $1.25.

THE JUMBO CHRISTMAS BOOK, edited by Edna Cahill. Plays, serious and comic, for every casting and staging situation. Baker's Plays, $1.25. Heuer, $1.25.

JUNIOR HIGH CHRISTMAS BOOK, by well-known authors. Christmas plays, readings, etc., for time-saving production. Baker's Plays, $1.25.

JUNIOR HIGH SCHOOL PLAYS, by Margaret Leighton. Includes play about New England faith, "When Mayflowers Bloomed in Plymouth" (2 boys, 3 girls, plays 15 minutes). Samuel French, Inc., $1.

JUNIOR PLAYS FOR ALL OCCASIONS, by Mildred Hark and Noel McQueen. Forty-three short children's plays for holidays and special days. Includes Christmas, Easter, Mother's Day. For lower and middle grades. Plays, Inc., $5.

THE JUST VENGEANCE, by Dorothy L. Sayers. 23 men, 10 women, 1 boy, 1 girl. Plays 2 hours, 30 minutes. Presentation of the atonement by God through Jesus Christ, using images and scenes, prose and verse. Difficult. Royalty: apply to Ann Watkins.

THE KHANUM AND HER TREASURES, by Grace Visher Payne. 6 women, 2 men. Plays 30 minutes. Set in today's Tehran, the play is a dramatization of the conflict between old and new Iran. Interesting background and tradition. Friendship Press, 50¢.

THE KINDLED FLAME, by Esther Baldwin York. 2 men, 2 women, extras. Plays 40 minutes. Interior set. A girl and her Roman family, living in Jerusalem at the time of the crucifixion, respond to the influence of Jesus. Baker's Plays, 50¢ (give author's name when ordering).

KING LEAR, by William Shakespeare. 20 men (doubling possible), 3 women. Plays full evening. Lear's inability to recognize true love brings him to destruction, but in his madness comes a regeneration through awareness of his own humanity. Pelican Books. Royalty: none.

KING SAUL AND THE WITCH OF ENDOR, by Edward Longstreth. Biblical chancel drama for reading or staged production. Available from author, $1.25. Royalty: inquire of the author.

A KING SHALL REIGN! by Marion Wefer. 2 men, 4 women, extras. Plays 20 minutes. Interior set. A mother grieving for her child, slain by Herod's soldiers, gives hospitality to travelers with a child. She has given shelter to Christ, and he is revealed to her. Samuel French, Inc., 60¢. Royalty: $5.

KING SOLOMON AND THE BEE, by Ray M. Cook. 6 boys, 4 girls, chorus. For ages 8–13. An original operetta from the famous legend. Union of American Hebrew Congregations, 50¢.

A KING WILL COME, by R. A. Dick. 9 men, 1 woman. The innkeeper, who has prepared a room for the King, does not realize that he has been born in his stable until the three kings come with their gifts. Evans Plays, 2*s*. Royalty: 25*s*.

THE KINGDOM OF GOD AND OTHER PLAYS, by G. Martinez Sierra. Four plays. College Book Service, $15.

KINGS IN NOMANIA, by Percival Wilde. 19 characters. Plays 90 minutes. Exterior set. The king, meeting the highest and lowest in his kingdom, spares the life of a condemned bootblack through understanding. Baker's Plays, 60¢. Royalty: $10.

KINGS OR BETTER, by Rabbis E. B. Borowitz, R. A. Soloff, and A. J. Wolf. 7 boys, 5 girls. For ages 5–12. A Purim play, in which King Ahasuerus disguises himself as a commoner at the instigation of Mordecai to meet with Haman. Very humorous. Union of American Hebrew Congregations, 35¢.

THE KING'S STANDARDS, by Costa Du Rels, translated by Helen A. Gaubert. 4 men, 2 women, extras. Interior set. The duality of closeness and conflict in the religious ministry regarding social work and modern justice. Three acts. Baker's Plays, $1.25. Royalty: $25.

KNEEL AT THE MANGER, words and music by Byron Carmony. Short cantata for Christmas. Nine gospel-style songs and scripture readings present the Christmas story from the evangelistic viewpoint. Eldridge, 50¢.

KNOWN BUT TO GOD. 5 women, 6 men. Plays 30 minutes. Five women, visiting the Tomb of the Unknown Soldier, each hear the voice of a different boy. For junior, senior high ages. Plays, Inc., 50¢.

LA MADRE, by Sister Mary Francis, P.C. 4 men, 8 women. 2 interior sets. Sister Teresa of Avila, a sixteenth-century nun, struggles to restore the old life of prayer to a convent influenced by the worldly. Samuel French, Inc., $1.25. Royalty: $25.

THE LADIES OF SOISSONS, by Sidney Cunliffe-Owen, adapted by Emmet Lavery. 12 men, 12 women (possible with 3 men, 13 women). Plays 2 hours. Three centuries in time are covered in this story of the Ladies of Soissons. Music, Song at the Scaffold. No changes in text permitted. Samuel French, Inc. (available only in manuscript). Royalty: $35–$25.

LADY OF THE MARKETPLACE, by Charlotte I. Lee. 14 women, verse choir, three wise men. Plays 20 minutes. Exterior set. Mexico, on Christmas Eve. Little Zela, too poor to have a white dress for the procession, finds pleasure in making a flower crown for the virgin. Baker's Plays, 60¢. Royalty: none if 8 copies purchased.

THE LADY WITH A LAMP, by Reginald Berkely. 20 men, 16 women, 2 children. Plays 2 hours, 15 minutes. Drama of Florence Nightingale's life in four acts. Samuel French, Inc., $1.25. Royalty: $25.

THE LAMB IN THE WINDOW, by Robert Finch. 6 men, 3 women. Plays 35 minutes. Reverend Mr. Edwards and his congregation are helped by the cleaning woman of the church. Harper, 50¢. Royalty: $5.

LAMP AT MIDNIGHT, by Barrie Stavis. 5 men, 2 women, 23 extras. Galileo's conflict between reason and faith. Dramatists Play Service, $1. Royalty: $25.

THE LARK, by Jean Anouilh, translated by Lillian Hellman. 19 men, 7 women. The life of Joan of Arc is told in flashbacks from her trial. She and France triumph over the minor demands of the institutions of the world. Requires simplicity and beauty of production, careful staging. Dramatists Play Service, $1.15. Royalty: $50–$25.

THE LAST DAYS, by James Brock. The Holy Week as a time of crisis. In the triumph of the entrance into Jerusalem, the inevitable progress to the end is begun. In *Modern Chancel Dramas*. Baker's Plays, $1.25. Royalty: $10.

THE LAST VICTORY, by Anne and Arthur Russell. 4 men, 5 women. Plays 25–30 minutes. A play about Joan of Arc shortly before she was captured by the British. At the latter part of the play she hears her saints' voices telling of her death. Not difficult. H. F. W. Deane & Sons, 1*s.* 9*d.* net. Postage, 2*d.*

THE LAST WORD, by James Broughton. 1 man, 1 woman. Plays 25 minutes. Interior set. A sophisticated couple in middle age await the coming of the bombs that will put an end to the world. The couple face one another as humans as they make an effort in their last moments to find the meaning of their existence. A parable of the last judgment. Baker's Plays, 60¢. Royalty: $10.

THE LEAST OF THESE, by Virginia Wilk Elicker. Plays 35 minutes. Dramatic and choric presentation of the appeal of the Have Nots of the modern world to the Haves for their rightful share in the world. Baker's Plays, 60¢.

THE LEFT-OVER REINDEER. 9 men, 5 women. Plays 30 minutes. A family promises to keep an iron deer in memory of the time long ago when a stern father and his children learned the meaning of Christmas. Closes with a recitation of "A Visit from St. Nicholas." Plays, Inc., 50¢.

LEGEND, by Percival Wilde. 1 man, speaker; 1 man, 1 woman, main pantomimists; 6 other pantomimists. The wish of Sister Ursula when she reaches heaven is to return to continue her work for mankind. Baker's Plays, 60¢. Royalty: $10.

THE LEGEND OF BABOUSHKA, by S. F. Cotton, music by Johan Shaufelberger. 15 men, 13 women, 8 children. A Nativity play. The legend of the peasant woman who is the Russian "Father Christmas" is recounted as she shelters the wise men and seeks the Christchild. Music of a Russian character. H. F. W. Deane & Sons, 2*s.* 6*d.* net (music available without charge from composer).

LEGEND OF THE CHRISTMAS ROSE, by Selma Lagerloff, adapted by Edith Quick and James Fluckey. Abbot Hans seeks a garden where the forest blooms even in the dead of winter to celebrate the birth of Christ. Music has been incorporated. Eldridge, $1.40 (purchase of 5 copies required).

THE LEGEND OF THE CHRISTMAS ROSE. 7 men, 3 women, female extras. Plays 10 minutes. Exterior set (road). For children. A shepherd girl finds a white rose to take as a gift to the Christchild. Opens with the coming of the wise men, closes with an angel chorus. Plays, Inc., 35¢.

THE LEGEND OF THE CHRISTMAS ROSE, by Edna Risque. 27 characters, extras. Christmas tableau in four scenes. Faith Press, 6*d.*

A LESSON FROM LUKE, by Earl J. Dias. 2 men, 5 women. Plays 20 minutes. Interior set. Judy, reading the Nativity story in Luke, recaptures her childhood feeling of Christmas. Baker's Plays, 60¢. Royalty: none if 6 copies purchased.

LET JUSTICE BE DONE, by Karin Asbrand. Flexible cast. Plays 8 minutes. From the story of Solomon. In *Easy Bible Story Dramatizations for Children.* Baker's Plays, $1.25.

LET MAN LIVE, by Par Lagerkvist. 10 men, 4 women. Fourteen historical characters recount the circumstances of their deaths, illustrating the moral that man should not judge. In *Religious Drama 3.* World, $1.65. Royalty: apply to the American-Scandinavian Foundation.

LET NOTHING YE DISMAY, by Dora M. MacDonald. 2 men, 2 women, extras. Plays 30 minutes. A pardoned criminal, old Randolph, returns to the old Randolph mansion for cheer at Christmas. Baker's Plays, 50¢.

LET US RECEIVE CHRISTMAS, by Miriam Baker. Variable cast. The entire church school participates in a Nativity pageant. Wetmore Declamation Bureau, 60¢.

LETTY'S CHRISTMAS PRODIGAL. 5 men, 6 women, extras. Plays 45 minutes. A man disguised as a tramp returns to court his old love and brings Christmas spirit to his hometown. Eldridge, 60¢.

LIFE'S CROSSROADS, by Cora G. Tichenal. 12 characters or more, chorus. Pageant, excellent for young people's groups in church. Eldridge, 50¢.

LIFT THINE EYES, by Marion Leonard Bishop. 8 women. Plays 30 minutes. Interior set. On Christmas Eve at the old ladies' rest home a nurse is aided in gaining the assurance to live her own life. Baker's Plays, 60¢. Royalty: none if 6 copies purchased.

THE LIGHT, by Bert and Malcolm Child. 12 men, 3 women. Plays 20 minutes. How the Maccabees' religious freedom fight has altered history. Anti-Defamation League of B'nai B'rith, 15¢.

THE LIGHT, by Leonard Young. 5 men, 1 woman. Plays 40 minutes. Mary and the Holy Grail influence the reconciliation of Peter (Jew) and Paul (gentile). Baker's Plays, 60¢.

THE LIGHT ETERNAL. Large cast. Plays 25 minutes. Easter candlelight service may be used at other occasions to illustrate reason for spreading gospel in the world. Eldridge, 60¢.

THE LIGHT ETERNAL, by Charles George. 5 men, 4 women. Designed for Catholic organization use, but may be produced by others. The disbelieving husband of a community schoolteacher and brother of Father Nolan has his sight restored in a stroke of lightning. Three acts. T. S. Denison & Co., $1. Royalty: $10.

THE LIGHT IN THE WINDOW, by Dorothy Clarke Wilson. 3 men, 5 women, carolers. Plays 40 minutes. Interior set. The light in Aunt Hope's window touches many people and gains a home for a disillusioned boy. Baker's Plays, 60¢.

THE LIGHT OF CHRIST, by Jean Lilyers. 8 boys and girls, singing choir. A church school Easter vesper service with all departments included. The ancient service of lights, symbolizing the return of the Light through the resurrection. Fortress Press, 10¢.

THE LIGHT OF MEN, by Kenneth Penfold. Variable cast. A Nativity play drawn from the medieval Cycles of York, Coventry, Chester, and Towneley, treating the mystery of the Incarnation. Simple, direct, and with humanity of approach. Includes production notes. Evans Plays, 2*s.* net. Royalty: 25*s.* each performance.

LIGHT OF THE WORLD, by Harold Bassage. Drama for the Epiphany season, which interprets "The Light, with which we are informed, through us, may bring Eternal Light to heal the darkness of the world." Seabury Press, 65¢.

LIGHT OF THE WORLD, by Brother Finian. 17 men, extras. Plays 40 minutes. Exterior set. Passion play in nine scenes. Portrays the men involved in the passion and death of Christ, those who stood in the light and those who remained in darkness. T. S. Denison & Co., 50¢ (purchase of 10 copies required).

THE LIGHT OF THE WORLD, by V. D. Peareth. 29 characters. Passion play in four scenes. Faith Press, 3*s.*

A LIGHT ON BEACON HILL, by Francesca Falk Miller. 2 men, 2 women, extras. Plays 30 minutes. Interior set. Through a small boy's faith a husband and wife are reunited on Christmas. Samuel French, Inc., 60¢. Royalty: apply to publisher.

THE LIGHT SHINES. A boy from India and a girl from Japan learn the "good news." For Christmas. Participants from all departments of church school. Augsburg, 10¢; 12 for $1.

LIGHT SHONE DOWN, song and story by Edna R. Worrell and Roger C. Wilson. 1 or 2 readers, choir, 15 for pageant cast. Plays 1 hour. Story of Light presented by Old and New Testament players. Nativity story is read; climax is the procession to the manger. Simple but effective. Eldridge, 50¢.

LIGHT UNTO ALL THE HOUSE, by Cathie Groeger. 9 players, 8–13 years. Plays 20 minutes. In a carpenter's shop the "miracle of oil" takes place and is seen as the natural result of kindness, faith, and loving labor. Union of American Hebrew Congregations, 25¢.

LIGHT UP THE WORLD, by Karin Asbrand. 7 characters. Plays 8 minutes. A verse playlet in which the Christmas star, the torchbearer, and the candlelighter illuminate the world. Seabury Press, 65¢.

THE LIGHT WITHIN, by Robert St. Clair. 7 men, 6 women, extras. Plays 2 hours. Interior set. In three acts with prologue and epilogue. A girl struggles to fulfill her devotion to Christian living in the face of poverty, tragedy, and personal infirmity. T. S. Denison & Co., 85¢ (purchase of 12 copies required).

THE LIGHTS OF CHRISTMAS, by Karin Asbrand. 12 girls and women, 14 years or older. Plays 45 minutes. Rehearsal of a Christmas pageant makes a change in a crabby old woman. Baker's Plays, 60¢ (purchase of 8 copies required).

LILIES FOR THE KING, by Lucy Hamilton Howard. 4 men, 2 women. Plays 30 minutes. Stewardship play for Easter or any season. The question of whether teen-agers understand the meaning of sacrifice is explored. Eldridge, 60¢ (purchase of 6 copies required).

LILIOM, by Ferenc Molnar, translated by Benjamin F. Glazer. 17 men, 5 women, 4 extras. Interior set. A man recounts his earthly sins in the Court of Heaven for a chance to return to earth and make an atonement to his love. The play on which the musical "Carousel" was based. Samuel French, Inc., $1.25. Royalty: $25.

A LITTLE BELL FOR SAN MARCO, by Michael Dines. 2 men, 4 women. An agnostic is willing to do anything for an Italian village except buy a bell for the church. A surprise ending finds both him and the village priest playing strange roles. One act. Evans Plays.

THE LITTLE BLUE ANGEL, by Edith Quick and James Fluckey. Large or small cast. Children's operetta of a little boy who pays a Christmas visit on a spoiled princess. Baker's Plays, $1.40 (purchase of 7 copies required). Eldridge, $1.40 (purchase of 7 copies required).

LITTLE FRIEND, by William Joyce Cowen. 6 men, 5 women, extras. 2 interior sets. Unable to bring her newborn brother to the church crèche to see the figure of the Holy Child, a little girl takes the Holy Child to see the baby. Samuel French, Inc., 75¢. Royalty: $10.

THE LITTLE LAME SHEPHERD, by Helen Roberts. 7 men, 2 women, extras. Plays 30 minutes. Lame David goes to the manger and is healed. Banner Play Bureau, 50¢ (purchase of 8 copies required).

LITTLE PEOPLE'S CHRISTMAS BOOK, by Clara J. Denton. Collection for lower grades. "The Angel's Song," "Christmas Dreams," "A Long-Ago Night," included. Baker's Plays, $1.

LITTLE PLAYS OF ST. FRANCIS, by Laurence Housman. Mostly men, 6–8 speaking parts average. Each plays about 30 minutes. Dramas of Francis of Assisi based on legend and history. Thirty-two plays in three volumes. Some plays available separately. Baker's Plays: volumes, $2; separate plays, 60¢. Royalty: single play, $5; for more than one, special arrangements necessary.

THE LITTLE POOR MAN, by Jacques Copeau, translated by Beverly Thurman. 25 men, 4 women, 2 male choruses. A drama about Francis of Assisi. In *Port-Royal and Other Plays*. Mermaid Dramabook. Royalty: apply to Annie Laurie Williams.

THE LITTLE RED APOSTLES, by Joy Anderson. All women. Interior set. The mother superior deals with problems from both within and without the convent. One act. Evans Plays.

THE LITTLE SHEPHERD, by Minta Meier. Speech choir. The young shepherd is not pleased at the idea of sharing a stable with a strange couple. Dramatic. Coach House Press, 90¢. Royalty: $10.

THE LITTLE SHEPHERD, by Barbara Stuart, music by Arthur Grantley. Pageant of the Nativity, a child's version. For primaries, beginners, and juniors. Eldridge, 50¢.

THE LITTLE SHEPHERD WHO WAS LEFT BEHIND, by Helen Roberts. 10 characters, extras. Plays 30 minutes. The traditional story dramatized. Banner Play Bureau, 50¢ (purchase of 4 copies required).

LITTLE STAR LOST, by George Crout. Plays 1 hour. The story of the Christmas star, hoping to shine again to bring eternal peace. Eldridge, 60¢ (purchase of 5 copies required).

THE LITTLE TOWN, by Pamela Sinclair. 3 speakers, children extras. Story of the Nativity in candlelight setting, revealed by hidden speakers. Children mime it. One act. Evans Plays.

LITTLE WOMEN. 9 women. Plays 30 minutes. Interior set. For junior and senior high. Adaptation includes the Christmas scene among others of the famous scenes of the original. Plays, Inc., 50¢.

LITTLEST ANGEL, by Helen M. Roberts. 14 speaking parts, extras, musician angels. Plays 30 minutes. A Christmas play for children set in the heavenly realms. Older angels are preparing for the birth of Christ. How Michael, the littlest, most mischievous angel, is chosen to go with Gabriel to earth is a beautiful and dignified story. Baker's Plays, 60¢ (purchase of 10 copies required).

THE LITTLEST ANGEL, by Charles Tazewell. 16 boys and girls, extras. The story of the small boy who becomes the unruly "Littlest Angel," and who gives to Christ something dear to him—a box of toys from his life on earth—which becomes the Christmas star. Heuer, 50¢.

THE LITTLEST SHEPHERD, by Florence Ryerson and Colin Clements. 9 men, 3 women. Plays 30 minutes. Exterior set. David, a little shepherd, stays to watch over the sheep when the older shepherds leave to follow the star of Bethlehem. David's wish to see the

Holy Babe is made possible by his guardian angel. Samuel French, Inc., 60¢. Royalty: $5.

LIVE WIRE CHRISTMAS BOOK, by Willis N. Bugbee. Collection includes: a tableau, "The Gleam of the Star Through the Ages"; "A Candle-lighting Exercise"; "Christmas Around the World"; and others. Eldridge, $1.

LIVING HYMNS, by Edith H. Willis and Edith Ellsworth. Large cast. Plays 1 hour or may be presented as four 20-minute programs. A chancel presentation for adults and children. Baker's Plays, 75¢.

THE LIVING LORD, by Mrs. Stanley R. Fisher. Large cast of children and adults, reader. Plays 20 minutes. Chancel setting for Easter pageant. In *Easy Bible Dramatizations for Children.* Baker's Plays, $1.25.

LOAVES AND FISHES, by Somerset Maugham, edited with an introduction by Gerald Weales. In *Edwardian Plays.* Mermaid Dramabook 25: cloth, $5.95; paper, $2.45.

LONELY ROAD, by T. C. Thomas. 2 men, 7 women. Plays 30 minutes. Interior set. Fleeing from the anger of Herod, Joseph, Mary and her baby ask for help at a humble home near Bethlehem. How the poor and dissatisfied family are changed by the Holy Family's visit is shown. H. F. W. Deane & Sons, 1*s.* 9*d.* net. Postage, 2*d.*

THE LONESOME BIBLES, by William H. Leach. 4 men, 4 women. Plays 20 minutes. Ezra is put in charge of the Bible booth at a church bazaar, for the women feel that he can pull no practical jokes there as he is apt to do. He does an original stunt by putting on display "the lonesome Bibles," which want homes. An effective lesson is learned. Eldridge, 60¢.

LONG AGO IN BETHLEHEM. 7 men, 10 women, extras. Plays 10 minutes. Exterior set. For middle grades. The innkeeper's greedy wife begins to understand the meaning of Christ's birth. Plays, Inc., 50¢.

THE LONG CHRISTMAS DINNER, by Thornton Wilder, revised for acting by Alexander Dean. 5 men, 7 women. Plays 30 minutes. Interior set. Ninety Christmas dinners are celebrated in this home, showing the changes and growth of the family. Samuel French, Inc., 60¢. Royalty: $10.

THE LONG ROAD TO BETHLEHEM, by Helen M. Roberts. 8 men, 3 women, optional extras. Two attendants of a wise man find that in giving their possessions to others they have given a gift to the Christchild. Eldridge, 60¢ (purchase of 6 copies required).

THE LONG VIEW—ON SOCIAL WORK, by Nora Stirling. Confrontation of problems of a growing community. Plays for Living.

A LOOK AT CHRISTIAN EDUCATION, by Nelle A. Holt. Tableaux for church schools; informs congregation of Christian education programs. Eldridge, 50¢ (purchase of 8 copies required).

THE LOST BOOK, by Dorothy Clarke Wilson. 2 men, 2 women, extras. Plays 25 minutes. Concerns the book of Law found in the temple in Hezekiah's time. In *Twelve Months of Drama for the Average Church.* Baker's Plays, $2.95.

THE LOST CHRISTMAS, by Edith Dalen. 6 women. Plays 20 minutes.

Neighborhood women who have lost the real meaning of Christmas are awakened by a new neighbor. Eldridge, 60¢ (purchase of 6 copies required).

THE LOST CHRISTMAS, by Bruce Kimes. 4 men, 3 women. Plays 35 minutes. Interior set. A blind and embittered woman, thanks to a strange gift, regains the true meaning of Christmas which she had lost. One act. Baker's Plays, 60¢. Royalty: $5.

THE LOST CHURCH, by Dorothy Clarke Wilson. 3 men, 8 women, 1 girl. Plays 35 minutes. Interior set. Projects the results for a community if the church were to be eliminated. Baker's Plays, 60¢.

THE LOST CROWN, by Dorothy Clarke Wilson. 4 men, 1 woman, extras (optional). Plays 20 minutes. Evangelistic appeal in a drama of Paul's defense before Agrippa, closely paralleling the scriptures. Particularly good for lenten services. In *Twelve Months of Drama for the Average Church*. Baker's Plays, $2.95.

LOST IN THE STARS, by Alan Paton, adapted by Maxwell Anderson. Paton's *Cry, the Beloved Country* in the form of a play. College Book Service, $7.50.

THE LOST PEOPLE, by Dorothy Clarke Wilson. 2 men, 2 women, extras (optional). Plays 30 minutes. Moses chooses to cast his lot with the children of God rather than reach for the throne of Egypt. The central subject of the play is "national righteousness." In *Twelve Months of Drama for the Average Church*. Baker's Plays, $2.95.

THE LOST STAR, by Walter Butts. 7 men, 4 women, extras. Plays 40 minutes. A flashback to the story of the Nativity helps a modern family find the Christmas star. Eldridge, 60¢.

THE LOST STAR, by Merlo Heicher and Robert St. Clair. 13 men, 6 women. The three kings, as punishment, lose the star that was guiding them and are brought by a miracle to Bethlehem. T. S. Denison & Co., 50¢ (purchase of 10 copies required).

THE LOST STAR, by Dorothy Clarke Wilson. 9 men, 5 women. Plays 30 minutes. Pageant play. The youngest wise man, filled with hatred of an enemy, loses the star he is following. Excellent musical background. Baker's Plays, 60¢.

LOURDES, by Louis N. Parker. 5 men, 5 women. 2 interior sets. Human dramas of the cures of the pilgrims and the meaning of Lourdes. Three acts. Baker's Plays, $1. Royalty: $25.

LOVE CAME AT CHRISTMAS, by Carolyn and Leonard T. Wolcott. Worship service for the participation of the family on the theme of God's gift of love. Abingdon Press. Package, 500.

LOVE NEVER DIES, by Elsa Debra. 2 speakers, 3 women, angel, 1 adult, choir. Dramatic Easter service, pageant type. Baker's Plays, 60¢ (purchase of 8 copies required).

THE LOVE OF RUTH, by Beatrice M. Casey. 4 men, 4 women. Plays 25 minutes. Interior set. The story of Ruth and Naomi with modern characters and setting. One act. T. S. Denison & Co., 50¢ (purchase of 8 copies required).

LOVE'S GIFT, by Florence J. Armstrong. 7 men, 4 women, chorus.

Plays 40 minutes. Pageant. An angel changes a shepherd girl's tears to Christmas roses as an offering to the Babe. Eldridge, 60¢ (purchase of 10 copies required).

LOWER THAN ANGELS, by Albert Johnson. 2 men, 1 woman. Drama Trio Play. An American's encounter with world responsibilities. Designed to be produced on bare or space stage with minimal furniture, simple costumes, and no hand properties. Available in manuscript from author, $1. Royalty: $10–$5.

THE LOWLY KING, by Martha Bayly Shannon. 3 men, 2 women, offstage chorus. Plays 30 minutes. The events of the Passover and Palm Sunday as seen in the home of Timon, a dealer in fruits and herbs. Baker's Plays, 60¢. Royalty: first performance, none; $1.50 each repeat.

LOYAL QUEEN ESTHER or NEVER BELITTLE THE POWER OF A LADY, by Lucille Sylvester. 12 boys, 4 girls (ages 12–16). Queen Esther and the familiar characters surrounding her in a romantic comedy with music. Includes parodies of well-known songs. Union of American Hebrew Congregations, 50¢.

LUCIFER AT LARGE, by Frank P. Ford. 5 men. Plays 40 minutes. Modern morality play. The struggles of the devil, set between heaven and hell. Samuel French, Inc., 60¢. Royalty: $5.

LUTE SONG, by Kao-Tong-kia, arranged by Will Irwin and Sidney Howard. 9 men, 6 women, extras. Plays full evening. A fifteenth-century Chinese play, with optional music. Love and faithfulness eventually bring reward to a dutiful wife. Dramatic Publishing Co., 90¢. Royalty: $35.

LUTHER, by John Osborne. 12 men, 1 woman, extras. Luther's training as a monk and his rebellion against the church abuses of his time. Excellent roles. May be simply staged in one setting. Evans Plays, 6*s*. 6*d*. Royalty: 6–5 *gns*.

MACADAM AND EVE, by Roger MacDougall. 3 men, 3 women. The immortal Macadam, personification of the first of men, is condemned to walk as a mortal, striving to overcome the instincts roused in him by the female descendants of his original partner. High in pace. Evans Plays. Royalty: $35–$25.

MACBETH, by William Shakespeare, commentaries and glossaries by George Skillan. 21 men, 6 women. Interior sets, exterior sets. The death and chaos that spring from the ambitious murder of a king, and the sensibility of Macbeth, his rule, and his death. Portrays the external evil of the council of witches and the internal evil of the ambition of Lord and Lady Macbeth. Samuel French, Inc., $2.

THE MADISON AVENUE PURIM, by Jacob Ostrow. Plays 25 minutes. For high school students. Tells the Purim story parodying radio, TV, and advertising tunes. Program is in Hebrew. Union of American Hebrew Congregations, 75¢.

THE MADMAN AND THE WRECKING CREW, by Florence Converse. 10 men, procession of women. Plays 40 minutes. A modern dialogue representing the implications of Christianity's ancient symbol.

Baker's Plays, 60¢. Royalty: $5 if admission is charged; none if not.

THE MADWOMAN OF CHAILLOT, by Jean Giraudoux, adapted by Maurice Valency. 24 men (may be doubled to about 15), 8 women. Plays full evening. Exterior sets, interior sets. The Madwoman leads the poor to protect the beautiful city of Paris, frustrating the madness of the world. Difficult. Dramatists Play Service, $1.25. Royalty: $50–$25.

MAGDA, by Ethel G. Rockwell. 7 men, 2 women, mob (heard but not seen). Magda, a Greek girl, and her betrothed, the disciple Thomas, come to an understanding of and devotion to the reality of the spiritual kingdom of Christ. Baker's Plays, 60¢. Royalty: $5.

THE MAGDALENE, by Ruth Laymon Kocher. 4 men, 3 women, 3 extra men. Plays 45 minutes. Interior set. Mary Magdalene during the final days of Christ's life: the trial, the crucifixion, and the resurrection. Baker's Plays, 60¢.

THE MAGIC SHOES. Play of Ireland giving atmosphere and facts of the country. Emphasizes world friendship. For lower and middle grades. Plays, Inc., 35¢.

THE MAGI'S GIFT, by C. M. Grubb. 5 men, 5 women, extras. Exterior set. An operetta in a medieval setting. Based, in part, on the old mystery of the shearmen and tailors. Two acts. Baker's Plays, $1.25 (purchase of 5 copies required).

THE MAID OF DOMREMY, by Joe Corrie. 4 men, 3 women. Plays 30 minutes. The early life of Joan of Arc, the faith and doubts of her parents, and, at last, her departure. Baker's Plays, 60¢. Royalty: $5.

MAJOR BARBARA, by George Bernard Shaw. 9 men, 7 women. 2 interior sets, 2 exterior sets. Major Barbara of the Salvation Army learns that the saving of souls must be accompanied by hypocrisy and the fillings of stomachs. Demonstrates the pace and barb of Shavian wit. Difficult to perform. Samuel French, Inc., 65¢. Royalty: $25.

MAKE HIS NAME GLORIOUS, by Dorothy Lehman Sumerau. The life of Lottie Moon, a missionary to China. Broadman Press, 50¢.

THE MAN BORN TO BE KING, by Dorothy Sayers. Variable casts. Twelve episodes of Christ's life. A cycle of broadcasts of the life of Christ, intended for those who are outside the churches and to whom Christ seems to have lost his appeal. Written for radio, no attempts to stage these plays should be made. Harper, $4.50. Royalty: apply to Ann Watkins. Baker's Plays, $4.50 (production restricted).

A MAN CALLED PETER, by Catherine Marshall, adapted by John McGreevey. 7 men, 8 women. Plays full evening. Outstanding play for production in church. Dramatic Publishing Co., 90¢. Royalty: $35.

A MAN DIES, by Ewan Hooper and Ernest Marvin. Large cast of young people. Plays 45 minutes. The Passion story presented in a modern setting. Prologue and three parts. Baker's Plays, $1.50. Royalty: $15. Film available: Association Films.

A MAN FOR ALL SEASONS, by Robert Bolt. 11 men, 3 women. Plays full evening. The tragedy of Sir Thomas More in a powerful and distinguished drama. Difficult. Two acts. Baker's Plays, $1.25. Royalty: apply to publisher.

THE MAN IN LEATHER BREECHES, by Rosalie Regen. One of a series of biographical dramas of peaceful people. Friends Book and Supply House, 15¢.

MAN IS OMEGA, by Nora Ratcliff. 6 men, 2 women, or 4 men, 4 women. A poet brings prayer to a futuristic state without ideals in this satire. One act. Evans Plays, 2*s*. Royalty: 25*s*. each performance.

THE MAN WHO FOUND THE KING. 7 men, 3 women. Plays 30 minutes. Exterior set. With no room in the inn, the innkeeper rents the stable manger. For junior high students. Plays, Inc., 50¢.

THE MAN WITHOUT A SOUL, by Par Lagerkvist, translated by Helge Kokeritz. 6 men, 6 women, extras. Interior sets, exterior set. A man finds humanity in love, and a desire to believe in the face of guilt and destruction. In *Scandinavian Plays of the Twentieth Century,* Series I. Princeton University Press (out of print). Royalty: apply to American-Scandinavian Foundation.

MANNEQUINS' DEMISE, by David Wolf Budbill. 4 men, 2 women, chorus of 4 men, 4 women. The Silent Man walks in a world of unimportant and chaotic chatter, and brings from an oath, and from death, a new life and a vision that he is still God. Baker's Plays, 85¢. Royalty: $15.

MANY THANKS. 10 men, 9 women. Plays 25 minutes. Interior set. For middle grades. Visitors from history and a group of school children convince Uncle Sam not to abolish Thanksgiving. Plays, Inc., 50¢.

MARIOT AND MARIETTE, by Preston L. Grover. 1 man, 2 women. She sold her hair to buy the watch for him; he bought her combs for the hair she had sold. A triologue. In *Jumbo Christmas Book.* Baker's Plays, $1.25.

MARTHA AND MARY, by Muriel and Sydney Box. 7 women. Plays 30 minutes. Interior set. Two women, shown between the time that they dispatch a messenger to Jesus and their realization that their brother is to be raised from the dead. Baker's Plays, 60¢. Royalty: $2.75.

THE MARVELOUS HISTORY OF ST. BERNARD, by Henri Gheon, translated by Barry V. Jackson. 22 men plus extras (doubling possible), 4 women, extras. Fourteenth- or early fifteenth-century costumes. Amid a host of miracles of faith and will, St. Bernard gives his life to God and succeeds in driving the devil from Mont-Joux. Sheed & Ward. Royalty: apply to publisher.

MARY FISHER AND THE SULTAN OF TURKEY, by Rosalie Regen. One of a series of biographical dramas concerning peaceful people. Written for the Society of Friends. Friends Book and Supply House, 15¢.

MARY MAGDALENE, by Maurice Maeterlinck, translated by de Mattos. A three-act play. College Book Service, $15.

MARY OF MAGDALA, by Ernest Milton. 15 men, 5 women, extras. Interior set. The life of the Magdalene is shown changed by her meeting with Christ and her decision to follow him. Three acts. Baker's Plays, $1. Royalty: $15.

MARY OF SCOTLAND, by Maxwell Anderson. 25 men, extras (some doubling possible), 6 women. Plays full evening. The conflict between Catholic Queen Mary of Scotland and her Protestant cousin, Elizabeth I of England. Very difficult. Samuel French, Inc., $1. Royalty: $25.

MARY'S QUEST, by Olov Hartman, translated by Eric J. Sharpe. 7 men, 7 women, chorus. Liturgical play. The night of the Lord's betrayal, its meaning shown through the act of breaking bread and pouring wine. Baker's Plays, 85¢. Royalty: $15.

MARY SMITH MEETS MR. PEOPLE. Mary has her outlook widened from that of an "all-American" by Mr. People. Human Relations playlet. Anti-Defamation League of B'nai B'rith, 15¢.

MARY STUART, by Friedrich Schiller, translated by Stephen Spender. 14 men, 4 women, extras. Interior sets, exterior set. The encounter between Queen Elizabeth and Queen Mary brought onto a level of personal conflict; portrays Mary's nobility of spirit. Faber & Faber. Royalty: apply to Peters & Ramsay.

MARY'S SON, by Sylvia Davidson. 4 women. A parallel of the story of Christ's trial and death in modern terms. Contemporary characters are counterparts of biblical figures. For Easter. H. F. W. Deane & Sons, 2*d*. Royalty: apply to publisher.

A MASQUE OF CHRISTMAS EVE, by W. Bradley. 24 characters, chorus. Plays 45 minutes. In verse introduces four Christmas carols, including music and accompaniment, and presents an ancient Christmas play. Abel Heywood & Sons.

THE MASTER BUILDER, by Henrik Ibsen, translated by Eva Le Gallienne. 4 men, 3 women, extras. The struggle between the desire for artistic fulfillment and the guilt in the soul of the aging master builder. In *Six Plays by Ibsen*. Modern Library: cloth, $1.95; paper, 85¢. Royalty: apply to Brandt & Brandt.

THE MASTER CAT AND OTHER PLAYS, by Dorothy Jane Goulding. Collection of six plays, includes "The Nativity." Production notes and helps included. Coach House Press, $3.50. Royalty: $10.

MASTER JOHN, by Rosalie Regen. One of a series of biographical dramas concerning peaceful people. Written for Society of Friends. Friends Book and Supply House, 15¢.

THE MASTER OF SANTIAGO, by Henry de Montherlant, translated by Jonathan Griffin. 7 men, 2 women. Interior set. A man sacrifices hopes of rebuilding his shattered wealth and of marriage for his daughter by submitting them to his severe view of his relationship to God. Needs strength, economy, and simplicity in production. In *The Master of Santiago and Four Other Plays*. Knopf. Royalty: apply to publisher.

A MATCH FOR THE DEVIL, by Norman Nicholson. 5 men, 4 women. Exterior sets. A moving verse-play of Hosea, visualizing him as a simple man, a baker, willing to bear the laughter of his neighbors when he takes back his unfaithful wife. Faber & Faber.

MAYBE EVEN HIGHER, by Isaac Loeb Perez, translated by Ida Lublenski Erlich. Valuable Jewish play, traditional. Everyman's Theatre (available in manuscript from publisher). Royalty: apply to publisher.

THE MEANING OF CHRISTMAS DAY, by Merlo Heicher. 5 men, 4 women. A group of young people decorating a Christmas tree for their church grow bored with the superficialities of celebration and learn in a unique manner the real meaning of Christmas Day. T. S. Denison & Co., 50¢ (purchase of 8 copies required).

THE MEANING OF EASTER, by Martha Mixer. 4 men, 11 women, junior choir, children. A girl, worried at her sister's illness, finds solace in the realization of Christ's power. In *Transparent Curtain Pageants for Easter*. Baker's Plays, $1.25.

MEDIEVAL MYSTERIES, MORALITIES, AND INTERLUDES, edited by Vincent F. Hopper and Gerald B. Lahey. Includes: "Abraham and Isaac," "Noah's Flood," "The Second Shepherd's Play," "The Castle of Perseverance," and "Everyman," with introductory and background materials for the period and the plays. Barron's Educational Series, $1.25.

THE MEGILLAHAH MUSICAL, by Carmelita Avery and Isabella R. Rips. 7 boys, 4 girls, chorus. Purim operetta, combining new lyrics with the melodies of well-known Hebrew songs sung by Purim characters. Union of American Hebrew Congregations, 50¢.

MEIGS BEST WORLD FRIENDSHIP SELECTIONS, compiled by Florence Wolcott. Dramatizations, recitations, novelties, for choral delivery, etc. For all ages, all missionary occasions. Eldridge, $1.

THE MEMBER OF THE WEDDING, by Carson McCullers. 6 men, 7 women. Plays full evening. The sympathy of a Negro mammy helps an adolescent girl adjust to her brother's marriage. For advanced production group. New Directions, $3. Royalty: $50–$25.

THE MERCHANT OF VENICE, by William Shakespeare. 17 men, 3 women, extras. Shakepeare's play of the law, prejudice, vengeance, mercy, the human heart. Difficult. Pelican Books. Royalty: none.

MERRY CHRISTMAS TO THE WORLD, by Karin Asbrand. About 45 participants. Plays 60–90 minutes. A goodwill pageant. Children from around the world sing songs of their countries and tell their Christmas customs, having come to America to find happiness and the Christmas spirit. Eldridge, 50¢.

MESSAGE OF A SONG, by Thurlene P. Singer. 3 men, 5 women. The dedication of a minister and his family to serving God and their fellowman. Eldridge, 50¢ (purchase of 8 copies required).

THE MESSAGE OF THE CHRISTMAS ANGELS, by Esther C. Averill. 4 men, 7 women, angel choir. Plays 40 minutes. The Christmas spirit tells of man's yearning for a savior. Baker's Plays, 60¢.

METAMORPHOSIS, by David Hargrove. 9 men, 1 woman (all-male cast possible). Plays 25 minutes. Joseph's rise from slavery to influence in Egypt. Pioneer Drama Service, 85¢. Royalty: none if 10 copies purchased. Purchase also grants rights for noncommercial production.

THE MIDNIGHT CLEAR, by Dorothy C. Allan. 1 man, 2 women, 1 boy, 1 girl, 2 angels. Plays 30 minutes. A group of street vendors on

Christmas show the possibility of happiness without great material fortune. Baker's Plays, 60¢.

MIDNIGHT IN THE DUNGEON, by Roy Pearson. 3 men. Interior set. From the tradition that Jesus and Barabbas spent the night before the crucifixion in the same dungeon. Stresses the universality of two ways of looking at life. Baker's Plays, 60¢.

MIDWINTER JOURNEY, by Joan Forman. 18 characters. No scenery. An explanation of the Nativity with its meaning set against the modern Christmas outlook. Evans Plays, 2*s.* net. Royalty: 25*s.* each performance.

THE MIGHTY DREAM, by Dorothy Clarke Wilson. Large cast. Mankind's struggle through time to create an ideal society. Emphasizes Christian brotherhood. Baker's Plays, 75¢. Royalty: first performance, none; $2.50 each repeat.

THE MIGHTY HUNTER, by Wolf Mankowitz. 2 men. The challenge of the Mighty Hunter to God ends in the building of the Tower of Babel. In *Five One-Act Plays.* Samuel French, Inc., $1.25. Royalty: $5 (not available in Canada).

MIMI LIGHTS THE CANDLE, by Edith Coulter. 1 man, 8 women. Plays 20 minutes. Interior set. For Christmas, but can be given at any time during the year. Concerns the Christchild's coming. Samuel French, Inc., 60¢.

MINOR MIRACLE, by Verne Powers. 4 men. Marooned on a raft are four men. Religious play. Harper, 50¢. Royalty: $5 if admission is not charged.

THE MIRACLE AT NAIN, by Ruth Cole Wareham. 5 women. Plays 20 minutes. Exterior set. A variety of characters with counterparts in the modern church seek Jesus, each for his own reason. Baker's Plays, 60¢.

A MIRACLE FOR CHANUKO, by Helen Fine, music by Dr. Moses J. Eisenberg. Large cast, including fairies, dolls, Chanuko figures. For ages 6–10. With music and verse. The little rag doll goes to the Israeli doll's party thanks to the magic of Mr. Nais. At the party, the dolls entertain. Union of American Hebrew Congregations, 75¢.

A MIRACLE FOR MARY, by Ruth Burdin. 4 men, 9 women. Plays 25 minutes. Exterior set. A legend that the old straw image of the virgin from an ancient European chapel once came to life and performed a miracle. Provides inspiration. Samuel French, Inc., 60¢. Royalty: $5.

A MIRACLE OF SAINT ANTHONY, by Maurice Maeterlinck. In a collection with five other plays. College Book Service (Modern Library), $7.50.

MIRACLE OF THE MADONNA, by Robert St. Clair. 4 men, 5 women, tableau characters, choir. From the suffering of a young girl stricken with polio comes a greater faith. Music may be recorded or performed live. Four scenes. Baker's Plays, 60¢. Royalty: $5.

THE MIRACLE WORKER, by William Gibson. 7 men, 7 women. Plays full evening. The story of Helen Keller and her teacher Annie Sullivan, and of the first break in Helen's silent, isolated world.

A play of teaching, seeking, and the realizations of human emotions. Eldridge, $1.25. Royalty: $50–$25.

MIRAGE, by David Morrison. 2 men, 2 women. Plays 30 minutes. Interior set. A man wrongfully imprisoned learns that people can inflict other sorts of suffering on one another. Baker's Plays, 60¢. Royalty: $5.

MIRAGE, by T. C. Thomas. 8 men, 9 women. Set on the top of the wall in Jerusalem, where the road to Calvary can be seen. Reactions of people of all ages and types watching the procession taking Christ to his crucifixion. H. F. W. Deane & Sons, 2*d.*

MISSILE OF REDEMPTION, by Mary Ann Klifetos. Voice choir, 10–50. Plays 20–45 minutes. Choralogue. The coming of the Christchild and its meaning, told strikingly and with simplicity. Baker's Plays, 60¢. Royalty: none if 10 copies purchased.

MISSION ACCOMPLISHED, by Gladys Baker Bond. A Human Relations playlet, concerning inclusion and exclusion in a birthday party. Anti-Defamation League of B'nai B'rith, 10¢.

MISSIONARY PROGRAMS FOR THE CHURCH. Twelve programs on world evangelism, God's love as theme. Eldridge, $1.

MR. CHRISTMAS, by John Randall. 4 men, 6 women. Interior set. Mr. Christmas and his strange friends teach spoiled and lonely Joan the true meaning of Christmas. Three acts. Samuel French, Inc., 60¢. Royalty: $5.

MR. SCROOGE FINDS CHRISTMAS, by Charles Dickens, from the story "A Christmas Carol." Plays 30 minutes. For junior and senior high students, also middle grades. Plays, Inc., 50¢.

MRS. SANTA CLAUS, by Margaret Parsons. 6 women. Plays 30 minutes. Interior set. A woman finds peace bringing Christmas joy to a homeless waif. In *Woman's Club Playbook.* Baker's Plays, $1.25.

THE MISUNDERSTANDING, by Albert Camus, translated by Stuart Gilbert. 2 men, 3 women. Plays full evening. A discerning play dealing with a crime which occurred because of mistaken identity. In *Caligula and 3 Other Plays.* Knopf, $5. Royalty: apply to Mrs. W. A. Bradley.

MODERN CHANCEL DRAMAS, by James Brock. Includes for Advent, "The Witness"; for Epiphany, "And Such a King"; for Lent, "The Human Condition"; for Holy Week, "The Last Days"; for Whitsuntide, "A Sound from Heaven." Baker's Plays, $1.25. Royalty: $10 each play.

A MODERN CHRISTMAS CAROL, by Ruth K. Baughman. 3 men, 3 women, 1 boy. Plays 15 minutes. Interior set. The well-known Christmas story written with modern language, setting. In *Celebrating Christmas.* Baker's Plays, $1.25.

MODERN PLAYS FOR SPECIAL DAYS, by Helen Louise Miller. One-act plays for special days, including Christmas, Mother's Day, Thanksgiving, Memorial Day, and others. For junior and senior high. Plays, Inc., $5.95.

THE MODERN THEATRE, edited by Eric Bentley. Inexpensive collection of works of important modern dramatists. In five volumes. These plays and playwrights for advanced companies. Vol. I: Büchner,

Verga, Becque, Brecht, Giraudoux, 95¢; Vol. II: De Musset, Ostrovsky, Schnitzler, Yeats, Brecht, 95¢; Vol. III: Gogol, Marc-Michel, Conrad, Anouilh, 95¢; Vol. IV: Fitch, Mitchell, Wilder, Saroyan, Loesser, $1.25; Vol. V: Gogol, Büchner, Ghelderode, Anouilh, O'Casey, 95¢. Anchor Books.

MODERN TREASURY OF CHRISTMAS PLAYS, edited by L. M. Brings. A collection of Christmas drama; all-purpose. T. S. Denison & Co., $4.50.

MONSIEUR SANTA CLAUS. 9 men, 7 women. Plays 25 minutes. Interior set. A French exchange student gives his friends the best Christmas gift of all, himself, in a Santa Claus suit. Plays, Inc., 50¢.

MONSIGNOR'S HOUR, by Emmet Lavery. 12 men, 2 women, extras. Plays 1 hour. Interior set. Set in the Vatican near the beginning of the next war. Tranquil, heartwarming. Samuel French, Inc., 60¢. Royalty: $5.

MOONSET, by Helen M. Clark. 6 men. Plays 30 minutes. Exterior set. After watching his brother die, a captain sees the war's futility and is taken to safety by a stranger. There he finds something to live for. Samuel French, Inc., 60¢.

MORE BLESSED TO GIVE, by Karin Asbrand. 4 women, Plays 15 minutes. Interior set. Mom gains her greatest pleasure from a new dress by giving it, for a bit of courage, to a girl soon to meet her blinded husband. In *Easy Church Plays for Women and Girls.* Baker's Plays, $1.25.

MORE PLAYS AND PAGEANTS FOR MANY OCCASIONS, by E. H. Emurian. Drama for worship. Includes "The Lord's Supper"; disciples' monologues are very good. W. A. Wilde Co., $2.50.

MORE RELIGIOUS PLAYS FOR WOMEN, by various authors. Includes two missionary plays, a stewardship play, two Christmas plays, an Easter play, a Mother's Day play. Baker's Plays, 75¢.

MORE STUNT PLAYS, by Tom Sullivan. Flexible casts. Collection of eleven sketches including "The Ladies' Aid Church Supper." Suitable for church programs and bazaars. Samuel French, Inc., $1.

MOSES, THE LAWGIVER, by Norman E. Nygaard. 4 men. Moses smashes the tablets after finding the people worshiping an image. In *The Bible Comes Alive.* Baker's Plays, $1.25.

THE MOST HEAVENLY HOSTS, by Elizabeth McFadden Wright. Large cast. Plays 35 minutes. Christmas play for the church school. The traditional Christmas story with background of familiar music. Allows participation of most church school members. Baker's Plays, 60¢.

MOTHER IN THE SHADOW, by Lillian Mortimer. 4 men, 10 women. A mother proves her love by sacrificing herself for the happiness of her child, first giving it to a foster home, then entering that home as a seamstress to again save the child. T. S. Denison & Co., 85¢ (purchase of 12 copies required).

MOTHER OF ALL LIVING. A play of Adam and Eve. In *Six Short Religious Plays.* Religious Drama Society of Great Britain, 70¢.

MOTHER'S APRON STRINGS. 5 men, 3 women. A play for Mother's Day.

Bill teaches others that Mother's "apron strings" help. Plays, Inc., 50¢.

MOTHER'S GIFT TO ANN, by Mildred Kerr. 8 women. Grandmother and Mother, when Ann packs for college, find her a real gift. Eldridge, 40¢ (purchase of 8 copies required).

MOTHERS, by Karin Asbrand. Series of tableaux introducing: "Nancy Hanks," "Whistler's Mother," "Gold Star Mother," "Madonna," and others. In *Easy Church Plays for Women and Girls.* Baker's Plays, $1.25.

MOTHERS AND HOME, by Samuel H. Cox. A service demonstrating respect and love for mothers, also devotional spirit and thanksgiving to God. Church school poems, music, recitations. Eldridge, 75¢ (purchase of 10 copies required).

MOURNING BEFORE MORNING, by Don M. Fearheiley. 3 men, 3 women. Plays 30 minutes. Interior set. A young man who has drifted from the church finds a realization of the Easter message in the death of his mother. Easter theme. Baker's Plays, 60¢. Royalty: $5.

THE MOUSE WHO WAS STIRRING, by Lenore Morgan. 3 men, 2 women, and the Mouse (either man or woman). Interior set. Santa is given new life in the hearts of the audience in a rollicking and rhythmical play with its base in the famous verse. For Christmas. Baker's Plays, 60¢. Royalty: $5.

MURDER IN THE CATHEDRAL, by T. S. Eliot. 10 men, 9 women. 3 interior sets. The martyrdom of Thomas à Becket, who, although tempted, refused to take temporal control of England. In verse. Baker's Plays, $1.25. Royalty: $35.

MUSEUM PIECE, by R. Tydeman. 8 characters. Religious drama that has won prizes and acclaim. Faith Press, 2*s.* 6*d.*

MUSIC IN THE VALLEY, by Dana Thomas. 8 men, 10 women. Exterior set. A play of faith and human hearts, happy enchantment and young love. Three acts. T. S. Denison & Co., $1. Royalty: $25.

MY FATHER'S BUSINESS, by Christine Hubbard Pickett. 6 men, 6 women, 1 child (2 extra women and voice of Jesus in epilogue). Plays 1 hour. Interior set. For Easter. The early home life of Jesus who, although he never appears, dominates the play. Concerns the problem of the elder brother studying at the temple or staying with his widowed mother in Nazareth. Baker's Plays, 60¢. Royalty: $5.

MY HEART'S IN THE HIGHLANDS, by William Saroyan. 13 men, 2 women. Plays full evening. The experiences and affections of small people dimly longing for a beauty they do not quite comprehend. Samuel French, Inc., $1. Royalty: $25.

A MYSTERY PLAY IN HONOR OF THE NATIVITY OF OUR LORD, by Robert H. Benson. 10 men, 6 women (all women if desired). Plays 30 minutes. A Christmas play in medieval fashion. A worship experience; particularly successful for Catholic audiences. McKay's Plays, 85¢. Royalty: $5.

NATHAN THE WISE, by Gotthold Ephraim Lessing, translated by William E. Steel. 11 men, 3 women. Exterior sets, interior sets. A play encouraging religious and racial tolerance, peace, and human generosity. Nathan the Jew is asked by the sultan whether the Muslim, Jewish, or Christian religion is the true one, and replies with a universalized version of Boccaccio's tale of the three rings and three brothers. In *Laocoon and Other Writings.* E. P. Dutton & Co., $2.25. Royalty: apply to publisher.

NATIVE SON, by Paul Green and Richard Wright. 17 men, 7 women. Racial injustice and Bigger Thomas. Adapted from the novel by Richard Wright. Samuel French, Inc.: available in manuscript from publisher; perusal script available for $2. Royalty: $50; $10 deposit is returnable.

THE NATIVITY, by Rosamond Kimball. 11 men, 1 woman, extras. Bible story selections of the Nativity arranged as a mystery play. Carols included. Adapted for young people. Baker's Plays, 60¢.

THE NATIVITY, by Ralph Marryott. Plays 20 minutes. A mystery play for Christmas, effective in the simplicity of the pageant. H. W. Gray Co., 40¢.

NATIVITY, by Nora Ratcliff. 15 men, 8 women. The shepherds, shown as real people in the activities of their daily lives, also become spokesmen for modern types in this Nativity play. Baker's Plays, 60¢ (give author's name when ordering). Royalty: $15.

NATIVITY IN STATUARY, by Harold C. Mason. 8 men, 1 woman, narrator, choir. Plays 25 minutes. Narration of the Christmas story made applicable to the achievement of peace in the world. In *Easy Christmas Grab Bag.* Baker's Plays, $1.25.

THE NATURE OF A GIFT, by D. L. Emblen. 7 men, 6 women, optional extras. Plays 40 minutes. Exterior set. The fantasy of a giant, an Alpine village on a Christmas day, and a key to the human heart. Baker's Plays, 60¢. Royalty: first performance, none; $5 each repeat.

THE NEIGHBORS, by Zona Gale. 2 men, 6 women. Plays 45 minutes. In modern costume. A friendless child comes under the care of "the Neighbors." Baker's Plays, 60¢. Royalty: $10.

NEVER TOO LATE, by Charles J. Ax. Play of the ministry of Christ. In *Bible Plays,* Book I, Christmas. Fortress Press, 75¢.

NEW BROOMS, by Frank Craven. 9 men, 4 women. Plays full evening. Age and youth in conflict. Samuel French, Inc., $1. Royalty: $25.

THE NEW-BORN KING, by Beryl Strugnell. Nativity play for a large number of children, ages 4–11. Unites children of the world's nations. Easy to rehearse. Baker's Plays, 85¢.

THE NEW TAX, by Charles J. Ax. Short Christmas play involving the innkeeper. In *Bible Plays,* Book I, Christmas. Fortress Press, 75¢.

NEW TESTAMENT MIMES, by J. G. Marash. Designed to give life and reality to biblical characters through pantomimes. For children. Baker's Plays, $1.25.

THE NIGHT BEFORE CHRISTMAS, by Charles George. 1 man, 3 women, 6 boys, 6 girls, extras. The transformation of a dreary home to a place of joy on Christmas Eve. An operetta. Baker's Plays, $1.25 (give author's name when ordering; purchase of 10 copies required).

THE NIGHT BEFORE CHRISTMAS, by Clement C. Moore. A reading with music. Baker's Plays, $1 (give author's name when ordering).

NIGHT COMES TO THE CITY, by Claire Boiko. Plays 10 minutes. A sort of idyll comes from a blending of the sounds of the city. Wetmore Declamation Bureau, 60¢.

NIGHT FALLS ON SPAIN, by Hazel H. Sholley. 3 men, 2 women. Plays 35 minutes. Interior set. Father Soreano remains a center of calm and courage, guiding his parishioners to safety through faith during the terrors of a rebellion. Baker's Plays, 60¢.

NIGHT OF RECKONING, by Nora Stirling. Demonstrates dramatically the fact that a hospital is a community institution. American Hospital Assoc.

THE NIGHTINGALE, by Dorothy Wright. Variable cast. Plays full evening. Fairy tale in the Chinese fashion, particularly suitable for Christmas; requires simplicity of production. Evans Plays, 6*s.* 6*d.* net. Royalty: 5–4 *gns.*

NIGHTS OF NOEL, compiled by Verne Powers. Wide range of Christmas plays, programs. Includes "The Vision," "A Child for a King," "Christmas Eve," "The Nature of a Gift," "A Certain Star." Baker's Plays, $2.25.

NINE NEW PLAYS FOR CHILDREN, by Rose Fyleman. Variable cast. Baker's Plays, $1. Royalty: $3 each play.

NO EXIT, by Jean-Paul Sartre, translated by Stuart Gilbert. 2 men, 2 women. Interior set. Sartre's concept of hell—three people locked together in a hotel room for eternity. They discover that they each must follow a set pattern of action, and that there is no escape from themselves or one another. In *No Exit and Three Other Plays.* Samuel French, Inc., $1.25. Royalty: $25–$20.

NO MORE CHRISTMAS, by Helen M. Roberts. Group of children and adults. Interior set. Two bitter, lonely women are changed in their determination not to celebrate Christmas by a dream of being Santa Claus to a group of children. Singing of carols incorporated. T. S. Denison & Co., 50¢ (purchase of 8 copies required).

NO ROOM AT THE INN, by Esther E. Olson. 2 men, 2 women. Plays 30 minutes. Malthar's first, imperfect lamp illuminates the manger on the night of Christ's birth. Baker's Plays, 60¢.

NO ROOM AT THE INN, by Dorothy Yost. 17 men, 5 women (choir). Plays 35 minutes. Interior set. The crowded inn, the Holy Family, the coming of the shepherds and the magi, in a drama for Christmas. Samuel French, Inc., 60¢. Royalty: $5.

NO ROOM AT THE INN. 15 men, 1 woman. Plays 30 minutes. Story prepared by junior high actors. Plays, Inc., 50¢.

NO ROOM IN THE HOTEL, by Dorothy Clarke Wilson. 6 men, 4 women. Plays 30 minutes. Only a newspaper reporter of the diverse group gathered at the hotel is affected by the appearance of a poor couple very like another couple refused room at an inn. Baker's Plays, 60¢. Royalty: first performance, none; $2.50 each repeat.

NO ROOM IN THE INN, by Lois W. Clarke. Variable cast (children or adult) as chorus of angels, optional choir. A beautiful retelling of the birth of Christ. Playing time varies with number of hymns used. Baker's Plays, 60¢ (give author's name when ordering).

NO ROOM IN THE INN, by Dora Boiteau Franc. 29 players, choir. A pageant of Christ's birth with its basis in Luke and Matthew. Cokesbury Press, 30¢. Package, 48.

NOAH, by Andre Obey, translated by Arthur Wilmurt. 5 men, 4 women, 8 men or women as assorted animals. Noah sets sail on the ark and discovers doubts amid his own family as to whether or not anything has been accomplished by the purging of the earth or Noah's attempts at saving mankind. Humorous touches are added by the assortment of animals. Noah remains the central, redeeming character of the play. Samuel French, Inc. Royalty: $25.

NOAH GIVES THANKS, by Eric Crozier. 4 men, 3 women, 4 children, optional extras. Plays 75 minutes. A celebration of the anniversary of a chapel and the seventeenth birthday of Noah, planned by the old folks, is interrupted by a minister and his wife, but rewarded by a small "miracle." Three acts. Baker's Plays, $1.50. Royalty: $15.

NOAH'S FLOOD, edited by Vincent F. Hopper and Gerald B. Lahey. 5 men, 4 women, women as gossips in audience. The medieval Noah pageant from the Chester cycle with introductory and background notes. In *Medieval Mysteries, Moralities, and Interludes.* Barron's Educational Series, $1.25. Royalty: apply to publisher.

NOBODY KNOWS, by Robert M. Healey. 3 men. Plays 30 minutes. Interior set. Concerns the production of a play about a racial incident in the South and the objections of a young Negro chosen within his school for a central role. Powerful and liberal in philosophy, but not offensive to its audience. Baker's Plays, 60¢. Royalty: $5.

NOBODY'S CHILD, by Mabel Crampton Cox. Reader, adults, children (large group). Plays about 30 minutes. Pageant of Christmas depicting the prophecy of Jesus' birth and the birth itself. The nurse, Nobody's Child, the Tramp, and the Rich Man attend the Christmas service. Eldridge, 60¢.

NOT BY MIGHT, by Archie Crouch. 5–7 men, 1–3 women. A family's choice between Christ and communism. Friendship Press, 50¢.

NOT MARTYRS, by Freda Collins. 9 men, 1 woman. The Diocletian persecution in North Africa in A.D. 303. Difficult historical play. Religious Drama Society of Great Britain, 34¢. Royalty: approximately $2.12.

NOT WITHOUT HONOR, by Elaine Walker Getzinger. 10 women. Plays 25 minutes. Interior set. Jealousy and doubt mark Jesus' return to Nazareth except for a young crippled girl who has faith in his power to heal her. T. S. Denison & Co., 50¢ (purchase of 10 copies required).

NOTHING IS IMPOSSIBLE, by Charles J. Ax. Play of the ministry of Christ. In *Bible Plays,* Book I, Christmas. Fortress Press, 75¢.

NOVELLIS, NOVELLIS, by John La Montaine. 2 sopranos, 1 alto, 2 tenors, 1 baritone, 1 bass baritone, 1 boy soprano, 3 children. A pageant opera of the Nativity story with prophets and characters from the Bible. G. Schirmer, Inc. Royalty: apply to publisher.

NOYE'S FLUDDE, by Benjamin Britten. Teen-agers and children, 1 bass, 1 contralto. An opera for church festivals at any season; concerns the story of Noah and the flood. Boosey and Hawkes. Royalty: apply to publisher.

THE NURSERY MAID OF HEAVEN, by Thomas Wood Stevens. 3 men, 6 women. Plays 45 minutes. Interior set. Simple novice Benvenuta, found in the outside world in a pitiable state, performs a miracle through her faith and adoration of the Christchild and "walks in the light." Baker's Plays, 75¢. Royalty: $10 if admission is charged; $5 if not.

NUTCRACKER SUITE, by Richter, music by Peter Ilich Tchaikovsky. 6 characters, variable extras. The music with a playlet. Opportunity for creative interpretation in ballet dances. Baker's Plays, $1.25.

O DISTANT LAND, by Stanley Richards. 7 men, 3 women, extras. Plays 30 minutes. In flashbacks, the childhood and struggles toward success of a playwright. Very worthwhile. Banner Play Bureau, 60¢.

O HOLY NIGHT, by Betty Grey Gruwell. 2 narrators, 2 choirs. Plays 1 hour. A choral pageant in pantomime with choirs of Nativity. Church aisles are used by wise men, shepherds, and choirs. Samuel French, Inc., 60¢. Royalty: apply to publisher.

O LITTLE TOWN OF BETHLEHEM. 8 men, 3 women, extras. Plays 25 minutes. Interior sets, exterior sets. The innkeeper's children try to make the Holy Family comfortable and the shepherd boys hear the message of the angel. Plays, Inc., 50¢.

O VALIANT HEART, by Evelyn Millard. 13 women. Interior set. Humor and pathos in the discipline and compassion of a suburban hospital. Three acts. Baker's Plays, $1.25. Royalty: $25.

O WORSHIP THE KING! Variable cast. A worship pageant composed of tableaux based on "As with Gladness Men of Old." Augsburg Press, 10¢.

OAKS OF MAMRE, by James D. Pendleton. 4 men, 1 woman. Plays 30 minutes. The conflict between Abraham and Sarah when the command comes to sacrifice Isaac, reflecting the twentieth-century conflict between faith and reason. Baker's Plays, 60¢. Royalty: $10.

THE ODD MAN. Teen-agers settle the rebuff of Mack, new to this section of the city, on the football field. A Human Relations playlet. Anti-Defamation League of B'nai B'rith, 15¢.

OEDIPUS AT COLONUS, by Sophocles, translated by David Grene. 20–30 men, 2 women, chorus (15), Elders of Colonus, extras. Oedipus, blind and exiled, is sought since the spot on which he dies will be sanctified. The tragedy of Oedipus' final search for redemption and his death. Very difficult. In *The Complete Greek Tragedies.* University of Chicago Press. Royalty: apply to publisher.

OEDIPUS THE KING, translated by David Grene. 6 men, 1 woman, 2 girls, 1 boy, chorus of 15, Theban elders, extras. The tragedy of Oedipus' search for truth, his discovery of his fate, and his final acceptance of responsibility. Very difficult. In *The Complete Greek Tragedies.* University of Chicago Press. Royalty: apply to publisher.

THE OFFENDING HAND, by R. F. Delderfield. 4 men, 4 women. Interior set. Problems and dangers of the current methods of handling juvenile delinquency. Dramatic. Baker's Plays, $1.25. Royalty: $25.

AN OLD ENGLISH CUSTOM, by Dora MacDonald. 15 men, 7 women, children. Plays 90 minutes. Interior set. Christmas pageant. Christmas celebrated in an English mansion. English customs, sixteenth-century, for a social evening at church. T. S. Denison & Co., 50¢ (purchase of 10 copies required).

THE OLD MAN OF THE MOUNTAINS, by Norman Nicholson. 5 men, 3 women, the Raven, the Beck (3 women's voices). Interior sets, exterior sets. The story of Elijah and the raven, transferred to the modern setting of the author's native Cumberland. Very lively verse and humanity of characterization. Faber & Faber. Permission for production required; inquire of Mercury Theatre.

THE OLD OLD STORY, by Helen Perry Curtis. 1 adult, from 12 to several hundred children. Christmas pageant in pantomime, movement, and tableaux to music. Accompanied by familiar carols. Angel, the only speaking role, may be played by an adult. Baker's Plays, 60¢.

OLD PINE TREE AND OTHER NOH PLAYS, translated by Makots Meda. A cycle of five Japanese Noh plays. Beautiful. Bison Books.

THE OLD RUGGED CROSS, Pantomime of the hymn, provided through the courtesy of the Rodeheaver Company. Eldridge, 50¢.

OLD TESTAMENT PLAYS, by Laurence Housman. Five Old Testament plays: "Abraham and Isaac," "Jacob's Ladder," "Ramoth Gilead," "The Burden of Nineveh," "Samuel the Kingmaker." Baker's Plays, $3.75. Royalty: apply to publisher.

OMAR, by Elliot Field. 7 men, 3 women. Plays 1 hour. Interior set. Two young people of Muslim background come under the influence of Christianity. Two acts. Baker's Plays, 60¢.

ON BORROWED TIME, by Paul Osborn. 11 men, 3 women. Plays full evening. A boy and his grandfather imprison Death in an apple tree. An excellent, very human fantasy. Difficult. Dramatists Play Service, $1. Royalty: $35–$25.

ON CHRISTMAS NIGHT, by Edna Risque. 19 characters, extras. 2 settings. Three scenes. Faith Press, 1*s.* 6*d.*

ON EARTH PEACE, by Karin Asbrand. 3 women, narrator, 2 extras (girls). Plays 15 minutes. Interior set. The birth of a grandchild ends the long feud between the families. In *Easy Church Plays for Women and Girls.* Baker's Plays, $1.25.

ON STAGE FOR TEEN-AGERS, by Helen Miller. Twenty-two one-act plays; something for all occasions. Plays, Inc., $4.

ON THE EVE OF HOLY WEEK, by Harold Bassage. An attempt to discover an answer to the question "Who is Christ?" crucifies him again but leads to a confession of sin and a new dedication. Good as a chancel drama or in readings. Seabury Press, 65¢.

ON THE HILL, by Edward Murch. 7 women. Those who care for a man about to be crucified learn of forgiveness at the time of the crucifixion. H. F. W. Deane & Sons, *5s.–6s.* Postage, *4s.*

ON THE ROAD TO EGYPT, by Mary R. Davidson. 3 men, 1 woman. Plays 30 minutes. May be given in chancel but more appropriately given in the parish house. In *Jumbo Christmas Book.* Baker's Plays, $1.25.

ON THE THIRD DAY, by Belford Forrest. 6 men, 5 women. Interior set. Easter play in three acts. Reverent drama of Jesus' appearance "on the third day." Baker's Plays, $1. Royalty: $15.

ONCE UPON A CHRISTMAS, by Alice Chadwicke. 7 women. Plays 35 minutes. Interior set. A strange Dr. Spirit brings her special brand of healing to one, long ill, on Christmas Eve. Baker's Plays, 60¢. Royalty: $5.

ONCE UPON A CHRISTMAS TIME, book and lyrics by Edith Sanford Tillotson; music by Ruth Dale. Mother tells a bedtime story of the Nativity in a young children's pageant. Eldridge, 50¢.

ONE FAMILY SINGS, adapted for stage by Sister M. Francis Borgia, O.S.F. 14 men, 25 women (flexible cast). The story and songs of the life of the Trapp family. May be done with simple drapery background. Baker's Plays, $1. Royalty: $1 minimum to $35 maximum based on 20% of gross receipts.

ONE FOOT IN HEAVEN, by Hartzell Spence, adapted by Anne Coulter Martens. 8 men, 9 women. Plays full evening. Pastor Spence and his family work to build a parish from a dilapidated parsonage. Dramatic Publishing Co., 90¢. Royalty: $25.

100 PLAYS FOR CHILDREN, edited by A. S. Burack. Includes in a general collection plays for Christmas, Easter, other special days, world friendship, character building. Plays, Inc., $6.50.

ONE NIGHT IN BETHLEHEM. 3 men, 5 women, extras. Plays 15 minutes. Exterior set. For middle grades. A woman's plan to offer her room in the inn to the couple from Galilee is spoiled by the greedy wife of the innkeeper. Plays, Inc., 50¢.

ONE NIGHT IN BETHLEHEM, by Karin Asbrand. 13 characters, angel chorus. Shows the Nativity scene and its effect on three thieves, one a small boy. Baker's Plays, 60¢.

ONE NIGHT IN BETHLEHEM, by Katherine S. Brown and Glenna Smith Tinnin. 17 men, 5 women. Interior sets, exterior sets. Simple settings and Old Testament costumes accompany a successful Nativity play. Prologue and five scenes. Samuel French, Inc., 60¢. Royalty: $5.

ONE RED ROSE, by Paul Hargan, adapted by Sister Mary Olive. 1 man, 6 women, extras (may be performed by small cast of girls). A human story of the need for salvation through love, involving the mother superior of an orphanage and a fifteen-year-old orphan. Contains stage directions. One act, eight short scenes. McKay's Plays, $1.25. Royalty: $15.

ONE STARRY NIGHT, by Karin Asbrand. 11 men, 5 women, chorus. Pageant in three parts: "The Message," "The Nativity," "The Token." Reverent and beautiful. Effective when presented in the church. Eldridge, 60¢ (purchase of 10 copies required).

ONE WITH THE FLAME, by Francesca Dunfey. 21 or 22 women (may be reduced to 14–15 by doubling, 11–12 by cutting). The destiny of Joan of Arc as witnessed through the eyes of women. Baker's Plays, $1. Royalty: $1 minimum to $35 maximum based on 20% of gross receipts.

ONE-ACT PLAYS FOR ALL-GIRL CASTS, by Marjorie Paradis. Twelve one-act plays for entertainment for junior and senior high schools. Plays, Inc., $3.

ONE-ACT PLAYS OF SPIRITUAL POWER, by Fred Eastman. A collection of ten plays relating to survival in the atomic age, and the creation of peace and brotherhood throughout the world. Baker's Plays, $3.25. Royalty: apply to publisher.

ONESIMUS, by A. T. Cadoux. 10 men, 2 women. Prologue, three acts, epilogue. A play on the story surrounding Paul's letter to Philemon. Baker's Plays, 85¢. Royalty: $10.

THE ONLY WAY, by Charles Dickens, adapted by Lt. Col. the Rev. Freeman Wills and the Rev. Canon Langbridge. 22 men (doubling possible), 4 women. A dramatization from *A Tale of Two Cities* which has had its place in the American theatre since the beginning of the twentieth century. Baker's Plays, $1.25. Royalty: $25.

OPEN SECRET, by Robert Adler, George Bellak, and Louis Ridenour. 7 men. Plays 30 minutes. An atomic bomb is dropped in the United States. Samuel French, Inc., 50¢. Royalty: $5.

THE OPEN WINDOWS, by Grace Kinyon. 10 women. Plays 45 minutes. The benefits of tithe giving shown in a pleasant play of a woman who shares part of whatever she has. Eldridge, 60¢.

OTHELLO, THE MOOR OF VENICE, by William Shakespeare. 8 men, 3 women. Othello, victim of the plotting of demoniac Iago, is tormented by doubt and fear and destroyed by jealousy. Only the remaining light of the dead Desdemona's love brings him realization and redemption. Powerful and extremely difficult tragedy. Cambridge Co. Royalty: none.

THE OTHER CROSS, by E. Harriet Donlevy. 3 men, 4 women, 3 male extras. Plays 25 minutes. Interior set. The family of John, the other man on the cross at Calvary, gains faith in life beyond death. Baker's Plays, 60¢.

THE OTHER ONE, by Arthur Ketchum. 3 men. Plays 30 minutes. The need of kindness and forgiveness among men is emphasized when the appearance of the Other One changes a vagabond's plans to victimize his youthful companion. Baker's Plays, 60¢. Royalty: $5.

THE OTHER SHEPHERD, by Dorothy Clarke Wilson. 7 men, 5 women. Plays 45 minutes. A shepherd about to leave his flock to consecrate his life to God stays instead to give shelter to Joseph and Mary. Baker's Plays, 60¢.

THE OTHER WISE MAN, by Henry Van Dyke, adapted by Pauline

Phelphs. 6 men, 2 women, reader. Plays 30 minutes. A man sells all he has to buy gems for the Christchild and sets out with the wise men. Baker's Plays, 60¢. Royalty: first performance, none if 7 copies purchased; $2.50 each repeat.

THE OTHER WISE MAN, by Henry Van Dyke, adapted by Harold G. Sliker. 19 speaking roles (doubling possible), speaking choir. Plays 1 hour. A choric drama of the fourth wise man whose search for Christ begins with the star and ends at the crucifixion. Baker's Plays, 60¢. Royalty: $5.

OUR CHRISTMAS HERITAGE, by Bessie M. Stratton. Variable cast. Plays 1 hour. The symbols of the Christmas decorations are brought to the altar by peoples of different lands. Baker's Plays, 60¢.

OUR GREATEST GIFT, by B. Margaret Voss. Large cast. Plays 1 hour. Interior set. The traditional Christmas scene is shown from the beginning of the Christian church to the present. Effective use possible for lighting, costume, and movement; optional choral speech; or rhythm choir. Baker's Plays, 60¢.

OUR LADY'S TUMBLER, by Ronald Duncan. 5 men. Plays 25 minutes. Set in chapel containing a statue of the Virgin. An acrobat offers his skills before the statue of the blessed Virgin. Treatment is effective, may be presented in hall or chancel. Faber & Faber. Royalty: apply to Margery Vosper.

OUR LEAN YEARS, by Fred Eastman. 8 men, 6 women. Plays 30 minutes. Interior set. A cooperative religious effort saves a home from financial collapse by practical measures. Baker's Plays, 60¢. Royalty: $5.

OUR TOWN, by Thornton Wilder. 17 men, 7 women, extras. Plays full evening. Bare stage with skeletal properties. The people of Grover's Corners, New Hampshire, seen in life, death, and the discovery of life made after death. The Stage Manager narrates the story of the town centering in the lives of Emily Webb and George Gibbs. The characters are seen against a backdrop of their social, religious, and philosophical traditions in a play of humor, pathos, and human universality. Baker's Plays, $1.25. Royalty: $25.

OUT OF DESPAIR, by Kitty McCann. Choral Easter reading. Universalizes the Easter message to free all men from despair. Baker's Plays, 60¢.

OUT OF THE BIBLE, by Lyman R. Bayard. Children's Day pageant. From a great Bible on the platform, Imagination and Religious Education call the biblical children. Baker's Plays, 40¢.

OUT OF THE DARKNESS, by John McGreevy. 4 men, 3 women, extras. Plays 30 minutes. Interior set. The guards at Christ's tomb deny the resurrection for money. T. S. Denison & Co., 50¢ (purchase of 7 copies required).

OUTSIDE THE DOOR, by Ruth Apprich Jacob. 4 men, 2 women. Interior set. A group of teen-agers, observing a beating, must decide whether or not to come forward as witnesses. Baker's Plays, 60¢.

OUTSIDE THE STABLE, by Freda Collins. 15 characters, crowd. For children. One continuous scene. Faith Press, 2*s.*

THE OUTSIDER, by Evelyn Neuenburg. 4 women. Interior set. A girl feels fear upon learning she is adopted. Baker's Plays, 60¢.

OUTWARD BOUND, by Sutton Vane. 6 men, 3 women. Interior set. The passengers of a ship, with the exception of two, are discovered to be dead and bound for an unknown destination. Religious in effect. Three acts. Samuel French, Inc., $1.25. Royalty: $25–$20.

THE PACKING OF THE HOME MISSIONARY BARREL. 10 women. Plays 30 minutes. A group of ladies learn a lesson in unselfishness in the midst of their charity work. Baker's Plays, 60¢.

A PAGEANT OF EASTER, by H. Alexander Matthews. Chorus. The Easter story with drama and music. H. W. Gray Co.: complete, $1.25; music, 50¢.

A PAGEANT OF JERUSALEM, by B. J. Hill. For advanced groups of junior- and intermediate-age children. Worthwhile. Religious Drama Society of Great Britain.

PAGEANT OF OUR LADY, by John J. Johnson and Aileen Shea. Large cast, doubling possible. Plays 40 minutes. Ten episodes of the life of Mary the mother from her childhood to her assumption into heaven. Baker's Plays, 75¢.

A PAGEANT OF PILGRIMS, by Esther W. Bates. Large, variable cast. Development of story through history. Baker's Plays, 50¢. Royalty: $10.

A PAGEANT OF THE HOLY NATIVITY, by W. J. Simmons. 23 characters, crowd. Eleven scenes, eight tableaux. For adults. Faith Press, 1*s*.

PAGEANT OF THE SINGING STARS, by Louis Wilson. 14 men, 20 women, 10 small girls. From a fantasy centering in Christ's birth the play moves through time and a betraying of the Christian ideal to a moment of elevated dedication. Baker's Plays, 60¢. Royalty: $5.

PAGEANTS AND PROGRAMS FOR SCHOOL, CHURCH, AND PLAYGROUND. Seven brotherhood programs. Nat'l. Recreation Assoc., 50¢.

PAPA WAS A PREACHER, by Alyene Porter, adapted by John McGreevey. 7 men, 8 women. Plays full evening. The joys and follies of the Rev. Porter and his family in home and church. Dramatic Publishing Co., 90¢. Royalty: $25.

PARABLE, by Ralph Stone. 3 women, 7 men, extras. The dream of an average housewife that she belongs to royalty in the middle ages. Comedy. One act. In *Circus, Parable and Construction.* Bethany Press, $1. Royalty: none if admission is not charged.

PARADE AT THE DEVIL'S BRIDGE, by Henri Gheon. 4 men, 3 women. Plays 20 minutes. Bare stage. A satire of that stubbornness that may cause a religious man's compromise with evil in the pursuit of a good end. Easy to act. In *St. Anne and the Gouty Rector and Other Plays.* McKay's Plays, $2.75. Royalty: $10 if admission is charged; $5 if not.

PARAMOUNT CHILDREN'S DAY BOOK. Collection for Children's Day, including pantomimes and playlets. Church school material. Baker's Plays, 40¢.

PARAMOUNT EASTER BOOK. Recitations, adult readings, etc., for all church school groups, with a program for the entire church school including suggestions for songs. Baker's Plays, 40¢.

THE PARAMOUNT MOTHER'S DAY BOOK. Dialogues, verse and prose playlets, etc. Baker's Plays, 30¢.

THE PARTY AT MOUNT YU, by Robert E. Fuerst. 2 men, 3 women, chorus. Plays 30 minutes. A teacher is reassured of her profession by viewing the enduring influences of a missionary in the village in Taiwan where she was born. Christmastime setting. Eldridge, 60¢ (purchase of 5 copies required).

THE PASSING OF THE THIRD FLOOR BACK, by Jerome K. Jerome. 6 men, 6 women. Interior set. The unsavory boarders of a Bloomsbury lodging house are influenced to lead better lives by the mysterious person who takes residence in the third-floor back. Three acts. Baker's Plays, $1.25. Royalty: $25.

THE PASSION FLOWER, by Jacinto Benavente, translated by John Garret Underhill. 6 men, 9 women, extras. 2 interior sets. A play, set in twentieth-century Castile, of revenge and family loyalty, jealousy, murder, and the closeness of love and hate. In *Contemporary Drama,* Vol. III. Charles Scribner's Sons, $3. Royalty: apply to publisher.

THE PASSION PLAY AT OBERAMMERGAU, 1900, edited by Lotte Eckener. German text with translation in English, illustrated with a series of the 1890's photographs. For Easter. College Book Service, $15.

PAST AND PRESENT, THREE SHORT PLAYS, by Clegg, Rands, and McArthur. Includes: "The Apple Tree" (a story of Caedmon), "Swords for the Innocent" (slaughter of the Innocents), "Gifts in the Stable" (Nativity cast by teen-agers). Religious Drama Society of Great Britain, 54¢. Royalty: apply to publisher.

THE PASTOR'S GUIDING HAND, by Lois M. Sandberg. 3 men, 4 women, reader. The pastor advises those who invade his privacy while practicing his sermon in the church. Easy to stage. Two acts. Baker's Plays, 60¢.

PATSY BECOMES A PILGRIM MAID, by Sadye A. Berman. 3 boys, 5 girls. Plays 15 minutes. A modern girl gains an appreciation of modern times. In *Plays for the Schoolroom.* Samuel French, Inc., $1.

PAUL AT CORINTH, by Edward Longstreth. Plays 1 hour. Biblical chancel drama suited to either reading or staging. $1.50. Royalty: inquire of the author.

PAUL AT DAMASCUS, by Edward Longstreth. Plays 1 hour. Biblical chancel drama for reading or staging. $1.50. Royalty: inquire of the author.

PAUL BEFORE KING AGRIPPA, by Norman E. Nygaard. 6 men, 1 woman. Paul speaks of Christ's and man's resurrection before King Agrippa. In *The Bible Comes Alive.* Baker's Plays, $1.25.

PAUL IN THE AREOPAGUS AT ATHENS, by Norman E. Nygaard. Paul tells the Greek philosophers of Christ's resurrection. Monodrama form. In *The Bible Comes Alive.* Baker's Plays, $1.25.

PAUL THOMPSON FOREVER, by Mordecai Gorelik. Plays 30 minutes. After death a man returns with the Investigator to determine his position in the afterlife. Baker's Plays, 60¢. Royalty: $5.

PEACE BE TO THIS HOUSE, by Dr. Charles M. Sheldon, adapted by Mary B. Harrison from the book *He Is Here.* 3 men, 1 woman.

Plays 30 minutes. The Stranger reunites a farmer and his son. Baker's Plays, 60¢.

PEACE I GIVE UNTO YOU, by Dorothy Clarke Wilson. 4 men, 1 woman. Plays 30 minutes. A telling of the story of the first Christmas with a relation to universal peace, set in the cottage of Joseph and Marta. Conveys the full emotional range of the story. Baker's Plays, 60¢.

PEACE IS AN OLIVE COLOR, by John W. Felton. 3 men, 1 boy, 1 voice. Plays 30 minutes. A GI, on guard duty for the UN, learns a new meaning of Christmas caring for an injured native boy. Baker's Plays, 60¢. Royalty: $5.

PEACE OF BETHANY, by Joan Brockelsby. 9 women. Plays 35 minutes. Mary and Martha during the time of the crucifixion and the resurrection. Abingdon Press, 35¢.

PEACE ON MARS, by Dorothy Clarke Wilson. 4 men, 2 women. Plays 30 minutes. Interior set. An exploration of man with all the tools to make a heaven he is unable to make. A messenger from the heavens proclaims God's love and the creation of life rather than death. Baker's Plays, 60¢. Royalty: $10.

PEACE TO EARTH, by Zella F. Soward and Rosemary Hadler. 2 girl readers, choir. Plays 45 minutes. Nativity pantomime for children. Baker's Plays, 50¢.

PEER GYNT, by Henrik Ibsen, translated by R. Farquharson Sharp. 15 women, 32 men, men and women extras (doubling possible). Exterior set, 1 interior set. Peer Gynt wastes his life in self-gratification, lies, and dreams, and compromises even with himself. He travels the world in search of his soul. Only the faith and love of Solveig may redeem him. E. P. Dutton & Co., $2.25. Royalty: apply to publisher.

THE PEOPLE VS. CHRIST, by Albert Johnson. 2 men, 1 woman. Bare stage with skeletal properties. A Drama Trio play. Christ is put on trial in modern terms and a sullen girl named Mary appears as the witness in his defense. She is examined about a recurrent dream, and in recounting it, the events of Christ's birth, life, and Passion are played out; the girl becomes Mary the mother, and two men take the parts of various characters surrounding his life. Poetic; touched with both humor and pathos; holds beauty and power. Baker's Plays, 60¢. Royalty: $10.

THE PEOPLE VS. THE PHARISEE, by T. N. Tiemeyer. 6 men, 2 women. Courtroom scene; may be simply staged. A Pharisee, made infamous by a parable told about him, asks that his case be given a fair hearing in the light of modern times. The audience finds itself on trial. Baker's Plays, 60¢.

THE PEOPLE WERE IN EXPECTATION, by Harold Bassage. An inquirer asks a congregation when Christ will come and learns that he will come when the inquirer prepares to receive him. A dignified selection for Advent. Seabury Press, 65¢.

THE PERFECT CAROL, by Aileen Sargent. 2 men, 2 women, 9 tableaux characters, village choir. Franz Gruber, inspired by the Christmas story in a quiet morning, gives the world "Silent Night." Baker's Plays, 60¢. Royalty: $5.

THE PERFECT GIFT, by Karin Asbrand. 6 women, carolers. Worried because they have little money for Christmas gifts, a group of girls realize that they can give service of far greater value. In *Jumbo Christmas Book.* Baker's Plays, $1.25.

THE PERSIANS, by Aeschylus, translated by Seth Benardette. 3 men, male chorus of 15 or 24, 1 woman. Exterior set. The shade of Darius repudiates Xerxes' rule of Persia. In *The Complete Greek Tragedies.* University of Chicago Press. Royalty: apply to publisher.

PERSON TO PERSON CALL, by Virginia Coigney. Individuals' confrontation with problems of community betterment. American Nat'l. Red Cross: perusal script, $2; kit of 6 acting scripts, $12.

PETER AT PENTECOST, by Norman E. Nygaard. Peter calls on the people of Jerusalem for repentance of their sins. Monodrama form. In *The Bible Comes Alive.* Baker's Plays, $1.25.

THE PETITION, by Margot Bryant. 4 men, 3 women, 1 boy. Interior set. A mixed group of characters is brought together in a courtroom to alleviate the burdens of George Windemere by distributing them among those gathered. As they are called on for sacrifices the people are seen as they really are. One act. Evans Plays, 2*s.* net. Royalty: 25*s.* per performance.

THE PETRIFIED FOREST, by Robert E. Sherwood. 16 men (doubling possible), 3 women, extras. Interior set. A gang of criminals holds a group of people prisoners at a desert bar and grill. An intellectual, sensitive man convinces a killer to shoot him so that his life insurance may help an innocent girl escape to find her dreams. A play of the death of individualism and hope in a fresh innocence. Dramatists Play Service. Royalty: $25.

PHILIP, THE DESERT EVANGELIST, by Norman E. Nygaard. 3 men. Two followers of Queen Candace are converted when they are told of Christ by Philip. In *The Bible Comes Alive.* Baker's Plays, $1.25.

PHILOCTETES, by Sophocles, translated by David Grene. 5 men, 15-man chorus. Set: entrance to cave. Attempts of the Greeks to persuade the marooned and agonized Philoctetes to aid them in winning the Trojan War with the Bow of Heracles. A study of pain, duty, selfishness, and honor, using the supernatural agent of the appearance of the demigod Heracles for its resolution. In *The Complete Greek Tragedies.* University of Chicago Press. Royalty: apply to publisher.

PICCOLA, by A. R. Wickens and Ruby M. Black. 2 boys, 2 girls. Interior set. Operetta. A poor peasant girl of France sets out her shoe, hoping for Christmas goodies; gratefully she finds in it a bird with a broken wing, which she believes to have been brought by the good saint. One act. Baker's Plays, 60¢ (purchase of 6 copies required).

THE PICNIC BASKET, by Nora Stirling. Problems of a mental patient in returning to normal response. Vocational Rehabilitation Administration (write publisher for free scripts, in limited supply).

PICTURES IN THE FIRE, by Anne Coulter Martens. 1 boy, 2 girls, chorus. Plays 10 minutes. The boy Lincoln sits before the fire that has his future in its flames. Baker's Plays, 25¢.

A PIECE OF SILVER, by Annabella Irwin. 3 men, 2 women. Plays 25 minutes. A family discovers that they already possess the things the piece of silver could have bought. Also included are a weary traveler and a mother and child needing shelter. Can be played by an inexperienced cast. One act. Eldridge, 60¢ (purchase of 5 copies required).

PILATE AND THE CROSS, by James J. Glade. 11 men, 7 women, extras. Plays 75 minutes. A very human, simple, and natural play of the crucifixion. Includes stage directions. McKay's Plays, $1.25. Royalty: $15.

PILATE, THE ROMAN GOVERNOR, by Norman E. Nygaard. Monodrama. Pilate feels his judgment of Christ as a judgment of himself. In *The Bible Comes Alive.* Baker's Plays, $1.25.

PILGRIM PARTING. 8 men, 6 women, extras. Plays 20 minutes. Despite their parents' arrangements for them to return to England, Miles and Comfort make their decision to stay. Plays, Inc., 50¢.

PILGRIMS OF THE WAY, by Dorothy Clarke Wilson. 4 men, 2 women. Plays 40 minutes. Exterior set. Saul of Tarsus before he is converted. Baker's Plays, 60¢. Royalty: first performance, none; $2.50 each repeat.

THE PILGRIM'S PROGRESS, by John Bunyan, adapted by Rodney Bennett. 4 men, 3 women, extras. Plays full evening. Simple sets. Baker's Plays, 85¢. Royalty: $15.

THE PILGRIM'S ROAD TO BETHLEHEM, by H. V. Lupton. 15 characters, crowd. 3 sets. For adults, a play for Christmas. Three scenes. Faith Press, 1*s.* 6*d.*

THE PILLARS OF SOCIETY, by Henrik Ibsen, translated by Una Ellis-Fermor. 10 men, 9 women, extras. Interior set. A man rises from a world ruled by corruption and scandal, and as a result of his experience decides to convert the pillars of society over to stand on freedom and truth. In *Three Plays by Ibsen.* Penguin Books. Royalty: apply to publisher.

PILOT LIGHTS OF APOCALYPSE, by Louis N. Ridenour. 12 men (or 7 men, 5 women). Plays 15 minutes. Atomic warfare seen in a vision of prophecy. One act. In *One Act Plays of Spiritual Power.* Baker's Plays, $3.25.

PINAFORE GONE PURIMDIG, by Adeline R. Rosewater. 5 boys, 1 girl, extras. A comedy with songs, chorus, and solo, that are Purim parodies of music from the Gilbert and Sullivan *H. M. S. Pinafore*; dances and much gaity. Union of American Hebrew Congregations, 25¢.

PING-PONG, by Arthur Adamov, translated by Richard Howard. 5 men, 2 women. Interior sets, 1 exterior set. The pinball machine becomes the center of the universe for a group of people in this examination of man's desperate pursuit of trivial and inanimate objects. Illustrates the futility of a mechanized civilization during religious and political strife. Grove Press. Royalty: apply to publisher.

THE PINK TELEPHONE, by Nora Stirling. The aid to dependent children program demonstrates an exciting challenge. American Public Welfare Assoc.: perusal script, $2; kit of 6 acting scripts, $12.

PINNACLE, by Evelyn Neuenburg. 4 women. Plays 30 minutes. Interior set. When a spinster daughter deceives her mother that she has found the perfect man, the mother, in an act of sacrifice, decides to force the daughter to make her own life. Baker's Plays, 60¢. Royalty: $5.

PIONEERS, by Mabel Gilmer. 3 men, 2 women. Plays 30 minutes. Farm people face nature's whims in 1843. Baker's Plays, 50¢. Royalty: $5.

PLANNIN' A CHRISTMAS PARTY, by Robert S. Hall. 5 men, 6 women. Plays 25 minutes. Interior set. Portrays a rural parsonage meeting; offers the chance for singing Christmas hymns, carols. In *The Easy Christmas Grab Bag*. Baker's Plays, $1.25.

A PLAY ON COVENANT, by Ruth Jacob. 8 men, 3 women, or 7 men, 4 women. Plays 30 minutes. Interior set. An attempt to explain covenant as minister and congregation offer question and interpretations, coming to an emphasis on faith. Easy to produce. Baker's Plays, 60¢.

PLAYBOOK. Plays for a new theatre by Lionel Abel, Robert Hivnor, Junji Kinoshita, James Merrill, and I. A. Richards, whose "A Leak in the Universe" is particularly fascinating. Humor is sophisticated; plays are representative of post-World War II drama. New Directions, $3.75.

PLAYETTE QUARTET. Four selections on missionary work and world friendship. "Mission to Paradise" (a girl with dreams of foreign service finds challenge in the Hawaiian Islands); "Widening Horizons," by Audrey McKim (a student missionary from Trinidad teaches a family in a Saskatchewan farmhouse that missions begin in the home); "The Reality," by Edith J. Agnew (churchwomen are more concerned with social standing of Alaska than with mission); "Together in Trinidad," by Constance Wagar (Indian, English, Negro, and Chinese girls live together in a dormitory; for girls in high school). Friendship Press, 50¢.

PLAYS AND PLAYLETS, by V. Whitman. Moody Press, $1.

PLAYS AS EXPERIENCE, by Irwin Zachar and R. A. Kimball. Fourteen one-acts for discussions of problems. Odyssey Press, $1.60.

PLAYS FOR GREAT OCCASIONS, by Graham DuBois. Twenty-four one-acts for special days, including Christmas, Easter, Thanksgiving, and others; includes portraits of famous men. For junior and senior high school students. Plays, Inc., $5.

PLAYS FOR HAPPIER HOMES, by Ruth C. and J. Edward Lantz. Small casts. A series of marriage-problem plays; excellent for discussion. Based on life experiences. Includes a sympathetic portrayal of the work of a Protestant pastor. Baker's Plays, $1.25.

PLAYS FOR THE CHURCH, by Committee of the Commission on Drama. A collection of eighty plays for advanced groups in churches. Nat'l. Council of Churches, Office of Publication and Distribution, 50¢.

PLAYS FOR THE SCHOOLROOM, by Sadye A. Berman. Includes "Patsy Becomes a Pilgrim Maid" for Thanksgiving. Samuel French, Inc., $1.

PLAYS FROM THE BIBLE, by Mary F. Holt. Old and New Testament characters depicted for young people, utilizing modern language. Baker's Plays, 75¢.

THE PLAYS OF EUGENE O'NEILL. Vol. I: "Desire Under the Elms," "Lazarus Laughed," "Strange Interlude," "The Moon of the Caribbees," "The Long Voyage Home," "The Rope," "Bound East for Cardiff," "In the Zone," "The Dreamy Kid," "Ile," "The Fountain," "Where the Cross Is Made," "Before Breakfast." Vol. II: "Ah, Wilderness!," "Marco Millions," "Gold," "Welded," "Diff'rent," "All God's Chillun Got Wings." Vol. III: "The Straw," "Beyond the Horizon," "The Hairy Ape," "The Iceman Cometh," "Days Without End," "Anna Christie," "The Great God Brown," "The Emperor Jones," "Dynamo." Random House: 3-volume set, $15; separate volume, $5.75.

PLAYS OF PERPLEXITY, by E. R. Hougham. Includes "Sensation on Budlegh Beacon," one-act play of a young man's search for a religion, in rhymed couplets, with an English tone; "Dead End," three-act play of living for the wrong goals. Religious Drama Society of Great Britain, 54¢. Royalty: "Sensation on Budlegh Beacon," approximately $1.48; "Dead End," approximately $5.92.

PLAYS, PAGEANTS, AND CEREMONIALS FOR THE CHRISTMAS SEASON. A Christmas collection for religious, social, and community performance. Nat'l. Recreation Assoc., 65¢.

THE PLOUGH AND THE STARS, by Sean O'Casey. 10 men, 5 women, 1 girl. Interior set, 1 exterior set. Residents of a Dublin tenement at the time of the 1916 Easter Week Rebellion. Death and pain result from their selfishness and their plundering during the violence. In *Three Plays.* Samuel French, Inc. Royalty: $25.

POETIC DRAMAS, by Alice Hunt Bartlett. Six leaders who envisioned world peace. College Book Service, $15.

POINT OF BEGINNING. The problem of minor compromises in honesty. Nat'l. Council of Churches, Office of Publication and Distribution, $1; production packet, $5.

POLYEUCTE, by Pierre Corneille, translated by Lacy Lockert. 10 men, 2 women. Interior set. Love and duty conflict in an old Roman setting as a young woman learns the nobility of her husband through his martyrdom for Christianity, and is converted to join him in death. In *Chief Plays of Corneille.* Princeton University Press, $5. Royalty: apply to publisher.

THE POOR MAN WHO DIED BECAUSE HE WORE GLOVES, by Henri Brochet. 3 men. Plays 15 minutes. The murder of the poor man who was thought rich brings the realization that love may bring good from evil. Good acting part. Technical production easy. In *St. Anne and the Gouty Rector and Other Plays.* McKay's Plays, $2.75. Royalty: $10 if admission is charged; $5 if not.

POSTSCRIPT TO PURIM, by Rabbis Eugene B. Borowitz and Arnold J. Wolf. 13 boys, 2 girls. The evening before his trial, Haman's friends try to free him. A very amusing trial follows. Union of American Hebrew Congregations, 35¢.

THE POTTER'S FIELD, by Phyl Steven. 8 men. Pilate and his son argue the wisdom of Jesus' arrest with the high priests, and Judas attempts to return the silver, but all is to no avail. H. F. W. Deane & Sons, 5*s* or 6*s*.

THE POTTING SHED, by Graham Greene. 6 men, 5 women. 3 interior sets. A man commits suicide in the potting shed and is resurrected; the miracle breeds the alienation of his son, and the destruction of his atheistic father's beliefs and his uncle's faith. Samuel French, Inc.: cloth, $3; paper, $1.25. Royalty: $50–$25.

THE POWER AND THE GLORY, by Graham Greene, adapted by Denis Cannan and Pierre Bost. 28 men, 9 women, extras. Plays full evening. A priest remains faithful to his calling and his people during the days of the Mexican Revolution, even at the cost of his life. Baker's Plays, $1.25. Royalty: $35.

THE POWERS THAT BE, by Sara McCarty and E. Clayton McCarty. 2 men, 4 women. Plays 15 minutes. Space set. Contrast of wishful thinking and reality in a fantasy. Uses stylization in space staging. Harper, 50¢ (purchase of 6 copies required).

PRELUDE, by F. E. M. Agnew. 6 women. Interior set. A Nativity play set in a Bethlehem eating house and bakery where Mary seeks lodging. There she meets Mary Magdalene and sees her baby, and is taken in by the innkeeper's wife, whose sympathy she gains. She leaves the bakery mistress discounting such fuss over the birth of a baby. English Theatre Guild, 2*s*.

THE PRELUDE TO DARKNESS, by Frederick Wahl. 2 men, 1 woman. Plays 30 minutes. A drama of the life of Johann Sebastian Bach. Banner Play Bureau, 50¢. Royalty: $5.

PRESENT PLEASURE, by Nora Stirling. A child faces the problem of adjustment in the home of foster parents. Child Welfare League of America.

PRIMARY CHRISTMAS PROGRAM BOOK, by Helen Stieve. A collection of playlets, choral readings, pantomimes, tableaux, etc. Baker's Plays, $1.

PRINCE OF PEACE, by Karin Asbrand. 5 women, chorus, shepherds (may be girls). Plays 15 minutes. Interior set. The Holy Family come to the inn, and the coming of the Messiah is told against a background of carols. In *Easy Church Plays for Women and Girls.* Baker's Plays, $1.25.

THE PRINCE OF PEACE, by E. Lawrence Gibson. 1 man, 2 women. Plays 25 minutes. Interior set. A fantasy in which a child's prayer brings a scarecrow to life, revealing him as the spirit of Christ come to the world in order to bring peace. Samuel French, Inc., 60¢. Royalty: $5.

THE PRINCESS POVERTY, by Francis de Sales Gliebe, O.F.M. 18 men, 4 women, extras. 7 sets. For staging or reading, a play of the life of St. Clare. Seventeen scenes. St. Anthony Guild Press, 50¢.

THE PRINCESS WHO COULD NOT BE MERRY, by Marion Holbrook. 6 men, 6 women. Plays 25 minutes. The little princess who has everything money can give finds happiness only when she is given friendship. In *Easy Christmas Grab Bag*. Baker's Plays, $1.25.

THE PRISONER RELEASED, by Stephen Chodorov. Deals with the imprisonment of deafness and solutions to its problems. Vocational Rehabilitation Administration.

THE PRODIGAL MOTHER, by Frances Blazer. 1 man, 2 women, 2 boys (teen-agers). Plays 35 minutes. Interior set. A mother is dominated by her love and her son does not understand. Emotionally intense. Baker's Plays, 60¢. Royalty: $10.

THE PRODIGAL SON, by Warren Kliewer. 3 men. Plays 20 minutes. A different approach to the timeless biblical story. In *Moralities and Miracles*. Golden Quill Press. Royalty: apply to the author, c/o the publisher.

THE PRODIGAL SON, by R. H. Ward. 4 men, 2 women. Plays 1 hour. The parable of the prodigal son in verse and mime. Actors need singing ability. May be produced in chancel. Baker's Plays, 85¢. Royalty: $15.

THE PRODIGAL SON COMES HOME, by Mary M. Parker. 5 men, 3 women. Plays 20 minutes. Interior set. The parable of the prodigal son in a dramatization somewhat enlarged for purpose of effect, but still maintaining a reverent spirit. T. S. Denison & Co., 50¢ (purchase of 8 copies required).

PROGRAMS FOR WOMEN'S GROUPS. For women's church groups, a play for each month of the year. Eldridge, $1.

PROLOGUE TO GLORY, by E. P. Conkle. 14 men, 7 women (extras), 5 extras. Plays full evening. Interior set. Historical. The early life of Lincoln, and the influence of Ann Rutledge. Samuel French, Inc., $1.25. Royalty: $25–$20.

PROMISE OF THE ANGELS, by Elaine Walker Getzinger. 2 men, 3 women. Plays 35 minutes. A woman of Bethlehem tries to gain audience to plead with Pilate, watches the crucifixion, and sees the open tomb, knowing the angel's promise fulfilled. Four scenes. T. S. Denison & Co., 50¢ (purchase of 5 copies required).

THE PROMISED ONE, by Martha B. Shannon. 6 men, 3 women, 2 children, choir, extras. Instrumental and choir presentation are combined with Bible readings and tableaux of adoration. Baker's Plays, 60¢. Royalty: none if 8 copies purchased.

THE PROMISED ONES, by Robert St. Clair. 4 men, 4 women. Plays 30 minutes. Gabriel's appearances to Zacharias and Mary. Two scenes. Baker's Plays, 50¢ (purchase of 8 copies required).

PROPHECY TO THE WIND, by Norman Nicholson. 5 men, 2 women. Exterior sets, interior sets. Four scenes and prologue, in verse. A contemporary man appears in the world of the future, which has returned to the primitive. Set in the author's native Cumberland. Living poetry, wit, and emotion. Faber & Faber. Permission for production required; apply to author's agent: Margery Vosper.

A PSALM OF THANKSGIVING, by Katherine Kester. 2 men, 2 women. Interior set. Survivors of a train wreck, some on the run, are brought the real meaning of Thanksgiving by the reading of a psalm. Samuel French, Inc., 60¢. Royalty: $5.

PUBLICAN AND SINNER, by L. M. Hollinshead. 3 men, 5 women, 1 boy, 1 girl. Plays 75 minutes. Pictures the possible lives and reactions of the disciples' families. Two acts. Baker's Plays, 75¢. Royalty: $5.

PULL DEVIL, PULL BAKER, by K. M. Baxter, music by Christopher de Fleming. 4 men, 1 woman, 2 choruses. Plays 1 hour. Verse and mime set to music. The parson shakes his complacent congregation by leading them in welcoming sinners from hell. Stylized. Actors must serve as singers. Baker's Plays, $1.95. Royalty: $15.

PULLMAN CAR HIAWATHA, by Thornton Wilder. 15 men, 18 women. Similar in theme and concept to Thornton Wilder's "Our Town." Acting experience not necessary. Samuel French, Inc., 60¢. Royalty: $10.

PUPPETS AND BIBLE PLAYS, by Josie Robbins and Marjory Bracher. A guide in making spool marionettes; also twelve biblical scripts. Fortress Press, $1.50.

PUPPY LOVE. 3 men, 4 women. Plays 30 minutes. Interior set. A dog helps to patch a lover's quarrel and secure a new job. For Christmas; junior and senior high ages. Plays, Inc., 50¢.

PURIM MERRY-GO-ROUND, by Rabbi Joseph Klein. 4 boys, 4 girls, extras. Characters of Purim introduce themselves in rhyme. Union of American Hebrew Congregations, 25¢.

PURIMNET, by Robert Wiener. 3 men, 3 women. A Purim parody on "Dragnet" featuring Sgt. Mordecai, a hood named Haman, and beautiful Esther; melodrama fused with laughter. Union of American Hebrew Congregations, 25¢.

PURLIE VICTORIOUS, by Ossie Davis. 6 men, 3 women. A hilarious comedy. Samuel French, Inc., $1.25. Royalty: $50–$25.

PUTTING FIRST THINGS FIRST, by Ethel D. Posegate. 3 women, 1 child. Plays 20 minutes. Interior set. A woman teaches others that the secret of successful living lies in putting "first things first" and in learning what things in life should come first. T. S. Denison & Co., 50¢ (purchase of 3 copies required).

THE QUEEN REPLIES, by Sister Marcelline, O.S.U. Narrator, 6 boys, 9 girls. A Christmas Eve miracle occurs in a children's hospital. Three acts. St. Anthony Guild Press, 75¢.

QUEM QUAERITIS, adapted by Amy Goodhue Loomis. In manuscript form for sophisticated adult casts. Vincennes University. Royalty: apply to adapter.

R. U. R., by Karel Capek, English version by Paul Selver and Nigel Playfair. 13 men, 4 women. Plays full evening. 2 interior sets. The story of the robots who take the world from man and find themselves unable to maintain their kind in order to keep it. Two robots begin again like Adam and Eve. Difficult to stage and perform convincingly. Samuel French, Inc., $1.25. Royalty: $25–$20.

RADIANT MORNING, by Anne Coulter Martens. 1 man, 5 women. Plays

20 minutes. The truth of Easter is revealed when the mothers of the crucified men meet. Dramatic Publishing Co., 50¢. Royalty: $5.

RADIO JERUSALEM, THE STORY OF JESUS, by Catherine Magee. 4 men or 4 women, verse choir. Plays 20 minutes. The story of Jesus in a modern setting, spanning the time from his twelfth year into his ministry. The narrator delivers the story as radio reports, while the choir delivers Bible passages. T. S. Denison & Co., 50¢ (purchase of 6 copies required).

RALLY DAY AND PROMOTION DAY TREASURY. A collection of monologues, playlets, tableaux, pageants, etc. Baker's Plays, 50¢.

THE RAVELED SLEEVE, by Helen P. Parker. 6 women. Plays 30 minutes. Interior set. Maternal love and sacrifice are shown in this play of a mother and her three grown daughters. Baker's Plays, 60¢.

READINGS AND RECITATIONS FOR SUNDAY SCHOOL AND CHURCH. Selections by various authors for Christmas, Easter, special days, for adults and children. Includes a dramatic monologue of four periods in the life of Mary. Eldridge, $1.25.

A "REAL" CHRISTMAS BOOK, by Helen Ramsey, Dorothy M. Shipman, and others. For church, school, or programs for the community. Collection for all grades; includes plays, dialogues, etc. Eldridge, $1.

THE REAL ST. GEORGE, by Rodney Bennett. For advanced intermediate and junior age-groups. Religious Drama Society of Great Britain.

RED CANDLES, by E. M. Clark. 5 boys, 7 girls, extras. Interior set. For grade school or students of junior high. Unusual carols and gay mood in this modern operetta. Two acts. Baker's Plays, $1.50 (purchase of 12 copies required).

THE REDEEMER'S ROBE, by Karin Asbrand. 1 man, 1 woman, 2 boys, 2 girls. Plays 10 minutes. Easter biblical play. In *Easy Bible Story Dramatizations for Children*. Baker's Plays, $1.25.

REHEARSAL-LESS EASTER COLLECTION, by Karin Asbrand. A collection for children: plays, pantomimes, services, etc. Baker's Plays, $1.

REHEARSAL-LESS FUN, by Karin Asbrand. A collection for all holidays, for all ages. Serious and comic. Baker's Plays, $1.25.

REINDEER ON THE ROOF. 5 men, 5 women. Plays 30 minutes. Interior set. For junior and senior high. In the face of disappointment caused by the backfiring of an elaborate Christmas display, Mother's candle in the window reminds everyone of Christmas' true meaning. Plays, Inc., 50¢.

RELEASE, by Dorothy Clarke Wilson. 6 men, 2 women. Interior set. Easter drama. Barabbas and two thieves await in a cell the judgment of Pilate. May be easily staged and costumed. Baker's Plays, 60¢.

RELIGIOUS DRAMA, introduced and selected by Marvin Halverson. Vol. I: "David" by D. H. Lawrence, "The Zeal of Thy House" by Dorothy Sayers, "The Bloody Tenet" by James Schevill, "For the Time Being" by W. H. Auden (Christmas), "The Firstborn" by Christopher Fry. Vol. II: Medieval Mystery and Morality, twenty-two plays. Vol. III: "Last Word" by James Broughton, "The

House by the Stable" and "Grab and Grace" by Charles Williams, "Santa Claus" by E. E. Cummings, "Let Man Live" by Par Lagerkvist, "Billy Budd" by L. O. Coxe and Robert Chapman, "The Gospel Witch" by Lyon Phelps, "It Should Happen to a Dog" by Wolf Mankowitz. Baker's Plays: Vol. I, $1.95; Vol. II, $1.55; Vol. III, $1.65. Royalty: apply to publisher.

RELIGIOUS DRAMA 2, selected and introduced by E. Martin Browne. Twenty-one complete medieval mystery, morality and miracle plays. Meridian Books, $1.45.

RELIGIOUS PLAYS FOR WOMEN, by various authors. Collection: a play for Christmas, Mother's Day, Easter, missionary, stewardship and general use. Plays are biblical and modern. Baker's Plays, 60¢.

REPORT TO HEROD, by Evelyn Neuenburg. 5 men, 3 women. Jotham recalls those he encountered in his search for the child destined to be king and they appear and tell their stories. Baker's Plays, 60¢. Royalty: $5.

REQUIEM FOR A NUN, by William Faulkner, adapted by Ruth Ford. 5 men, 2 women. A play of Temple Blake's guilt, torment, and finding of truth. Has great power. Samuel French, Inc., $3.95. Royalty: $50–$25.

THE RESURRECTION. Easter service. Selections of the Bible arranged in mystery play form, with accompaniment of Easter carols and Bach's Passion music. Samuel French, Inc., 60¢.

THE RESURRECTION, by Rosamond Kimball. 12 men, 3 women, voice of Jesus. Easter tableaux in four scenes. Baker's Plays, 60¢.

THE RETICENT ONE, by E. P. Conkle. 6 women. Plays 30 minutes. Interior set. Women awaiting the directions of the Voice of the Overseer in the Supernal Waiting Room gossip about one woman until that woman is called directly to God because of the beauty of her soul. Baker's Plays, 60¢. Royalty: $5.

A RETRIEVED CHRISTMAS, by Mabel C. Allwy. 5 women, extras. Plays 25 minutes. Interior set. A woman repents of a selfish mourning after her son's death and takes a little girl in her home at Christmas. T. S. Denison & Co., 50¢ (purchase of 5 copies required).

THE RETURN OF CHANDRA, by Dorothy Clarke Wilson. 4 men, 3 women. Plays 45 minutes. Interior set. A young student returns to his native India from America disillusioned with Christianity and finds, through a dramatic series of incidents, his faith returning. He recommits himself to serving his people. Baker's Plays, 60¢ (available in television form; inquire of the publisher).

THE RETURN OF THE PILGRIMS, by Lois Bole. 3 boys, 7 girls. A family of Pilgrims makes a return to modern Thanksgiving. Eldridge, 40¢ (purchase of 10 copies required).

THE RETURN OF THE PRODIGAL, by Hankin. In *Edwardian Plays.* Hill & Wang: cloth, $5.95; paper, $2.45.

THE RETURN OF THE PROPHETS, by Edward Longstreth. Plays 30 minutes. Biblical chancel drama. Royalty: inquire of the author.

REVERIE, by Percival Wilde. 4 men, 3 women, 8 children or more can play all parts. A vision in the fireplace brings the guilt for Ex-Governor Harkness' estrangement from his children back to him. Baker's Plays, 60¢. Royalty: $10.

RHINOCEROS, by Eugene Ionesco, translated by Derek Prouse. 6 men, 4 women, extras. Interior, exterior sets. A play of individualism and mass conformity, intuitive morality and rational relativism. The people of a small French town, with the exception of one little man, are caught up in a mass hysterical metamorphosis into rhinoceroses. A farcical allegory with accompanying satire and a very serious undertone. Difficult. In *Rhinoceros and Other Plays.* Grove Press, $1.95. Royalty: apply to Margaret Ramsay.

RICHARD III, by William Shakespeare. 35 men, 3 women. Exterior, interior sets. The deformed but powerful Richard plots his way to the throne by eliminating all those in the succession before him; his world crumbles when he has obtained the crown, and he comes to death in Bosworth Field. Tragedy. Very difficult. Cambridge Co. Royalty: none.

RING, CASTLE BELL, by Edith Quick and James O. Fluckey. Plays 90 minutes. A musical play of a plot to free prisoners in Greenwood by keeping the bell from tolling until midnight on Christmas Eve. Contains a pageant, organized by the troubadour within the play. Eldridge, $1.40 (purchase of 7 copies required).

THE RING OF SOLOMON, by Ben Aronin, piano accompaniment by Samuel Adler. 9 characters, priests, Levites, extras. Plays 1 hour, in 6 scenes and epilogue. Operetta for junior high. Solomon learns that once Evil is used as a slave it becomes master, and he also learns the meaning of the words "My trust is in Thee, O Lord." Union of American Hebrew Congregations, 75¢.

RING OUT WILD BELLS, by Alfred Lord Tennyson. Tennyson's poem set to music to be sung or recited. Baker's Plays, 60¢.

THE RISEN CHRIST, by Jean Lilyers. 8 children, singing choir. Children interpret the Easter story as, in Christ's time, they have heard it. Strong worshipful quality. Fortress Press, 10¢.

RIZAL OF THE PHILIPPINES. Gives information about, and atmosphere of, the islands. World-friendship play for junior high schools. Plays, Inc., 50¢.

THE ROAD TO BETHLEHEM, by Donna Colley. 3 men, 6 women. Exterior set. Nativity. A blind girl is cured by the star of the shepherds and her selfish sister is led to the manger. Samuel French, Inc., 60¢. Royalty: $5.

THE ROAD TO BETHLEHEM, by Ann Claire Gilbert. 7 men, 6 women, choir. Plays 40 minutes. A treatment of Christ's birth from the angle of human interest, encompassing a wide range of characters. Eight scenes. T. S. Denison & Co., 50¢ (purchase of 8 copies required).

THE ROAD TO EMMAUS, by James Forsyth. 14 men, 6 women, extras. An Easter play starting at the garden and moving through the day, ending with the assurance at Emmaus. William Heinemann, Ltd. Royalty: apply to Margery Vosper.

THE ROAD TO EMMAUS, by Sister Mary Francis, P.C.C. 6 men, 2

women. Exterior set. Reuben and Cleophas, after discovering Christ has died like a common criminal, meet the risen Christ on the road and break bread with him unknowingly. Samuel French, Inc., 60¢. Royalty: $5.

THE ROAD TO EMMAUS, by Paul Nagy, Jr. 3 men, 1 woman. Plays 30 minutes. Two men meet a stranger on the road who is recognized as the Christ when he breaks bread. Baker's Plays, 50¢.

THE ROBE, by Lloyd Douglas, adapted by John McGreevey. 19 men, 9 women, extras. Plays full evening. Marcellus through possession of "the robe" gains a devotion to faith. Worthwhile, holds much beauty. Dramatic Publishing Co., 90¢. Royalty: $25.

THE ROBE AND THE THORN, by Conrad Carter. 2 men, 2 women. Interior set. After the crucifixion a Roman soldier gives Christ's robe to the Jewish girl he loves. She yields it to a centurion to give to Christ's mother, but Mary treasures the thorn she has found in the robe's folds. Evans Plays, 2*s.* net. Royalty: 25*s.* per performance.

THE ROCK, by Mary P. Hamlin. 8 men, 3 women. Plays 1 hour, 45 minutes. 2 exterior sets. Four scenes; a character examination of Simon Peter, so powerful a spiritual message as to be capable of changing lives. Samuel French, Inc., 75¢. Royalty: $10 if admission is charged; $5 if not.

ROGER WILLIAMS AND MARY, by Albert Johnson. 2 men, 1 woman. Plays about 40 minutes. Bare stage with minimum properties. A Drama Trio play. The story of Roger Williams and his wife and their struggle for religious freedom, understanding, and the realization of their dream of a new land. Narrator takes many parts. May be produced in a chancel. Friendship Press, 75¢. Baker's Plays, 75¢.

ROMEO AND JULIET, by William Shakespeare. 17 men, 4 women (also attendants). Interior, exterior sets. The story of the "star-cross'd" lovers and the two warring families whose hate was resolved by their death. The power and beauty of a lyrical Shakespeare. Very difficult. Pelican Books. Royalty: none.

ROOM FOR A KING, by Betty Smith. 10 men, 7 women (many minor female parts). Plays 30 minutes. The innkeeper grudgingly gives room in the stable, then is awakened by the coming of the shepherds and wise men. Eldridge, 60¢ (purchase of 8 copies required).

ROOM FOR ONE MORE, by Anna Wright, adapted by William Davidson. 8 men, 8 women. Plays full evening. The story of two people who take in homeless children. Very warm and human. Dramatic Publishing Co., 90¢. Royalty: $25.

A ROOMFUL OF ROSES, by Edith Sommer. 3 men, 5 women, 1 child. The readjustments in the psychological makeup of a home when a visit is paid by a child of a broken home. Dramatists Play Service, $1. Royalty: $50–$25.

THE ROSARY, by Edward E. Rose. 5 men, 4 women. 2 interior sets, 1 exterior set. The character of Father Kelly, understanding and sympathetic, appeals especially to Catholic audiences. Religious and moral appeal. Four acts. Samuel French, Inc., $1.25. Royalty: $25–$20.

THE ROSE AND CROWN, by J. B. Priestley. 4 men, 3 women. Short play. A probing insight into human nature is revealed in this story of a stranger who enters a public bar to take one of the "regular" customers. The problem is: which one should he take? One act. Samuel French, Inc. Royalty: apply to publisher.

ROSES FOR THE KING, by Hazel F. Bailey. 2 men, 3 women, children. Christmas fantasy, appealing to all ages. A simple, beautiful, and gentle message in a world of continual warfare. Baker's Plays, 60¢.

THE RUNAWAY SLAVE, by Freda Collins. A good play based on the book of Philemon. In *Five More Christian Plays.* Religious Drama Society of Great Britain, 50¢.

RUTH, by Annabel Lawrence. 7 men, 3 women. Plays 1 hour, 45 minutes. Interior, exterior sets. Biblical story of Boaz and Ruth. Easy to produce. Three acts. T. S. Denison & Co., 85¢ (purchase of 7 copies required).

SABOTAGE, by Hellem, Valcros, and D'Estoc, translated by Anne Tridon. 2 men, 2 women, 1 child. Labor's struggle against capital, and a tragedy growing from the destruction of property. One act. In *Still Another Book of Miniature Plays.* Baker's Plays, $1.25.

SACRED ROMANCE, by Sister Mary John, O.S.F. 4 young men, 4 young women, 2 small boys, 2 small girls, 5 tiny girls (doubling possible). A high school boy and girl learn the meanings and beauties of the clerical life from a priest; background of twelve dramatic episodes and tableaux. Full notes for production. St. Anthony Guild Press, 75¢.

THE SACRIFICE OF ISAAC, edited by Robert Schenkkan and Kai Jurgensen. In *Fourteen Plays for the Church.* Rutgers University Press.

THE SACRIFICE OF ISAAC, edited by Switz and Johnston. In *Great Christian Plays.* Seabury Press.

THE SAINT, by A. Beatrice Knowles. 14 men, 14 women, extras. Plays 30 minutes. Interior set. Learning that the three wise men have no gifts for the Christchild, Nicholas gives them gifts to take and earns the name "Saint Nicholas, Giver of Gifts." Baker's Plays, 60¢. Royalty: $5.

ST. ANNE AND THE GOUTY RECTOR AND OTHER PLAYS, by Henri Gheon and Henri Brochet, translated by Marcus S. and Olive R. Goldman. Small casts. Collection of seven plays of saints of southern France, possessing both comedy and tragedy in a religious vein. McKay's Plays, $2.75.

ST. FELIX AND HIS POTATOES, by Henri Brochet. 3 men. Felix prays for the safety of his potatoes and a thief and his accomplice are unwittingly involved. In *St. Anne and the Gouty Rector and Other Plays.* McKay's Plays, $2.75. Royalty: $10 if admission charged; $5 if not.

ST. FRANCIS BRINGS BETHLEHEM TO GRECCIO, by Sister Mary John. Large or small cast. Plays 1 hour. Francis of Assisi recreates the

Nativity in a rocky hillside cliff to give peasants a Christian spirit in the midst of their Christmas revels. Baker's Plays, 60¢.

ST. FRANCIS OF ASSISI, by J. A. Peladan, translated and adapted by Harold John Massingham. A five-act play. College Book Service, $10.

SAINT JOAN, by George Bernard Shaw. 25 men, 2 women, extras. Interior, exterior sets. Joan, a simple, naïve, and somewhat tomboyish girl with a dash of military genius is given stature by her tremendous faith and boundless dedication and honesty. She is seen as the victim of the conflict between the medieval church and the rising states of Europe, embodied in characters of great pettiness. Baker's Plays, 65¢. Royalty: $25.

ST. MICHAEL COMES TO SHEPHERD'S BUSH, by James Parish. 3 men, 1 woman. Plays 30 minutes. Interior, exterior sets. Two bits of glass, the spearhead of St. Michael and a bit of the devil's tail, are taken from a shattered cathedral window as souvenirs by Eustace. The devil, according to tradition, is transfixed on the spearhead of St. Michael. Baker's Plays, 60¢. Royalty: $5.

THE SAINTS' RETURN, by Esther Willard Bates. 10 men or women. Plays 40 minutes. Single set. The saints lose heart and leave earth, then are brought back when human courage reaches them on the road to heaven. Baker's Plays, 60¢. Royalty: $5.

SAMPLE SET OF MORE THAN 40 PLAYS. Jewish plays for children. A collection for Purim, Chanuko, Passover, Shovous, etc. Union of American Hebrew Congregations, $5.

SANCTUARY, by Robert Duce. 7 women. Plays 35 minutes. A story from John 8. Independent Press. Royalty: apply to publisher.

SANCTUARY, by Phoebe M. Rees. 7 women. Plays 35 minutes. Interior set. Historical. Reactions of various women, including several dispersed nuns, during the French Revolution. Baker's Plays, 60¢. Royalty: $5.

THE SANDBOX, by Edward Albee. 3 men, 2 women. Short play. A "theatre of the absurd" play depicting a funeral. One act. Dramatists Play Service, $1.25. Royalty: $10 (available only for amateur performances for nonsegregated audiences).

SANTA CLAUS, by E. E. Cummings. 2 men, 1 woman, 1 child, extras. Plays 15 minutes. A modern morality play with Santa Claus and Death as the two figures of the allegory. Knowledge without understanding takes love from the world, and separated from love, persons do not exist. For advanced players. Brandt & Brandt. Royalty: $20.

SANTA'S NEUROSIS, by R. W. Sherman. Variable cast. Plays 75 minutes. Santa is convinced by a series of scenes shown him by psychiatrists that adults are not creating a mockery of Christmas. Spiritual undertone in the comedy. Eldridge, 60¢ (purchase of 8 copies required).

THE SAUSAGE MAKER'S INTERLUDE, by Henri Gheon. 5 men, 2 women, 3 children. Plays 20 minutes. A comedy with satirical overtones about a machine which turns on the man who invented it and devours him. In *St. Anne and the Gouty Rector and Other Plays.* McKay's Plays, $2.75. Royalty: $10 if admission is charged; $5 if not.

SCAPEGOAT, by Nora Ratcliff. 3 men, 4 women, extras. Plays 30 minutes. Interior set. The witchcraft superstitions and the tragedy of their application to a poor old woman. May be very moving. H. F. W. Deane & Sons, 2*d.*

THE SCARECROW, by Percy MacKaye. 10 men, 6 women. Interior set. The devil and a woman blacksmith give life to a scarecrow and introduce him as Lord Ravensbane into a Massachusetts community. The scarecrow attains humanity when he discovers his origin and destroys himself. A unique treatment of salvation from the supernatural through love, with some difficult stage effects. Samuel French, Inc., $7.50. Royalty: $25.

THE SCARLET RIBBON, by Alberta Hawse. 8 men, 6 women, narrator. Plays 90 minutes. An unusual and easy-to-rehearse Christmas selection. Baker's Plays, 60¢ (purchase of 9 copies required).

SCATTERED SHOWERS, by Nora Stirling. 3 women, stage manager. Three mothers and their preschool children react in a crisis according to their varying interpretations of discipline. Nat'l. Assoc. for Mental Health. Royalty: none for first performance with purchase of production packet; $2.50 for following performances if admission is charged; $1 if not.

SCROOGE, by Charles Dickens, adapted by Daily Paskman. 9 men, 2 women, 1 boy. The adaptation of *A Christmas Carol* performed by Lionel Barrymore for a recording. One act. English Theatre Guild.

THE SEAMLESS ROBE, by Esther C. Averill. 1 man, 5 women, extras. Plays 40 minutes. Exterior set. The mystery of Christ's robe, which seemed almost a part of him. Eldridge, 60¢.

A SEARCH FOR CHRISTMAS, by Esther B. Stricker. 2 men, 2 women, extras. Plays 25 minutes. A young man and his family search for the real meaning of Christmas, ringing doorbells and asking questions, and coming to both revelation and reward. Baker's Plays, 60¢.

SEARCH FOR THE SAVIOUR, by Jean M. Mattson. 10 men, 6 women, extras. Plays 35 minutes. Interior, exterior sets. The meaning of Christ's life is realized after his death; Luke and Matthew set out to learn all they can from those who remember him, acquiring the truth of the story of Christmas. Four scenes. T. S. Denison & Co., 50¢ (purchase of 10 copies required).

THE SEARCHING WIND, by Lillian Hellman. 11 men, 3 women. Plays full evening. Compromise and confusion in politics, and personal relations that lead to war. Dramatists Play Service: perusal script available from the publisher, $2; returnable deposit, $10. Royalty: $50–$25.

THE SEASON'S GREETINGS, by Hebe Elsna. 4 men, 4 women. Interior set. A family with troubles interrupts their parent's quiet Christmas Eve, and all problems are eventually solved. Light tone with sentimental undertone. Baker's Plays, $1.25. Royalty: $15.

THE SECOND MARRIAGE OF SANTA CLAUS, by John Kirkpatrick. 3 men, 4 women. Plays 30 minutes. Interior set. A family is caught up in commercialism and petty arguments around Christmastime, except for Emmy and her young man. Emmy's elopement with Santa Claus brings hope of a Christmas someday free of commercialism. Samuel French, Inc., 60¢. Royalty: $5.

THE SECOND SHEPHERD'S PLAY, anonymous. 4 men, 2 women, 1 boy (age 14–18). Interior, exterior sets. The medieval play; the first part of the play a rollicking comedy of Mak's theft of one shepherd's sheep, the second part leading to the Nativity. From the Townley manuscript, Wakefield Cycle. Meridian Books. Royalty: apply to publisher.

THE SECOND SHEPHERD'S PLAY, anonymous, edited by E. M. Browne. Religious Drama Society of Great Britain.

THE SECOND SHEPHERD'S PLAY, anonymous. In *Fourteen Plays for Church*. Rutgers University Press.

THE SECOND SHEPHERD'S PLAY, anonymous, edited by A. C. Cawley. In *Everyman and Other Interludes*. E. P. Dutton & Co.

SECOND SPRING, by Emmet Lavery. 25 characters. Various scenes. The story of Cardinal Newman of Oxford, his friend and sometime opponent Cardinal Manning, and a search for beauty and truth. Three acts, prologue, epilogue. Samuel French, Inc., $1.25. Royalty: $25–$20.

THE SECOND THANKSGIVING, by Effa Preston. 4 men, 4 women. Plays 20 minutes. An Indian attack in 1622 ends happily when a family shares in Thanksgiving. T. S. Denison & Co., 50¢ (purchase of 7 copies required).

THE SECRET, by Evelyn Neuenburg. 8 women (3 bit parts). Plays 30 minutes. Interior set. Three women love the same man. One, plain and semi-invalided, maneuvers the situation and wonders if she has done right. Baker's Plays, 60¢. Royalty: $5.

THE SECRET CHANUKAH, by Gladys D. Kauffman. 10 characters, 4 newscasters, torchbearer, extras. A rabbi and his family in their efforts to celebrate Chanukah in the U.S.S.R. Given as a television newscast. Union of American Hebrew Congregations, 25¢.

THE SEDUCER, by Søren Kierkegaard, adapted by Myraney Pipes. 5 men, 5 women. From the story "The Diary of the Seducer." In two acts, fifteen scenes. Gerald Duckworth and Co. Royalty: apply to publisher.

SEED OF ADAM AND OTHER PLAYS, by Charles Williams. For advanced players. Collection: "Seed of Adam" (Nativity), "The House by the Stable" (Christmas), "Grab and Grace" (a sequel to "The House by the Stable"), "Death of Good Fortune" (morality play for Christmas). Oxford University Press, $1.40. Royalty: apply to publisher.

SEEING THE STAR, by Alberta Hawse. 5 men, 3 women. Plays 1 hour. A play of putting Christ back into Christmas. Three acts. Recommended. Baker's Plays, 60¢.

THE SEEKING YEARS, edited by John M. Gunn. Contemporary themes for college-age youth, easily produced. Bethany Press, $1.50.

THE SEFER MOBILE, by Shirley Simon. 10 boys, 7 girls. For Chanuko or Jewish Book Month. An easily produced playlet to increase interest in libraries, schools, and Jewish books. Union of American Hebrew Congregations, 25¢.

SELECT DRAMAS FOR CHILDREN'S DAY. A collection of three plays: "The Blue Stone," "God's Loving Purpose," "In the Household of Zaccheus." Eldridge, 30¢ (purchase of 12 copies required).

SEND OUT THY LIGHT, by Dorothy Clarke Wilson. 11 characters, extras. Plays 50 minutes. Interior set. The center of religion in the church of the present is pointed out, and the direction of the church of the future indicated. Baker's Play's, 60¢.

SENSATION ON BUDLEGH BEACON, by E. R. Hougham. The search for religion of a young man. In rhymed couplets and with an English setting. In *Plays of Perplexity*. Religious Drama Society of Great Britain, 54¢. Royalty: approximately $1.48.

THE SEPARATIST, by Mary P. Hamlin. 6 men, 3 women. Plays 30 minutes. The story of Pilgrim William Brewster. Samuel French, Inc., 50¢. Royalty: $5.

SERGEANT SMITH RETURNS, by Dorothy Clarke Wilson. 4 men. Interior set. A father who has served in World War I returns symbolically to his son, wounded in World War II, and offers his experience from the objective view of another world. In *One Act Plays of Spiritual Power*. Baker's Plays, $3.25. Royalty: $5.

SERJEANT MUSGRAVE'S DANCE, by John Arden. 13 men, 2 women. Plays full evening. The subject of violence is explored in this exciting epic play. Grove Press. Royalty: apply to Theatrework, Ltd.

THE SERVANT AT THE INN, by Helen Roberts. 8 men, 5 women. Plays 30 minutes. Martha, a servant, offers the Holy Family room in the stable despite her master's displeasure; as the shepherds and kings offer their gifts she offers her gift of service. Banner Play Bureau, 50¢ (purchase of 13 copies required).

THE SERVANT IN THE HOUSE, by Charles Rann Kennedy. 5 men, 2 women. Interior set. A mysterious oriental visitor unites a house divided against itself and brings redemption—spiritual, social, and economic. Universal brotherhood in a religious and very well-written stage play. Samuel French, Inc., $1.25. Royalty: $25–$20.

SEVEN MIRRORS, by ten students of Immaculate Heart College, edited by Emmet Lavery. Large cast, doubling possible. Seven versions of Mary, each representing a portion of the world, women's assistance in the achievement of man, and man's relationship to God. Samuel French, Inc., $1.25. Royalty: $25–$20.

SEVEN PLAYS, Vol. I, by Michel de Ghelderode, introduction by George Hanger. Includes: "Chronicles of Hell," "Barabbas," "The Women at the Tomb," "Pantaglieze," "The Blind Men," "Three Actors and Their Drama," "Lord Halewyn," with selections drawn from the Ostend Interviews. Hill & Wang: cloth, $4.50; paper, $1.95.

SEVEN PLAYS FOR CHILDREN, by various authors. Collection: Christmas (four plays), Easter, worship appreciation and morality plays. Religious Drama Society of Great Britain, 60¢.

SHADOW AND SUBSTANCE, by Paul Vincent Carroll. 6 men, 4 women. Interior set. A narrow and authoritarian canon causes an incident over a schoolteacher's book and brings to death the one person for whom he cares—a serving girl who sees visions—breaking himself in the process. Irish drama. Dramatists Play Service, $1.25. Royalty: $35–$25.

SHADOW OF A CROSS, by Frances Bowyer. 13 men, 8 women, extras if wanted. In Christianity's years of formation a young Nazarene gathers a following with a doctrine of nonviolence. Has power, range for character development. Three acts. Baker's Plays, $1. Royalty: $1 minimum to $35 maximum based on 20% of gross receipts.

SHADOW OF THE CROSS, by Ellen Jane Lorenz and Herman von Berge. Reader, 5 voices, extras, singers. Ten shadow scenes in a pageant of Passion Week. Eldridge, 50¢.

SHADOW OF THE MINE AND OTHER PLAYS OF THE COAL FIELDS, by Leo B. Pride. Collection of seven plays of the miners of southern Illinois, for home missions. Samuel French, Inc., $1.75.

THE SHEPHERD OF BETHLEHEM, by Janet Knox. 8 boys, 8 girls or adults, 3 children. Plays 35 minutes. A shepherd scoffs at the idea of the birth of the Savior in a stable until Mary's faith and the rescue of the child from Herod's soldiers change his mind. T. S. Denison & Co., 50¢ (purchase of 10 copies required).

THE SHEPHERD WHO STAYED, by Stuart Hunter. 4 men, 2 women. Plays 25 minutes. Interior set. A realistic treatment of the story and significance of Christ's birth, told with beauty. T. S. Denison & Co., 50¢ (purchase of 6 copies required).

THE SHEPHERD WHO STAYED AWAY, by John McGreevey. 3 men, 3 women, extras. Plays 30 minutes. Interior set. Ammon finds acceptance of God and a cure for his son's illness by coming to the Babe. Baker's Plays, 60¢. Royalty: $5.

THE SHEPHERD'S CHRISTMAS. Plays 50 minutes. Junior high operetta. Rebirth of the Christchild in modern times. Optional use of carols. Eldridge, $1.25 (purchase of 4 copies required).

SHEPHERD'S PIE, by Stephen L. Caiger. 4 men, 4 women. Plays 1 hour. A play concerning fund-raising for the church. SPCK. Royalty: apply to publisher.

THE SHEPHERD'S PLAY OF THE PRODIGAL SON, translated by George Barker. Plays 30 minutes. An old Mexican folk drama with a quality of the medieval. University of California Press, $1.75.

THE SHEPHERD'S STAR, by Janet Katherine Smith. 14 men, 8 women, chorus, extras. Plays 90 minutes. The Nativity in seven scenes from the annunciation to the adoration. Baker's Plays, 75¢. Royalty: $10 if admission is charged; $5 if not.

SHEPHERDS ABIDING, by Dorothy Clarke Wilson. 3 men, 4 women. Plays 55 minutes. Exterior set. The song of the angels works wonders in a thief and between two estranged shepherd brothers. Baker's Plays, 60¢.

THE SHEPHERDS AND THE WISE MEN, by Leroy Phillips. 10 men, 2 women, 1 child, women's choir. Plays 40 minutes. The shepherd's journey following the star, and their joining of the wise men and the Holy Family in Bethlehem. T. S. Denison & Co., 50¢ (purchase of 7 copies required).

THE SHEPHERDS BROUGHT A SONG, by Lenore Morgan. 1 man, 2 women, extras. Plays 45 minutes. Bare stage. A disillusioned Roman governor and his wife come to a realization through the babe born in Bethlehem. Baker's Plays, 60¢. Royalty: $5.

THE SHINING STAR, by Lettice Cuttle. 30 players. A Nativity play from the biblical account, in two scenes, set in the inn at Bethlehem and on a hillside. Cokesbury Press, 35¢. Package, 48. $3.50 for set of 12.

A SHIRT A SIZE TOO SMALL, by Barbara Kay Davidson. A play pointing out the need for improvements in the child welfare programs. National Council on Crime and Delinquency: perusal copy, $2; kit of 6 acting scripts, $12.

THE SHOE ON THE OTHER FOOT, by Ben Adam. 3 men, 2 women. Plays 30 minutes. Suspense drama of the "golden rule." Banner Play Bureau, 50¢. Royalty: $5.

THE SHUSHAN HEART, by Helen Fine, music by Dr. Moses J. Eisenberg. Plays 35 minutes. A robot who desires a heart in a fun presentation with catchy music. Union of American Hebrew Congregations, 75¢.

SIGHT TO SEE, by Karin Asbrand. 9 women. A woman gains humanity when she reads the Bible as she is going blind. In *Easy Church Plays for Women and Girls.* Baker's Plays, $1.25.

SIGN OF A STAR, by Aileen Fisher. 6 men or women, singing chorus (or records). Plays 20 minutes. Heaven is excited on the eve of the fulfillment of God's prophecy. Baker's Plays, 60¢. Royalty: none if 6 copies purchased.

THE SIGN OF JONAH, by Gruenter Rutenborn. 7 men, 3 women. Plays 1 hour. Man's predicament when he refuses to meet God where God has chosen to meet him, with biblical, contemporary, and existential implications. May be produced with technical simplicity; also good as a reading. Lutheran Student Assoc. of America. Royalty: apply to publisher.

SILENT NIGHT, by Ada Goepp. 3 men, 3 women. Plays 25 minutes. Interior set. A family's minor disputes are softened by the coming of snow and carols, and the family is seen as kind and spiritual. For Christmas. Baker's Plays, 60¢. Royalty: $5.

SILENT NIGHT, by Leslie Hollingsworth. 4 boys, 5 girls. Plays 25 minutes. Good version of the story of "Silent Night." Plays, Inc., 50¢.

SILVER BEADS, by Sister Marcelline, O.S.U. Narrator, 10 boys, 7 girls, angel chorus. 2 sets. For grammar school children. Children meet in a cave outside Bethlehem to plot to help a rebel leader. This is followed by the scene of the Nativity. Three acts. St. Anthony Guild Press, 75¢.

THE SILVER CORD, by Sidney Howard. 2 men, 4 women. 2 interior sets. A mother's too-possessive and self-centered love, and its effects on her grown sons. Samuel French, Inc., $1.25. Royalty: $25–$20.

THE SILVER STAR OF CHRISTMAS, by Esther B. York. 3 men, 5 women. 2 interior sets. Nativity play. The handmaiden of Herod's queen sets out to the manger in order to worship the Messiah. T. S. Denison & Co., 50¢ (purchase of 8 copies required).

THE SILVER TASSIE, by Sean O'Casey. 18 men, 5 women. Interior sets, 1 exterior set. A crippled hero becomes a reminder of the war. "The Lord hath given and man hath taken away." Second act is expressionistic, the others semi-realistic. A bitter condemnation of war, containing a comic contrast with the full power of the tragic situation. In *O'Casey: Selected Plays.* Braziller. Royalty: apply to publisher.

THE SILVER TRUMPET, by Elliot Field. 11 men, 7 women. Plays 90 minutes. Interior set. A pastor's choice between staying with the people of a mill town or seeking success in a larger assignment. Baker's Plays, 60¢.

THE SILVERED ROPE, by Jay Sigmund and Betty Smith. 3 men, 2 women. Plays 15 minutes. Interior set. The last hours of Judas Iscariot when, on the first Good Friday, a goat breeder is host to a strange visitor. T. S. Denison & Co., 50¢ (purchase of 5 copies required).

SIMEON (The Faithful Servant), by Philip F. Day. 7 men, 2 women, extras. Plays 30 minutes. Exterior set. Through Simeon the hope of the Jews in the coming of the Messiah is shown. For Christmas. Baker's Plays, 60¢. Royalty: $5.

SIMON, CALLED PETER, by Pearl Neilson. Plays 1 hour. The remorse of Peter during the time between his denial of Christ and Christ's meeting with the disciples after the resurrection, with a revelation, in conversation, of the crucifixion. One act. Eldridge, 50¢ (purchase of 9 copies required).

SIMON PETER, by Irene Caudwell. 16 characters. A sacred drama of the Passion. Faith Press, 2*s*. 6*d*.

SIMON, THE CROSS BEARER, by Dorothy L. Marshall. 4 men, 1 woman. Plays 30 minutes. Interior set. A maker of crosses, working to fulfill his wife's material ambitions, realizes that he may have gained success at the cost of others' suffering. Baker's Plays, 60¢.

SIMON THE LEPER, by Dorothy Clarke Wilson. 4 men, 4 women. Plays 1 hour. Exterior set. Simon, cured by the Master, learns the difficulty of continuing with Christ's work. Baker's Plays, 60¢.

SIMPLE CHANCEL DRAMAS, by Hazel F. Bailey. Plays for special church days and occasions, emphasizing spiritual quality and ease of production. Minimum expense. Baker's Plays, $1.25.

A SIMPLE LITTLE AFFAIR, by George Herman. 9 men, 5 women. Bare stage. Memories of the past show a wedding as an act of courage showing hope for the future. Baker's Plays, 60¢. Royalty: $5.

SING CHRISTMAS, by Margaret Douglas Chamberlin. Large cast. A piano tuner shows a group of high school carolers the origins of their songs. Nine short scenes. Baker's Plays, 75¢.

SING THE SONGS OF CHRISTMAS. 21 men, 4 women, 19 male or female extras. Plays 35 minutes. Musical pageant of the origins of some favorite Christmas carols. Plays, Inc., 50¢.

SIR TOMMY'S PILGRIMAGE, by D. M. Davis. 17 children. Pageant-play with music. A vision appears to Sir Tommy who cannot go out in quest of the Grail. Baker's Plays, 30¢.

SISTER BEATRICE, by Maurice Maeterlinck, translated by Bernard Hall. 2 men, 9 women, 1 girl, 1 boy, extras. Interior set. A beautiful lyric treatment of the thirteenth-century miracle play of a young sister who leaves her convent because of love, and whose place is taken by an image of the virgin come to life. Samuel French, Inc. Royalty: $25.

SISTER CRAVEN, by Stuart Ready. 10 women. Interior set. A good woman returns from death to help the elderly ladies now living in her former house. Baker's Plays, $1.25. Royalty: $25.

THE SITE, by John Whitney and Geoffrey Bellman. 5 men. Plays 25 minutes. Far better to give oneself completely to the power of religion than try to gain it when it is almost too late. In *Coventry Porch Plays*. Baker's Plays, $1.25. Royalty: $10.

SIX CHARACTERS IN SEARCH OF AN AUTHOR, by Luigi Pirandello, English version by Edward Storer. 13 men (doubling possible), 6 women, 1 boy, 1 girl. Six characters gain a life of their own and invade the rehearsal of another play, each striving for an existence that he must, but cannot, have. Their actions, due to their independence, exceed the intent of their author, and as a consequence all comes to confusion. In *Naked Masks*. E. P. Dutton & Co. Royalty: apply to publisher.

SIX PLAYS OF STRINDBERG, translated by Elizabeth Sprigge. Strindberg writes in tones of the faith that grows from what appears to be futility. Doubleday, $1.25.

SIX SHORT RELIGIOUS PLAYS, by Arlett, Buchanan, and others. Contains: "Mother of All Living" (about Adam and Eve), "A House in Capernaum" (Christ's life in part), "This Rock" (about Peter). Religious Drama Society of Great Britain, 70¢.

SIX STEPS SLOWLY, by Elizabeth Blake. The problems of a heart patient returning to his family and attempting to resume a normal life. Health Education Unit, Heart Disease Control Program (no charge).

THE SKIN OF OUR TEETH, by Thornton Wilder. Large cast. Plays full evening. The history of man within the context of a single family. Samuel French, Inc. Royalty: $50.

THE SLAVE MAID OF ISRAEL, by Mary S. Hitchcock. 12 men, 11 women, extras. Plays 2 hours. Interior set. From the biblical story of Elisha healing the leper Naaman. T. S. Denison & Co., 85¢ (purchase of 12 copies required).

A SLEEP OF PRISONERS, by Christopher Fry. 4 men. Interior set. Four soldiers are held prisoner and disgusted with war. Each has a biblical dream acted by all four; the dreams concern Adam and Cain and Abel, David and Absolom, Abraham and Isaac, and Shadrac, Meshac, and Abednego. Written for chancel presentation, difficult. Dramatists Play Service, $1.25. Royalty: $25.

SMALL SHOES AND SMALL TULIPS. Children's play for world friendship;

gives facts and customs of Holland for lower and middle grades. Plays, Inc., 35¢.

SMALLEST OF ALL, by Sister Mary Francis, P.C. 4 men, 4 women, extras. Interior, exterior sets. The "beautiful lady" appears to a little girl in the small town of Lourdes in this play of St. Bernadette. Focus is upon "the Lady." Baker's Plays, $1.25. Royalty: $25.

A SMELL OF CINNAMON, by George Herman. 4 men, 8 women. Plays full evening. Interior set. A cardinal and the real devil's advocate examine the case of Mother Mary Francis Clarke, a candidate for canonization, and unearth a truth about sanctity. Samuel French, Inc., $1.25. Royalty: $25–$20.

SNAKES AND EGGS, book and lyrics by Robert D. Hock, music by Robert Rogers. 5 men, 5 women (may be more). All musical review, much of its content satiric, based on the seven deadly sins. Barbed humor with content thoughtful and sometimes moving. Basis in Old Testament writings. First given at Union Theological Seminary, New York City. Baker's Plays, $1.50. Royalty: $50 (apply to publisher for information on music).

SO IT'S CHRISTMAS AGAIN, by Karin Asbrand. Small or large cast of grammar school children. Plays 15–30 minutes (depends on music used). The annunciation, the revelation, the Nativity, the adoration. Baker's Plays, 25¢.

SO SHE MADE A NOVENA, by Carl Delozier. 2 men, 4 women. Interior set. A Roman Catholic play. After the failure of her novenas to bring her a husband, Katie Bryan throws out St. Joseph's statue; at that time her husband is found. Baker's Plays, 60¢.

SO THE BLIND MAY SEE, by Charles J. Ax. In *Bible Plays,* Book I, Christmas. Fortress Press, 75¢.

SO THIS IS BLISS, by Albert Johnson. 7 men, 7 women, extras. A young man, attempting to decide between college and marriage, is allowed by his parents to run a home and a business for a day. Unusual comedy. Heuer, 75¢. Royalty: $10.

SOCIAL HELPS FOR CHURCH WORKERS, by various authors. A collection of plays, games, party suggestions; for all ages. Baker's Plays, $1.25.

THE SOLDIER CITY, by Helen W. Munro. 4 boys or girls, chorus. Plays 40 minutes, cutting possible. Story of a gallant town suitable for Memorial Day programs. Baker's Plays, 60¢.

SOLDIERS OF THE CROSS, by Max William Koetter. 8 men. Plays 30 minutes. Interior set. A play of the way to salvation, with its center in the Easter events; is producible at other times of the year. Baker's Plays, 60¢.

SOLILOQUY ON THE SOUNDS OF EASTER, by John W. Felton. 2 men, 1 woman, narrator and pantomimist (either male or female). Plays 20 minutes or longer, depending on music used. Simple to produce. Easter as the time of discovery of love and faith. Baker's Plays, 60¢. Royalty: $5.

SON OF STEPHEN, by Clyde Cruse. 3 men, 3 women. Plays 30 minutes. Interior set. David, son of Stephen, the first Christian martyr, is involved in Saul's conversion to Christianity. Baker's Plays, 60¢.

SONG AT THE SCAFFOLD, by Gertrud von le Fort, adapted by Emmet Lavery. 4 men, 9 women, or 3 women, chorus. Sixteen nuns who go to death in the French Revolution reveal a truth about martyrdom. Three acts. Baker's Plays, $1.25. Royalty: $25.

A SONG IN THE NIGHT. 6 men, 5 women, male extras. Plays 30 minutes. Exterior set. Christmas play for junior and senior high students. The innkeeper learns compassion in a forceful recounting of the Christmas story with dramatic stage effects. Plays, Inc., 50¢.

A SONG IS BORN, by Matilda Rose McLaren. 3 men, 2 women, 1 boy, extras, choir of boys. The events leading to the writing of "Silent Night," and the moment of spirit it gave to the lives of the villagers. Good for combination of music and drama. Art Craft, 60¢ (purchase of 5 copies required).

SONG OF GLORY, by Anne Coulter Martens. 6 men, 6 women, extras. Plays 30 minutes. A strange angel establishes the true spirit of Christmas as that of the birthday of Christ when she appears in a Christmas pageant. Includes a presentation of the Nativity. One act. Heuer, 50¢.

THE SONGS OF CHRISTMAS, by Martha Bayly Shannon. Large cast. Plays 1 hour. Interior set. May be shortened or lengthened. Stories and tableaux based on carols. Baker's Plays, 60¢.

SONS OF ADAM, by P. J. Lamb. 5 men, 4 women, A four-part meditation on the Nativity. Baker's Plays, $1.25. Royalty: $15.

A SOUL IN FINE ARRAY, by Michael Casey. 9 women. Interior set. A nun, having learned that she is dying, must still find a reason for her death. Baker's Plays, 60¢. Royalty: $5.

A SOUND FROM HEAVEN, by James Brock. Large cast. The conversion of three thousand on the day of Pentecost marks the Christian church's beginning. In *Modern Chancel Dramas*. Baker's Plays, $1.25. Royalty: $10.

THE SOUNDS PROLONG, by Ray M. Cook. 2 men, soloists, choir. Plays 16 minutes. A cantata depicting Jewish ideals in America, using the sounds of hammer (justice), bell (freedom), and song (brotherhood) in the dramatization. Union of American Hebrew Congregations, 50¢.

SOUP, SAND, AND SAGEBRUSH, by Maude Hickman. 1 man, 7 women. Plays 45 minutes. The story of a frontier missionary and his family. Three acts. Eldridge, 60¢.

SPARK IN JUDEA, by R. F. Delderfield. 10 men, 3 women. Interior set. A drama of the Passion emphasizing the political aspect; Christ is the "harmless philosopher" who is one problem among many in the day of the governor of Samaria and Judea. Baker's Plays, $1. Royalty: $25.

THE 'SPECIALLY GOOD CHRISTMAS BOOK, by Helen Ramsey, Willis N. Bugbee, and others. A collection for all ages: plays, monologues, pantomimes, etc. "The First Christmas," a pantomime, is included. Baker's Plays, $1.

SPIRIT AND THE TRUTH, by Frank New. 2 men, 3 women. Interior set. An Easter play, but may be used for all occasions. Set in a room in the house of Pilate, who, after the crucifixion, is impressed through a woman's faith with what Jesus will mean to mankind's future. Evans Plays, 2*s.* net. Royalty: 25*s.* per performance.

THE SPIRIT OF CHRISTMAS, by Mary Ring Fagan. Six Christmas programs providing something for all grades through high school. Some parts have lines, some parts are in the background of the pageantry. Balanced with both religious spirit and joy of Christmas entertainment. Baker's Plays, 60¢.

THE SPIRIT OF CHRISTMAS GIVING, by Claudia Harris. 17 characters. Interior set. A boy who has much luxury learns in a dream the value of sharing. T. S. Denison & Co., 50¢ (purchase of 8 copies required).

SPIRIT OF CHRISTMAS TIME. A pageant of Christmas with carols, tableaux, foreign Christmas songs, etc., from Christ's birth to the present. Eldridge, 50¢.

SPREADING THE NEWS, by Lady Gregory. 7 men, 3 women. Plays 30 minutes. An Irish comedy demonstrating the way gossip grows. Baker's Plays, 60¢. Royalty: none in United States.

SPRING'S MIRACLE. Easter program for primary and junior ages, with songs and exercises. Eldridge, 30¢.

THE STABLE BOY. Plays 15–20 minutes. Good Bible message play, with production notes. One act. Concordia, 40¢.

THE STABLE MANGER, by Jessie Powell. 4 or more men, 3 or more women. The incarnation and its significance to varying types of people. Baker's Plays, 60¢. Royalty: $10.

THE STAR AND THE SIXTH, by Olga Cossi. 3 men, 7 women. Plays 20 minutes. Exterior set. A modern, sophisticated teen-ager learns the true meaning of Christmas and gains contentment when he learns to understand "The Sixth." Eldridge, 60¢ (purchase of 10 copies required).

THE STAR GAZER, by John W. Felton. 3 men, 1 woman. Plays 25 minutes. Interior set. A contrast of the world of modern science with the simplicity of the day of Christ's birth; lightened with a touch of romance. Baker's Plays, 60¢. Royalty: $5.

STAR IN THE EAST, by Karin Asbrand. A little girl's desire to join the wise men in the adoration of the baby king. Pageant for younger people or adults with the five main parts played by children. Eldridge, 60¢.

THE STAR IN THE WINDOW. 4 men, 3 women. Plays 30 minutes. Interior set. For junior and senior high students. Otto is surprised to find an unusual Christmas star shining in his shop window where he had displayed a plain tinsel one. Plays, Inc., 50¢.

STAR LIGHT, STAR BRIGHT, by Maude Hunter. 3 speaking parts, speaker, choral readers, choir. The meaning of "the star" for a child, a youth, an adult. Art Craft, 60¢ (purchase of 24 copies required).

THE STAR OF FRANCE, by Eva A. M. Jones. 2 men, 3 women, 7 children. Plays 30 minutes. Interior set. A play for Christmas. A woman of France, taken from her home and husband in the course of war, has a vision of Joan of Arc and a realization of country and God. Baker's Plays, 60¢.

STAR OF LIGHT, by Karin Asbrand. Large cast. 3 men (all women may be used). Plays 30 minutes. Effective candlelight pageant for Christmas (or may be given any time during the year). Eldridge, 60¢ (purchase of 8 copies required).

STAR OF SPLENDOR, by Barbara Hart, edited and arranged by Cam Floria. Plays 45 minutes. A Christmas cantata honoring Christ and his star, come as salvation for the world. Eldridge, $1.25 (purchase of 10 copies required).

STAR OF WONDER, by Effa E. Preston. 8 men, 8 women, 1 boy. Plays 30 minutes. Interior set. A grouchy couple, stranded at a small railroad station when their car breaks down, learn the true Christmas meaning when the star of Bethlehem brings scenes of the Nativity to them. T. S. Denison & Co., 50¢ (purchase of 8 copies required).

STAR OVER BETHLEHEM, by Joan Selby-Lowndes. 8 characters, choir. Plays 50 minutes. A simple, yet moving, Christmas play by a well-known children's author. Faith Press, 1*s.* 6*d.*

STAR SONG, by Wendy LaBere. For advanced intermediate and junior age groups. Religious Drama Society of Great Britain.

STAR SONG AND OTHER ONE-ACT PLAYS, by Florence Ryerson. Collection of six plays for all seasons. Includes "The Triumph of Job." Samuel French, Inc., $2. Royalty: $5.

A STAR TOO FAR, by Don Fearheiley. 3 men, 2 women. A Christmas play about the reconciliation of father and a son. Broadman Press, 35¢.

STATE OF SIEGE, by Albert Camus, translated by Stuart Gilbert. 24 men (chorus included), 10 women (chorus included). Exterior, interior sets. The Plague and Death, his feminine companion, establish a totalitarian regime over Cadiz through fear and depersonalization; at last one man sacrifices himself to save his love and free the city. In *Caligula and Three Other Plays.* Knopf, $5. Royalty: apply to publisher.

STATE OF THE UNION, by Howard Lindsay and Russel Crouse. 11 men, 6 women. Plays full evening. Political satire containing a strong challenge for a Christian spirit in society and a sense of personal integrity and morality. Dramatists Play Service, $1. Royalty: $50–$25.

STATION Y-U-L-E, by Karin Asbrand. Christmas selections presented as if they were in a radio talent program. In *Jumbo Christmas Book.* Baker's Plays, $1.25.

STEPHEN D., by James Joyce, adapted by Hugh Leonard. Flexible cast. A play of great and haunting power and beauty; a dramatization of *A Portrait of the Artist as a Young Man* and *Stephen Hero.* Evans Plays, $1.25 plus postage. Royalty: $50–$25.

STEPHEN, THE FIRST MARTYR, by Norman E. Nygaard. 7 men, extras. The stoning of Stephen because of his restatement of belief in God. In *The Bible Comes Alive.* Baker's Plays, $1.25.

THE STEWARD'S DAUGHTER. Plays 20 minutes. Good Bible message play, with complete production notes. One act. Concordia, 40¢.

STILL SHINES THE STAR, by Karin Asbrand. Large cast, choir. Three modern young people, forced to take shelter in a deserted stable, dream of the Nativity. Eldridge, 60¢ (purchase of 8 copies required).

A STORM IS BREAKING, by Jim Damico. 1 man, 1 woman's voice, 1 boy. Exterior set. Comedy. Courage and faith give a boy unrealized strength, revealing his stature. Baker's Plays, 60¢. Royalty: $5.

STORY BOOK PURIM, by Lillian S. Freehof. 8 boys, 6 girls. A playlet of fancy. Queen Esther is aided by Alice in Wonderland, Humpty Dumpty, and Little Red Riding Hood, among others. Union of American Hebrew Congregations, 25¢.

THE STORY OF ARTABAN, THE OTHER WISE MAN, by Henry Van Dyke, adapted by Robbins and Nordoff. 2 men, speech chorus, soloist. From the story "The Other Wise Man"; a Christmas play with music. Artaban would have joined the other wise men, but was destined to seek Christ among the world's suffering and to find him elsewhere. Piano and percussion accompaniment. Eldridge, $1.50.

STORY OF CHRISTMAS, by Grace B. Perry. Pageant in pantomime with Christmas carols for background music and readings from the scriptures; makes a simple but effective production. Eldridge, 60¢.

THE STORY OF CHRISTMAS IN MIME, by E. Martin Browne. 15 men, 9 women. Plays 35 minutes. A biblical recounting entirely in pantomime from Isaiah's prophecy to the wise men's return. Sheldon Press.

THE STORY OF EASTER, words and music by R. M. Stults. A cantata of the Easter story. Eldridge, 75¢.

THE STORY OF HANUKKAH, by Eleanor Goff and Harry Anik. Two-volume dance pageant; Hanukkah traditions and the Maccabees' story. Anti-Defamation League of B'nai B'rith, $2.50.

THE STORY OF JEREMIAH, by John Hunter, Norman Spooner, and Vera Allen. Large cast, singers and actors. Plays 1 hour. The biblical story with modern language and music. Episcopal Society for Cultural and Racial Unity. Royalty: apply to publisher.

STRANGE VICTORY, by Evelyn Neuenburg. 1 man, 2 or 3 women. Plays 30 minutes. Interior set. The mother of Giuseppi Verdi, her child, and a servant girl hide from soldiers in the bell tower of the church. The servant, supernaturally sensing the music surrounding the baby, gives her life so that the mother and child may live. Baker's Plays, 60¢. Royalty: $5.

THE STRANGER, by Elizabeth George Speare. 3 men, 2 women, 1 boy. Plays 30 minutes. Interior set. The coming of a young Nazarene carpenter to take lodging for the night changes the bitterness of Mattathias and alters the life of his family. Baker's Plays, 60¢.

A STRANGER IN BETHLEHEM, by Charles George. 3 men, 3 women. Plays 40 minutes. A tramp helps a family in Bethlehem, Pennsylvania, to understand the happiness of celebrating Christmas with those things provided by God. Baker's Plays, 60¢.

THE STRANGER OF VALLENSKA, by Michael Dines. 14 characters, extras. The Jews of a Russian village in 1859 take Joseph Ben Gabrial, who does not know the meaning of his own powers, for the

Messiah; the Elders examine him. Evans Plays, 2*s*. net. Royalty: 25*s*. per performance.

A STRANGER PASSES, by Joseph Carlton. 6 men, 5 women. Plays full evening. Interior set. A stranger straightens the lives of a selfish American family, reuniting them about the mother. Baker's Plays, 75¢. Royalty: $10.

STRICTLY FEMININE, by Lyda Nagel. Collection includes: "Proud Is the Heart" (a broken romance), "Bright Is Tomorrow" (about a selfish daughter and devoted mother), "The Mother Part" (a woman's foolishness in trying to conceal her age), "Miracle for Three" (a girl yields her love to another), "The Dark Corner" (a generous heart overcomes the hatreds that follow war). Baker's Plays, $1.25. Royalty: each play, $5.

THE STRONG ARE LONELY, by Fritz Hochwaelder, adapted by Eva Le Gallienne from the French version by Richard Thieberger and Jean Mercure. 20 men, extras. Interior set. In a Jesuit missionary colony for the Indians in the Buenos Aires of 1767, the Father Provincial struggles between his vows of obedience and his convictions. Powerful emotionally. Two acts. Samuel French, Inc., $1.25. Royalty: $35–$25.

STUDY IN COLOR, by Malcolm Boyd. 2 Negro men, 1 white man. Short plays. Three plays treating the problem of race relations in different ways. Each one act. Episcopal Society for Cultural and Racial Unity. Production kit and royalty information available.

THE STUMBLING BLOCK, by Mary E. Glazener. Paul's final visit to Jerusalem, and his arrest. Broadman Press, 75¢.

THE SUMMONING OF EVERYMAN, adapted by John Baird. 18 men, 5 women. Plays 1 hour. Blank verse. Adaptation of the old morality play of Everyman's journey to the grave after his calling by Death; effective in its simplicity. Samuel French, Inc., 60¢. Royalty: $5.

THE SUMMONING OF EVERYMAN, adapted by Warren Kliewer. 2 men. Plays 20 minutes. Adaptation of the old morality play in modern terms. In *Moralities and Miracles.* The Golden Quill Press. Royalty: apply to the author, c/o the publisher.

THE SUMMONING OF EVERYMAN, adapted by Herbert Payne. Samuel French, Inc.

A SUNDAY SCHOOL CHRISTMAS PROGRAM, by Jean Mattson. 8 men, 7 women, 2 children, 3 choruses, narrator. Plays 30 minutes. A child's impressions of Christmas, in and out of church school; presents both traditions and modern ideas, and points up that Christ is Christmas. Eldridge, 60¢ (purchase of 5 copies required).

THE SUNKEN BELL, by Gerhart Hauptmann, adapted by Charles H. Meltzer. 6 men, 3 women, 2 boys, 5 girls (age 16), extras. Interior, exterior sets. During the middle ages, a war is being waged by the elves and fauns against the spread of Christianity. One man from the Christian world tries to live in the realm of nature worship, and is ultimately destroyed by the conflicting forces. The struggle of the spirit, of desire and duty, of a man isolated from others. In *Seven Modern Plays.* Houghton Mifflin Co. Royalty: apply to publisher.

SUPERSONIC PURIM, by Helen Fine, original music by Dr. Moses J. Eisenberg. 3 girls, 12 boys. Plays 35 minutes. A fanciful play with music holding the spirit of Purim. Spacemen come to the aid of Queen Esther. Union of American Hebrew Congregations, 75¢.

SUSAN AND GOD, by Rachel Crothers. 5 men, 6 women. 3 interior sets. A comedy of a woman whose fad is a new "religion" which is practiced in her home and which reforms her at last. English Theatre Guild, 10*s.*

THE SWEET POTATO VINE, by Barbara Kay Davidson. Sympathetic and constructive treatment of the problems of unmarried mothers. Plays for Living.

THE SWORD AND THE SCROLL, by Thomas R. Atkins. 9 men, 3 women, extras (doubling possible). Christians await the whims of a mad Nero. Baker's Plays, 75¢. Royalty: $10.

SYMPHONY OF EASTER. Music of Beethoven arranged for choirs in an Easter cantata. Eldridge, $1.50; $3 for set of 100 librettos.

THE TABLE, by Jay Leipzig. 5 boys, 5 girls, a voice. Plays 20 minutes. The table in a second-hand shop gets its wish to witness a seder. A review of seder symbols and meanings. Three acts. Union of American Hebrew Congregations, 25¢.

THE TABLE SET FOR HIMSELF. 3 men, 5 women, 1 boy. Interior set. Based on the Irish legend that every Christmas Eve the Christchild comes to the earth to learn how he is being remembered. One act. Baker's Plays, 95¢. Royalty: $10 if admission is charged; $5 if not.

TAKE THIS MAN, by Gordon Jaynes. 4 men, 1 woman, extras. A man is crucified for an idea in a play characterized by deep thought. One act. Baker's Plays, 60¢. Royalty: $5.

TARDY APRIL, by Louis Wilson. 1 man, 4 women. Plays 30 minutes. Interior set. Missionary activity of church women in a play about fund-raising and nostalgic romance. Baker's Plays, 60¢.

TELL IT TO THE WIND, by Edward Murch. 7 women. Exterior set. The shepherds leave the scene of the Nativity and are told by an angel to spread the news of their coming to find the Christchild. Baker's Plays, 60¢. Royalty: $5.

TELL IT WITH TRUMPETS, by P. W. Turner. Collection includes: "6:15 to Eternity," "Passion in Paradise," and "Mann's End." Plays occupy the area between drama and evangelism. Baker's Plays, $1.50. Royalty: $25.

TEN GOOD CHRISTMAS PANTOMIMES, by Ethel Eldridge. Pantomimes to accompany familiar hymns and songs, recitations. Includes "Silent Night," "Little Town of Bethlehem," etc. Music included. Baker's Plays, 75¢.

TEN PANTOMIMED HYMNS, by Ida Belle Lull. Definite and effective directions given for each pose for various well-known hymns, such as "Jesus Loves Even Me," "Blest Be the Tie That Binds," "Let the Lower Lights Be Burning," and others. Eldridge, 75¢.

TEN STIRRING BIBLE PLAYS, by Margaret Parsons. A younger folk's collection, easily dramatized. Contains the plays "Samuel," "Daniel and the Lions," and others. Eldridge, $1.

THE TERRIBLE MEEK, by Charles Rann Kennedy. 2 men, 1 woman. Plays 50 minutes. An unknown woman, a Roman captain, and a soldier on the night after the crucifixion. Intended to be presented in darkness except at play's end. One act. Samuel French, Inc., 60¢.

THE TERRIBLE MISS DOVE, by Frances Patton. The high qualities of a schoolteacher live on in her pupils. Very well written and very human. Edna Means Dramatic Service, 65¢.

THANK YOU, GOD, FOR EVERYTHING, by L. M. Hollinshead. 4 men, 3 women, a voice. Plays 30 minutes. Interior set. Children's fantasy. A blind girl is given her sight by two guardians sent to earth to watch over her, and is disappointed that her dreams have not come true until she learns that shadows make the sun brighter. Baker's Plays, 60¢.

THANKFUL FOR WHAT? by Effa E. Preston. 4 girls, 4 boys. Plays 20 minutes. Interior set. The children of one family realize their blessings when they learn of another boy's Thanksgiving without dinner. T. S. Denison & Co., 50¢ (purchase of 7 copies required).

THANKSGIVING PLAYS AND WAYS, by Lettie Van Derveer. A collection of four playlets. Eldridge, 85¢.

THANKSGIVING PROGRAM BOOK. Collection includes four playlets: "Two-fold Harvest," exercises, songs, etc. Eldridge, 40¢.

THAT FELL ARREST, by Lesbia Scott. 2 men, 3 women. Plays 30 minutes. Interior set. A modern morality play in which a young girl, under anaesthetic, dreams of the hereafter and of what her life has prepared for her there. H. F. W. Deane & Sons, 2*d.*

THAT HEAVEN OF FREEDOM, by Dorothy Clarke Wilson. 5 women. A schoolgirl returns to her village in India and finds service. Friendship Press, 50¢.

THAT HOME IN NAZARETH, by Dorothy Clarke Wilson. 3 men, 2 women, offstage voice. Plays 40 minutes. A semi-allegorical sketch of the need of divine presence in the home; an imaginary story of the effect of Jesus on those who knew him daily. In *Twelve Months of Drama for the Average Church*. Baker's Plays, $2.95.

THEN WILL SHE RETURN, by Lesbia Scott. Large cast. Basis in Ecclesiastes 4:18. In a small parish in England a pastor and his wife work out their aspirations. Religious Drama Society of Great Britain, approximately 28¢. Royalty: approximately $5.92.

THERE SHALL BE NO NIGHT, by Robert Sherwood. 3 men, 4 women. Finland's struggle against the attempt of communism to destroy democracy. Filled with power. Dramatic Play Service, $1. Royalty: $35–$25.

"THERE WAS A MAN . . ." by Maxwell Silver. 13 men, 1 woman, chorus, extras. A dramatization by a scholar of the Book of Job, which emphasizes doctrines of the book important to modern times. Nine scenes. Union of American Hebrew Congregations, $1.

THERE WAS ONE WHO GAVE A LAMB, by Annette Mason Ham. 11 boys,

3 girls, angel chorus. Traditional carols support a musical Nativity. Eldridge, $1 (purchase of 6 copies required).

THERE'S A SONG IN THE AIR, by Paul Nagy, Jr. Variable cast. A service for Christmas which strives to create something original, minimize rehearsal, and use as many people as possible, particularly younger people. Baker's Plays, 60¢.

THESE ARE NOT CHILDREN, by Jerome Alden. A family life drama centered around mentally retarded children. Vocational Rehabilitation Administration (write publisher for free scripts, in limited supply).

THEY CAME BEARING GIFTS, by Elizabeth H. Emerson. 3 men, 5 women, angel. The box in which the wise man brought frankincense to the Christchild is found while Elath is cleaning house, and Mary tells its story. Baker's Plays, 60¢.

THEY FOUND CHRISTMAS, by Lois R. Boli. Children, chorus. Plays 30 minutes. A boy and girl, in search of Christmas, are shown its true meaning by the Christmas Lady. Eldridge, 50¢ (purchase of 5 copies required).

THEY MADE A PATH, by Helen Kromer. Large cast (doubling possible). The spread of Christianity from the time of Paul until modern times. With prologue and epilogue; individual scenes can be used separately. Friendship Press, 75¢. Royalty: none.

THEY MOVE ON, by Gregory Page. 6 men, 4 women, extras. Six souls to be assessed before the celestial magistrate: a financier, a preacher, a nun, an urchin, a dancer, and a dictator. In the climax the recorder reveals himself as Pilate. Evans Plays, 2*s.* net. Royalty: 25*s.* each performance.

THEY THAT SIT IN DARKNESS, by Dorothy Clarke Wilson. 10 men, 8 women. Plays 30 minutes. Miriam, an outcast of Bethlehem, finds the light in Christ's coming. Baker's Plays, 60¢. Royalty: first performance, none; $2.50 each repeat.

THEY THAT WALK IN DARKNESS, by Willard S. Smith. 8 men, 2 women, extras. Plays 35 minutes. Exterior set. A blind girl is given sight by Jesus at the time of the Passover meal in the upper room. T. S. Denison & Co., 50¢ (purchase of 6 copies required).

THEY WANTED A LEADER, by Sam Bate. 5 men, 3 women. A group of Jews await the coming of Ben Israel, a prince of the House of David, to lead a revolt against Herod and Rome; they witness instead the Palm Sunday entry of Jesus. H. F. W. Deane & Sons.

THE THIEF AND THE HANGMAN, by Morton Wishengrad. 8 men, 1 woman. Who is to be hangman when society itself is the thief? In *One Act Plays of Spiritual Power*. Baker's Plays, $3.25.

THINE SHALL BE THE GLORY, by Dr. Charles M. Sheldon, adapted by Mary B. Harrison. Variable cast. Plays 50 minutes. From the book *He Is Here*; the story of a teacher who has tried to pass, in addition to the local board requirements, a part of Christ's conceptions of the true life to her students. Baker's Plays, 60¢.

THE THIRD DAY, by Karin Asbrand. Plays 1 hour. Pageant for Easter, for adults and children. A mother without faith after the injury of her child dreams three visions, of living flowers and candles, and of the resurrection. She wakes with new faith in her child's recovery. Eldridge, 60¢ (purchase of 10 copies required).

THE THIRD DAY, by Sidney Carver. 4 men, 5 women. The reactions of those close to Jesus, with particular emphasis on Barabbas, on the first Easter Sunday. Evans Plays, 2*s.* net. Royalty: 25*s.* per performance.

THE THIRD WINDMILL BOOK OF ONE-ACT PLAYS, by Margaret Wood. A collection of six plays, includes "The Road to Damascus." Heinemann Educational Books, 7*s.* 6*d.*

THIRTY FAMOUS ONE-ACT PLAYS, edited by Bennett Cerf and Van H. Cartmell. A collection of plays by Barrie, Strindberg, Saroyan, Millay, Shaw, and Schnitzer among others. Modern Library, Inc., $2.95.

THIS FREEDOM, by Elliot Field. Part I deals with freedom's coming to America; Part II examines the meaning of freedom by picturing America deprived of Constitution and Bill of Rights. Baker's Plays, 75¢. Royalty: first performance, none; $2.50 each repeat.

THIS IS MY CHURCH, by Clarence M. Waite. 4 men, 7 women, 2 soloists, organist. Plays 1 hour. An older woman finds a new outlook in visiting the church she knew as a young person. Eldridge, 60¢ (purchase of 10 copies required).

THIS IS THE END, by Ken Taylor. 4 men, 2 women. Plays 30 minutes. The meaning of life in the face of death; a deep examination from the standpoint of the observation that "Everyone's death is entertainment for almost everyone else." In *Coventry Porch Plays.* Baker's Plays, $1.25. Royalty: $10.

THIS IS THE WORD, by P. W. Turner. 3 men, male and female chorus. God's association with man through the entire biblical story, in five visual presentations to be given in the place of a sermon. "Word Made Flesh" included also. Baker's Plays, $1.25. Royalty: $10.

THIS NIGHT SHALL PASS, by Dorothy Clarke Wilson. 2 men, 1 woman. Plays 25 minutes. Exterior set. Love conquers the hatred between a man and a youth. Set on a ruined city hilltop. Baker's Plays, 60¢. Royalty: noncommercial acting rights for one performance free if 3 copies purchased; $2.50 each repeat.

THIS ROCK, by Alan Poole. 4 men, 2 women. A simple play set the day after the crucifixion, in which Peter struggles to realize that Christ loved and forgave him. Baker's Plays. Royalty: $5.

THIS THINE HOUSE, by Marion Wefer. 9 men, 2 women, 3 children. Plays 30 minutes. A pastor's successful efforts to make his a "community church." Friendship Press, 50¢.

THIS UNION UNDER GOD, by Albert Johnson. 2 men, 1 woman. Bare stage, with minimum properties. A Drama Trio play. A lyrical saga of Abraham and Mary Lincoln through their strange romance and storm-filled years as President and first lady. Available in manuscript from author, $1. Royalty: first performance, $10; $5 each repeat.

THIS WAY TO CHRISTMAS, by Leota Summerhays. 5 men, 2 women. Plays 40 minutes. Interior set. An elf learns with the help of the

Good Nicholas to do for others with joy in this fantasy of the bringing of the first Christmas tree to the children. One act. Samuel French, Inc., 60¢. Royalty: $5.

THIS WAY TO THE TOMB, by Ronald Duncan, music by Benjamin Britten. 5 men, 2 women (doubling possible). Plays 2 hours. Part I: a verse story of God's search for a saint; Part II: a satire of present-day religiosity. Music ranges from a capella choral music to experiments in the jazz idiom. Faber & Faber. Music rental: Boosey and Hawkes. Royalty: apply to Ninon Tallon-Karlweis.

THE THISTLE IN DONKEY FIELD, by Richard Tydeman. 5 men, 3 women. Mankind, the thistle, reacts to the possible destroyer of the world, the donkey. One act. Evans Plays, 2*s.* net. Royalty: 25*s.* per performance.

THOR WITH ANGELS, by Christopher Fry. 8 men, 3 women. Plays 90 minutes. Set in A.D. 600; a poetic recounting of the legend of Hoel, teacher of Christianity to the partly barbaric Jutes. Both beautiful and difficult. Dramatists Play Service, 75¢. Royalty: $25.

THOU ART PETER, by Maryann Manly. 8 men. Plays 30 minutes. Exterior set. Peter dedicates himself to the service of God out of a consciousness of his failures. Baker's Plays, 60¢. Royalty: $5.

"THOU FOOL!" by Paul Heckel and Bradway Rogers. 5 players. Plays 10 minutes. A big businessman, too busy and self-centered to help others, has a revelation of life's true values in a conversation with his own soul. Eldridge, 60¢.

THOU SHALT NOT LIE, by Franz Grillparzer, translated by Henry H. Stevens. 13 men, 1 girl, extras. 1 interior set, exterior sets. A kitchen-boy for the Gallo-Roman bishop Gregory of Chalons goes to rescue the nephew of the bishop from the Frankish chieftain Count Kattwald under a promise to tell nothing but the truth. Underlying theme of relative truth and the limitations of perfection in human beings. Register Press. Royalty: apply to publisher.

THREE CHURCH DRAMAS, by Olov Hartman. These three plays effect a return to the intimacy of drama and worship: "Prophet and Carpenter" (concerns Jonah), "The Crown of Life" (about Adam, Eve, and Satan), "The Fiery Furnace" (explores dictatorship). The participation of the congregation is required. Fortress Press, $3.50. Royalty: apply to publisher.

THE THREE FACES OF EASTER, by Anne Coulter Martens. 3 men, 7 women, extras. Plays 30 minutes. Interior set. A girl watches and learns from a rehearsal of an Easter pageant: the children and their eggs and bunny, older people and their parade and fashions, and finally the emergence of the true meaning. She joins the pageant choir to sing a hymn of triumph. A teen-age play with modern focus. Baker's Plays, 60¢.

THE THREE MARYS, by Karin Asbrand. 5 women, angel chorus. Plays 15 minutes. Interior set. Mary the Mother, Mary Magdalene, and the Other Mary seen at the times of the crucifixion and the resurrection. In *Easy Church Plays for Women and Girls.* Baker's Plays, $1.25.

THREE MEDIEVAL PLAYS. Includes: "Everyman," "Master Pierre Pathelin," "Coventry Nativity Play." Heinemann Educational Books, 7*s*. 6*d*. net.

THREE PLAYS, by Gabriel Marcel. The Christian existentialist's first American collection of plays. Hill & Wang, $3.75.

THE THREE SISTERS, by Anton Chekhov, translated by Stark Young with Catherine Alexander Burland and Richard O'Connell. 9 men, 5 women. 2 interior sets, 1 exterior set. Three sisters stranded by the death of their father are presented as profound character studies. Samuel French, Inc., $1.25. Royalty: $25–$20.

THREE TOWNELEY PLAYS, adapted by Dennis Hamley. Modern versions of three plays of the medieval mystery cycle, with special appeal to children. Heinemann Educational Books, 4*s*. 6*d*.

THREE WISE MEN, by Dorothy C. Allan. 6 men (doubling possible), chorus. Plays 40 minutes. The magi, coming to the Christchild, have a vision of the cross and learn that it is a beginning; not an end. Baker's Plays, 60¢.

THE THREE WOMEN OF THE NATIVITY, by Mary Russell. 2 men, 7 women. Plays 25 minutes. Play centering on Elizabeth, Anna, and Mary, the three women who were concerned in the Nativity. Baker's Plays, 60¢.

THROUGH A GLASS DARKLY, by Ruth E. Bell. 6 men, 4 women, quartet. Plays 30 minutes. Interior set. A young minister in his first pastorate invites the members to his study to discuss informally a plan for the betterment of the community; many come, with chaotic results. Baker's Plays, 60¢. Royalty: $5.

THROUGH A GLASS, DARKLY, by Stanley Richards. 4 men, 3 women. Plays 40 minutes. The attitude of intolerant Aaron, an orthodox Jew, is changed when his son brings home a Scottish-Presbyterian bride. Banner Play Bureau, 60¢. Royalty: $10.

THUNDER ROCK, by Robert Ardrey. 6 men. Plays 2 hours. A lighthouse keeper, who lives in the past, becomes a leader who brings new order from the chaos of the world. Dramatists Play Service, $1. Royalty: $25.

THUS IT IS WRITTEN, by Paul W. Gooch. 26 actors, choir. The biblical Nativity readings of a family are enacted. Two acts. Eldridge, 75¢ (purchase of 10 copies required).

THY KINGDOM COME, by Florence Converse. Large cast. Plays 1 hour. The Roman soldiers guarding the tomb of Christ encourage four children to talk of their master and later dream of the crucifixion. The play ends with the coming of the angels to roll aside the stone. Baker's Plays, 60¢. Royalty: $5 if admission is charged.

THY WILL BE DONE, by Robert J. Murphy, C.S.P. and Cecelia Lenz. 11 men, 7 women. 2 interior sets, 3 exterior sets. The heart of Gallus, who feels he is putting to death a guiltless man, is probed at the time of Christ's crucifixion. He, in time, becomes a Christian. Baker's Plays, 60¢. Royalty: $10.

TICKET TO TOMORROW, by Nora Stirling. Parents and teen-aged children tackle their problems with conflict and resolution. Health and Welfare Division, Metropolitan Life Insurance Co.

THE TIDINGS BROUGHT TO MARY, by Paul Claudel, translated by Wallace Fowlie. 4 men (plus extras), 3 women (plus extras). 1 interior set, exterior sets. A woman infected with leprosy gives good for evil and maintains, like Christ, love, faith, and charity. The play closes about the time of Christ's birth. Bound with "Break of Noon." Henry Regnery Co.: cloth, $4.75; paper, $1.10. Royalty: apply to publisher.

TIDINGS OF JOY, by Elizabeth McFadden. 6 men, 2 women, 4 boys, 4 girls, extra children. Plays 40 minutes. A young couple is threatened with being evicted on Christmas Eve, and is befriended by a group of carolers and others touched by the spirit of Christmas. Three acts. Baker's Plays, 60¢. Royalty: $5.

TIDINGS OF PEACE, by Karin Asbrand. 7 characters. Plays 30–45 minutes. Four travelers are given food and water by an unknown boy who tells of others turned from an inn centuries before; the innkeeper finds room for these four. Eldridge, 60¢ (purchase of 7 copies required).

TIGER AT THE GATES, by Jean Giraudoux, translated by Christopher Fry. 15 men, 6 women, 1 girl. Exterior, interior sets. Hector, having become disgusted with the glorification of war, struggles to prevent the start of the Trojan War; play shows a man's struggle against destiny. Samuel French, Inc., $1.25. Royalty: $50–$25.

TIJL FOUNDS UTOPIA, by Jan Naaykens. A call for understanding among nations. Netherlands Centre of the International Theatre Institute.

A TIME FOR LOVE, by Gwen Holly Simpson. 3 men, 7 women, extras. Two Roman Catholic nuns are dedicated to the rehabilitation of the residents of a war-ravaged Pacific island. Play-within-a-play tells the Christmas story. Includes stage directions. McKay's Plays, $1.25. Royalty: $10.

A TIME OF MINOR MIRACLES, by Jack Blacklock. 6 men, 3 women. Plays 30 minutes. Interior set. A news commentator, embittered and refusing to believe, recognizes his consequent loneliness when a group seeks shelter in his home on Christmas Eve after a bus breakdown. Baker's Plays, 60¢. Royalty: $5.

A TIME TO BE BORN, by P. D. Cummins. 8 men, 3 women, 3 children. Nativity play with originality. Produced on Christmas Eve, 1951 and 1953, by BBC television. H. F. W. Deane & Sons, 2*d.*

THE TINIEST CHRISTMAS TREE, by Anne Coulter Martens. 11 children, carolers. Plays 15 minutes. A sick girl's Christmas is happier because of a tiny tree. Baker's Plays, 25¢.

THE TINKER, by Fred Eastman. 4 men, 3 women. Interior set. Comedy with spiritual power. A family anxious for material possessions but financially limited is joined by a genial tinker with a different kind of values; their outlooks invite conflict, with flashes of humor. Three acts. Baker's Plays, $1. Royalty: $15.

THE TINSEL FAIRY, by George Crout. 50–100 children. The meaning of the Christmas ornaments is revealed when from children's imaginations the tinsel fairy comes to life to help trim the tree. Eldridge, 50¢ (purchase of 6 copies required).

TO BEAR THE MESSAGE, by Irma Russell Cruse. 6 men, 5 women, choir. Plays 1 hour. A man's remembrance of past Christmases convinces John and Trudy to try to bring people the true Christmas message with their program. One-act play-pageant. Eldridge, 60¢ (purchase of 8 copies required).

TO BETHLEHEM, by Edna Risque. 14 characters, children. A Christmas play in four scenes with a tableau. Faith Press, 6*d.*

TO HEAR THE ANGELS SING, by Pearl Neilson. 5 adults, 15 children (ages 10–16). Plays 1 hour. Interior set. A family's preparation for Christmas without the mother, and the question if mother will get "to hear the angels sing." Three scenes. Eldridge, 50¢ (purchase of 10 copies required).

"TO MEET THE KING" AND THREE OTHER PLAYS, by H. C. G. Stevens. 2 men, 2 women, voice. Interior set. Contains a famous play of "mother love," concerning a son's air race crash. H. F. W. Deane & Sons.

TO TEMPER THE WIND, by Elizabeth Blake. Deals with the problem of family unity and sense of security while Mother is hospitalized. Nat'l. Council on Homemaker Service: perusal script, $2; kit of 6 acting scripts, $12.

"TO THINE OWN SELF . . ." by Helen Kromer. 5 women. Plays 30 minutes. Missionary play. A woman becomes blind and for the first time understands the light of service. A very strong play. Baker's Plays, 60¢.

TO US A SON, by J. Paul Faust. 3 men, 7 women, extras. Plays 30 minutes. Interior set. Believing that they have heard the instruction of God through their son, the innkeeper and his wife bring Mary and Joseph to the stable. Baker's Plays, 60¢.

TO YOU A SAVIOUR, by Betty Prevender and Rita Gowal. Narrator, 8 tableau parts (no speaking), 2 choirs (1 speaking, 1 singing). Choric pageant with eight tableaux. The virgin Mary in her appearances through the ages. The speaking choir offers the opportunity for pantomime and solo. Baker's Plays, 60¢. Royalty: $5.

TOBIAS AND SARA, by Paul Claudel, translated by Adele Fiske. 7 men, 2 women, 1 dog, 1 fish. Plays full evening. Based on the apocryphal Book of Tobit, a love story relating to a divine plan. In *Port-Royal and Other Plays.* Hill & Wang. Royalty: apply to Librarie Gallimard.

TOBIAS AND THE ANGEL, by James Bridie. 8 men, 8 women. 1 interior set, 3 exterior sets. A dramatization of the apocryphal Book of Tobit with a touch of perverse concoction; has grace and distinctive style. Baker's Plays, $1.25. Royalty: $25.

TOLERANCE IN ACTION, edited by Annette Smith Lawrence. A collection of plays, radio plays, etc. for junior-senior high students. Includes: "The Unerring Instinct" by Thornton Wilder and "Haven of the Spirit" by Morrill Denison. American Unity, $2.

TOMORROW IS A DAY, by Nora Stirling. 3 or 5 women, 1 girl (teen-age), 1 or 2 boys (teen-age), stage manager. Plays 30 minutes. A mother does not understand the needs of love and help for her shy daughter until a neighbor shows her that understanding is important. One act. Play cannot be given within fifty miles of New York City. Nat'l. Assoc. for Mental Health. Royalty: none for first performance if production packet is purchased; $2.50 each repeat if admission is charged, $1 if not (pay to American Theatre Wing Community Plays).

TONGUES IN TREES, by Jay Mann. 2 boys, 2 girls, or 3 boys, 1 girl. Plays 20 minutes. Illustrates the right to one's own religion, and its celebrations rather than another's; a boy has a dream showing the disrespect of bringing a Christmas tree into his home and the rightness of celebrating Chanuko. Union of American Hebrew Congregations, 25¢.

TOUCH OF A SHADOW, by John W. Felton. 6 men, 1 woman. Play for Easter. A man's shadow touches those about him in his life; it remains to affect them after his death, those who have been touched repeating his actions. The influence of a great man is broad and reaches out to touch generations. Baker's Plays, 60¢. Royalty: $5.

A TOUCH OF LILAC, by Lyda Nagel. 6 women. Interior set. At Christmas a nurse becomes disgusted with the doctor's wealthy and insincere clientele. In contrast is one woman who thinks of her family's welfare. Baker's Plays, 60¢. Royalty: $5.

A TOUCH OF THE POET, by Eugene O'Neill. 7 men, 3 women. Plays full evening. An attempt to match illusion with reality is made by an Irishman; his only background is a nineteenth-century myth of Massachusetts. Yale University Press, $3.75.

A TOWN IS BORN, by Tom Sayer, adapted by W. Guthrie Piersel, Ph.D. 6 men, 1 girl. Interior set. A little girl moves a group of five experts traveling on a train to construct a dream town from her make-believe copy of her poverty-stricken one, and, to the rising sound of Christmas carols, the dream town becomes real. Baker's Plays, 60¢. Royalty: $5.

THE TOWN THAT COULDN'T HAVE CHRISTMAS, by Helen M. Clark. 3 men, 6 women, 2 boys, 2 girls. Plays 30 minutes. Interior set. Christmas is blotted out of a town because of its selfishness when a little old lady comes begging and warns that Christ will not celebrate Christmas in such a place; it is returned years later, when the town repents its selfishness and makes the Christchild supreme. Eldridge, 60¢.

THE TRAGEDY OF JOB, anonymous, adapted by Horace Kallen. 5 men, 3 women or men, chorus. Exterior set. The book of Job arranged as a Greek tragedy, with its basis in the Revised Standard Version of the Bible. Hill & Wang. Royalty: apply to publisher.

THE TRAGICAL HISTORY OF DOCTOR FAUSTUS, by Christopher Marlowe. 36 men (doubling possible), 6 women (doubling possible), 1 boy, extras. Exterior set, interior sets. Multiple staging. The tragedy of Faustus, who sells his soul for twenty-four years of earthly power and delight to Mephistopheles, who collects. A blending of medieval and Elizabethan drama. Washington Square Press. Royalty: none.

TRANSPARENT CURTAIN PAGEANTS FOR CHRISTMAS, by Martha Mixer.

A collection of three pageants for all ages to participate in with beauty and meaning of the season, yet requiring minimum rehearsal. Baker's Plays, $1.25.

TRANSPARENT CURTAIN PAGEANTS FOR EASTER, by Martha Mixer. Three pageants for the Easter season. Baker's Plays, $1.25.

THE TRAVELLER, by Robert Finch. 9 men, 2 women. Plays 25 minutes. Interior set. In a modern treatment of the good Samaritan story a stranger and a holdup man meet at night, and there is disaster. T. S. Denison & Co., 50¢. Royalty: $5.

THE TRAVELLERS, by Rex Frost. 7 men, 4 women. Interior set. At a tavern on the road to Jericho the ruler attempts to convince other travelers to set out with him to seek someone who will change their lives. Only the merchant and the potboy accompany him in the light of the star, to become perhaps the only three wise men in the world. Samuel French, Inc., 60¢. Royalty: $5.

THE TRAVELLING MAN, by Lady Gregory. 1 man, 1 woman, 1 boy. Plays 25 minutes. A mother turns a stranger from her door, resenting the intrusion, only to realize that he was the world's King. Baker's Plays, 60¢. Royalty: $5.

A TREASURY OF CHRISTMAS PLAYS, edited by Sylvia E. Kamerman. Forty modern and traditional one-acts, arranged by age-groups. The Christmas story, fantasies, legends; arranged in groups by age for lower grades through senior high. Plays, Inc., $5.

A TREE ALONE, by Heidy Mayer. 1 boy, 5 girls, extras. The benefits of planting trees are presented in a playlet with a happy tone. Union of American Hebrew Congregations, 25¢.

A TREE IN YOUR LIFE, by Rabbi Leo J. Stillpass. 10 children. Two American children in Israel's Union Forest dream the trees come alive. Singing, dancing the hora included. Union of American Hebrew Congregations, 25¢.

A TREE THEY WANT! by Rabbi Robert I. Kahn. 2 men, 2 women, 1 boy (9), 1 girl (7). The question of Christmas trees in a Jewish home is the subject of a family argument; treatment has both humanity and impact. Union of American Hebrew Congregations, 25¢.

THE TRIAL, by Robert J. Crean. 3 men, 6 women. Plays 30 minutes. The trial of a cloistered nun who is accused of turning her back on her family and the needy in seeking a life of prayer and sacrifice. Very effective reading program. A morality play. Baker's Plays, 60¢. Royalty: $15.

THE TRIAL OF JEANNE D'ARC AND OTHER PLAYS, by Edward Garnett. Collected with letters from noted people referring to the plays published here for the first time. College Book Service, $20.

THE TRIAL OF JESUS, by John Masefield. 20 men, 12 women. Poetic choruses, allegorical figures, and the appearance of Christ himself distinguish this Passion play. Three acts. Baker's Plays, $1. Royalty: $15.

THE TRIAL OF ST. PAUL, by Edward Longstreth. Plays full evening. 1 set. Biblical play. Three acts. Royalty: apply to the author.

THE TRIUMPH OF JOB, by Florence Ryerson. 10 men, 3 women, extras. Plays 40 minutes. 2 sets. An adaptation of the story of Job which strives to compress and clarify contradictory elements while maintaining the beauty and spirit of the original. In *Star Song and Other One-Act Plays.* Samuel French, Inc.: volume, $2; separately, 60¢.

THE TRIUMPH OF THE DEFEATED, by Fred Eastman. 5 men, 14 women. Plays 30 minutes. A pageant involving Paul, Luther, W. L. Garrison, Wagner, Susan B. Anthony, Galileo; presented in symbolic fashion. Samuel French, Inc., 50¢. Royalty: $5.

THE TROUBLE WITH THE CHRISTMAS PRESENTS, by Mary P. Hamlin. 10 men or women. Plays 25 minutes. Interior set. Humorous yet spiritual. Three acts. Samuel French, Inc., 60¢. Royalty: $5.

TURN TO THE EAST, by Karin Asbrand. 7 women. At Christmastime an estranged family is reunited by a group of women working at the church. In *Jumbo Christmas Book.* Baker's Plays, $1.25.

'TWAS THE FIGHT BEFORE CHRISTMAS, by Anne Coulter Martens. 4 men, 4 women. A boy settles a dispute between two families before playing the role of "Brotherly Love" in a church pageant. Comic elements. Eldridge, 60¢.

'TWAS THE NIGHT BEFORE CHRISTMAS, by Lee Hendry. 1 man, 1 woman. Plays 35 minutes. Interior set. Small problems give comedy to this play as two parents prepare for Christmas but do nothing to mar the spirit of peace. The play ends with "Adeste Fidelis" played at midnight. One act. Samuel French, Inc., 60¢. Royalty: $5.

TWELFTH NIGHT AT MOULDERBY HALL, by Gertrude Knevels and Marie N. Van Doren. 8 men, 5 women, extras. Plays 30 minutes. A Twelfth Night revel in sixteenth-century England, depicting all the joy and ceremony of that festive occasion. Baker's Plays, 60¢.

TWELVE ANGRY MEN, by Reginald Rose, adapted by S. Sergel. 15 men or women. Plays full evening. Interior set. A jury room setting for moral and immoral action. Dramatic Publishing Co., 90¢. Royalty: $35.

THE TWELVE DAYS OF CHRISTMAS. 30 men (doubling possible), 28 women. The English Christmas carol dramatized. Plays, Inc., 50¢.

TWELVE DAYS OF CHRISTMAS, by Edna Buttolph and Charlotte Perry. 25–90 children (aged 6–13 or high school students). Musical playlet with pantomime of the old English song. Eldridge, 75¢ (purchase of 5 copies required).

TWELVE MONTHS OF DRAMA FOR THE AVERAGE CHURCH, by Dorothy Clarke Wilson. Short religious plays written for simpleness of production and in fulfillment of a need in religious education, well suited for the Sunday evening service. Baker's Plays, $2.95.

TWENTIETH CENTURY LULLABY, by Cedric Mount. 5 men, 3 women. Plays 30 minutes. The events of a man's life, from birth to death, condensed into one half-hour and told with potent satire and a conclusion of new hope. One act. Baker's Plays, 60¢. Royalty: $3.75.

TWENTY-MINUTE BIBLE PLAYS, by Edna Watson. Eight dramas, appealing and correct biblically. Eldridge, $1.

TWO CEREMONIAL PROGRAMS FOR THANKSGIVING. Ceremonies for church use; simple Thanksgiving presentations. Nat'l. Recreation Assoc., 15¢.

TWO MOTHER'S DAY PROGRAMS, by Jean M. Mattson and Ruth Blackwell. Includes: "Mothers and Daughters Through the Years" (16 actors or fewer, narrator; six scenes. Mothers and daughters are seen through several generations); "Along the Path" (reader, cast of adults or children; verse portrayal of the important events of marriage and motherhood). Baker's Plays, 60¢.

TWO RELIGIOUS DIALOGUES, by J. Paul Faust. Includes: "The Eve of Christmas" (3 readers; organ interludes); "In the Garden, a Cross" (2 readers; organ interludes). For Holy Week. Baker's Plays, 60¢.

TWO SAINTS PLAYS, by Leo Lehman and Robert Gittings. Includes: "Man's Estate," by Robert Gittings; "St. Chad of the Seven Wells," by Leo Lehman. William Heinemann, Ltd.: cloth, 8*s.* 6*d.*; paper, 4*s.* 6*d.*

TWO STRANGERS FROM NAZARETH. 5 men, 5 women. Plays 20 minutes. Interior set. For Christmas. A shepherd, having loaned money to a friend, cannot pay his own taxes. He offers to guide a weary couple to Bethlehem, and his wife fails to understand until she sees the part he is playing in the wondrous events of that night. Plays, Inc., 50¢.

THE TWO-IN-ONE HALLOWEEN-THANKSGIVING BOOK, by various authors. Collection includes sketch "Crusader for the Day" by Helen Ramsey, which concerns Sarah Hale, who worked to nationalize Thanksgiving in the 1850's. Eldridge, 85¢.

UNCLE TOM'S CABIN, by Harriet Beecher Stowe, adapted by George L. Aiken. 21 men (5 Negro), 6 women (4 Negro), 1 boy (Negro), 2 girls (1 Negro). Interior sets, 1 exterior set. A treatment of the famous melodrama with development of character and sympathy for both North and South. Six acts. Samuel French, Inc., 75¢. Royalty: none.

UNDER MILK WOOD, by Dylan Thomas. 17 men, 17 women. Plays full evening. The lives of the residents of a Welsh village are examined in the twenty-four hours of their living. A beautiful verse treatment; has humor, pathos, and an essence of humanity. Samuel French, Inc., $1.35. Royalty: $50–$25.

UNDER ONE ROOF, by Helen Kromer. 3 men, 2 women, 4 children. Plays 30 minutes. Interior set. A good play for home missions. Two Puerto Rican families struggle to improve their condition in a New York apartment house. Difficult characters drawn with sincerity. Friendship Press, 50¢.

THE UNDERTAKING, by Patricia Vought Schneider. 2 men. Plays 30 minutes. A prize-winning satire concerning the problems of burying a prophet. Abingdon Press. Royalty: apply to publisher.

UNERRING INSTINCT, by Thornton Wilder, edited by Annette Smith Lawrence. Prejudice interpreted with originality; using of red, blue, and green lights as symbols. (Included in the same volume is "Haven of the Spirit" by Morrill Denison.) American Unity, $2.

UNITED NATIONS PLAYS AND PROGRAMS, by Aileen Fisher and Olive Rabe. Plays and programs concerning the United Nations for a wide range of ages. Plays, Inc., $3.75.

THE UNLIGHTED CROSS, by Dorothy Clarke Wilson. 6 men, 7 women, 2 boys. Plays 35 minutes. Interior set. Parallel between the necessary contact of electricity and a lighted church cross and of Christ and his church. Baker's Plays, 60¢.

THE UNSEEN HOST, by Percival Wilde. 3 men. Plays 25 minutes. Interior set. A play about a dying French soldier (he does not actually appear) who has seen the angels of Mons. Emphasizes the tragedy of war. One act. Baker's Plays, 60¢. Royalty: $10.

UNTO THE END, by Wilfred Grantham. 6 men, 4 women. Interior set. In an inn outside Jerusalem a rich man, a harlot, a centurion of Rome, Barabbas, and a stranger (who, as a boy, had played with Jesus) react to one another and to the events of the crucifixion. Evans Plays, 2*s*. net. Royalty: 25*s*.

UNTO THE LEAST OF THESE, by Martha Mixer. The king and his court in an old English village come out to see the Christchild, but he passes unnoticed. Unselfish Jan alone finds the Child to take him to those who have need of him. In *Transparent Curtain Pageants for Christmas*. Baker's Plays, $1.25.

UNTO THY DOORS, by Rollin W. Coyle. Narrator, 5 men, 3 women, singing choir (optional), extras (for tableau). Simple to stage. A chorus integrated with the drama is a feature of this short yet effective recounting of the first Christmas. Baker's Plays, 60¢. Royalty: none if 8 copies purchased.

UNTO US, by Claracy L. M. Waldrop. 2 readers. Tableaux tell the Christmas story. Broadman Press, 35¢.

UNTO US A CHILD IS BORN, by Carrington and Rule. 10 men, 2 women, narrator. Pantomime accompanied by a narrator reading the Bible Christmas stories. Abingdon Press, 25¢. Package, 25.

"UNTO US IS BORN—A SAVIOUR," by Paul Simpson McElroy. Cast, 1 to 50. Verse treatment of the Christmas story with inclusion of appropriate music. In *Jumbo Christmas Book*. Baker's Plays, $1.25.

UNTO US THE LIVING, by Harold G. Sliker. Variable cast, 2 choirs (speaking and singing). Tableaux of the dispossessed of today, with commentary added by the choirs. Harper, 50¢. Royalty: $10 if admission is charged; $5 if not.

THE UNVEILING, by Gwendolyn Downes. 12 characters. A mystery play for Christmas. Faith Press, 2*s*.

UNWASHED HANDS, by Pearl Neilson. 8 men, 2 women. Plays 1 hour. Exterior set. Christ's trial, crucifixion, and resurrection, focusing on the guilt of Pilate. Five scenes. Eldridge, 50¢ (purchase of 8 copies required).

THE UPLIFTED CROSS. New incidental music accompanies a dramatic and symbolic Easter pageant. Eldridge, 50¢.

THE UPPER ROOM, by Monsignor R. Hugh Benson. 8 men, 3 women, chorus. A presentation of the Passion with the human emotions involved in it; designed for a stage of limited space. Easy to produce. Three acts. Baker's Plays, 85¢. Royalty: $5.

THE UPROOTED, by Basil Beyea. The problems of itinerant families treated dynamically. Nat'l. Travelers Aid Assoc.: perusal script, $2; kit of 6 acting scripts, $12.

THE VAGABOND, by T. B. Morris. 5 boys, 7 girls (ages 8–17). A little girl, a vagabond and papist in Reformation England, holds her faith and experiences a small miracle in the reuniting of her family and their acceptance of her crippled friend. H. F. W. Deane & Sons, 2*d.*

THE VALIANT, by Holworthy Hall and Robert Middlemass. 5 men, 1 woman. Plays 40 minutes. Interior set. The story of a man's sacrifice so that his sister may keep a memory to love. Very successful, moving. Baker's Plays, 95¢. Royalty: $10.

VALLEY FORGE, by Maxwell Anderson. 32 men, 3 women. Plays full evening. George Washington faces the possibility of defeat with courage at Valley Forge. Samuel French, Inc., $1. Royalty: $25.

THE VELVET GLOVE, by Rosemary Casey. 5 men, 5 women. Interior set. Comedy. The mother superior and others of a convent school hatch a plot to dissuade the bishop from discharging a slightly liberal young teacher. Three acts. Baker's Plays, $1.25. Royalty: $50.

VERBA CRUCIS, by Paul Nagy, Jr. Minister, acolyte, quartet. Plays 30 minutes or longer, depending on music used. A philosophy of life in death in the seven words spoken by Christ. Baker's Plays, 60¢.

VERDICT OF ONE, by Helen Kromer. 11 men, 5 women, 3 men or women. Plays 90 minutes. Edward is found guilty, by implication, of a murder because he did not act to stop the tendency toward it. By manipulation of his denial of God he was helping to make a world where Christ is the only answer, consummate in mass murder. Baker's Plays, 85¢. Royalty: $15.

A VERY COLD NIGHT, by Dennis J. Winnie. 2 men, 1 voice. Plays 10 minutes. Interior set. Two men seated around a warm stove discuss whether they would rise to offer their seats to anyone else. The men represent the thieves crucified with Christ, and his approaching footsteps end this short, effective play. Awarded first prize in the religious plays contest that was sponsored by the Union Theological Seminary, New York City. Baker's Plays, 60¢. Royalty: $5.

A VIEW FROM THE BRIDGE, by Arthur Miller. 9 men, 2 women, extras. A parallel to violent ancient myths; the story of a pair of illegal Sicilian immigrants and a man in love with his orphaned niece, who in turn loves one of the Sicilian boys. The uncle's attempts to separate the lovers lead to violence and death in a play of powerful love, jealousy, desire, and hate. Dramatists Play Service, $1.25. Royalty: $50–$25.

THE VIGIL, by Ladislas Fodor. 18 men, 6 women. Plays 90 minutes. Interior set. In a small-town courtroom, on the night between Good Friday and Easter Sunday, the Easter story is acted out in modern setting. Three acts. Baker's Plays, $1.25. Royalty: $35.

THE VISION, by William Grandgeorge. 7 men, 7 women, carolers (optional). Plays 35 minutes. Interior set. A cobbler announces he has seen a vision, and that Christ promised to visit his shop before Christmas. Has both beauty and a compassionate treatment of the subject. Baker's Plays, 60¢. Royalty: first performance, none; $5 each repeat.

THE VISION OF SIR LAUNFAL, by James Russell Lowell, adapted by Audrey Bradbury. Choral speaking drama. Lowell's poem dramatized. Expression, $1.

THE VISIT, by Friedrich Duerrenmatt, adapted by Maurice Valency. 25 men, 5 women, 2 children. Plays full evening. A rich woman offers a fortune to a town in economic difficulty in return for the life of the man who was responsible for her expulsion from the town years before. Samuel French, Inc., $1.25. Royalty: $50–$25.

THE VOICE OF MOSES, by Elizabeth H. Emerson. 2 men, 3 women. Plays 20 minutes. The conflict between the taking by Moses of a wife not of his race and the refusal and final acceptance of her by his brother and sister. A revelation of the need for generosity and self-sacrifice regardless of race or religion. Based on Numbers 12. McKay's Plays, 85¢. Royalty: $5.

THE VOICE THAT FAILED, by Effa E. Preston. 5 men, 6 women. Plays 20 minutes. Interior set. Solinda, planning for a career as a concert singer, loses her voice when her sister dies. She dedicates herself to hospital aide work, becoming a shining example. One act. T. S. Denison & Co. (purchase of 8 copies required).

VOICES, by Elizabeth T. Shrader. Variable cast. Dramatic worship service. A play of man's suffering and the help of man to man in a universal setting. Baker's Plays, 60¢.

VOICES OF MASS AND CAPITAL A, by James Schevill, music by Andrew Imbrie. 4 men, 3 women. A voice play for concert readings about humanity in the architecture of modern cities. Musical score for piano, flute, double bass and 3 singers. Friendship Press, 75¢. Music available from the composer. Royalty: none if music not used except for broadcast performances. If produced on radio or television apply to author.

THE WAIT, by Marlene Brenner. 6 women. Plays 30 minutes. Interior set. Powerful drama. The good and the bad reveal themselves in a group of women as they wait for news of those buried in a mine disaster. Baker's Plays, 60¢. Royalty: $5.

WAITING FOR GODOT, by Samuel Beckett. 4 men, 1 boy. Two tramps waste their lives waiting for the coming of someone who will explain their lives' meaning, but he never comes. An expression of futility in life without the existence of faith. Grove Press, $1.25. Royalty: $50–$25.

WAKE TO THUNDER, by Don M. Fearleiley. The meaning of Easter to individuals. One act. Broadman Press, 50¢.

THE WAKEFIELD MYSTERY PLAYS, edited by Martial Rose. The entire cycle of thirty-two plays in an acting edition, in language for a modern audience, with notes. Evans Plays, $1.95. Royalty: apply to publisher.

THE WANDERER, by R. H. Ward. Large cast. The story of the human soul wandering through the ages; set in a church. The soul finds that freedom can be won only within itself. Prologue, three acts. Baker's Plays, $1.50. Royalty: $15.

THE WARNING, by Charles J. Ax. Plays 20 minutes. A play for the lenten season in simple language. In *Bible Plays,* Book II, Easter. Fortress Press, 75¢.

A WAY FOR ALL, by Frances Hole Underwood. Large cast. Plays 25 minutes. Interior set. A Nativity story with well-known carols. Uses modern language and some scriptural passages. Baker's Plays, 60¢.

WAY OF THE CROSS, by Karin Asbrand. 5 men, 4 women, angel chorus, children. An Easter pageant of religious nature; may be used with illuminated cross. Includes full instructions. Eldridge, 60¢.

THE WAY OF THE CROSS, by Henri Gheon, translated by Frank de Jonge, foreword by Dom Thomas Becquet, Benedictine monk of Amay. 2 men, 3 women; or 3 men, 3 women. The fourteen stations of the cross revealed by a reciter, and the story of the crucifixion presented by the characters of the Passion. Beautiful when read, or may be staged. In *The Mystery of the Finding of the Cross* (especially written for the Benedictine monks of Amay). Baker's Plays, $1.25 (give author's name when ordering). Royalty: $10 if admission is charged, $5 if not.

THE WAY OF THE CROSS, by Dorothy Clarke Wilson. 8 men, 6 women, 4 children. Plays 40 minutes. A man to whom Easter means little becomes involved with the events of Good Friday and Easter morning, and comes to understand a new meaning of the resurrection. Baker's Plays, 60¢.

THE WAY TO THE KINGDOM, by Barbara Johnson. 3 men, 3 women, extras. A biblical youth drama based upon Christ's raising of the dead daughter of Jairus. Four beggar children, through the promises of the dying Judith and the miracle of her resurrection, feel the power of Christ. Samuel French, Inc., 60¢. Royalty: $5.

WE HAVE SEEN THE LORD, by Forrest G. Walter. Easter cantata in simple vocal style. Eldridge, $1.50. Set of 100 librettos, $3.

THE WEAVERS, by Gerhart Hauptmann. In *Seeds of Modern Drama.* Dell, 75¢.

WEDDING ANNIVERSARY CELEBRATIONS, by Beatrice Plumb. Collection of skits, celebration ideas, etc. T. S. Denison & Co., $2.75.

THE WELL OF DOTHAN, by Frances Blazer. 4 men, 1 woman, 2 boys. Plays 35 minutes. Joseph, the favorite of his father Jacob, is isolated from his brothers by his dreams of kingship. He repents, having learned from his father that a man's life is shaped by the little things he does for good or evil. Baker's Plays, 60¢. Royalty: $10.

THE WELL OF THE SAINTS, by John Millington Synge. 4 men, 3 women, male and female extras. Exterior sets. Irish drama. Martin and Mary, both blind, live happily together until a wandering saint gives them sight; then they separate, embittered with what they see of themselves, one another, and the world. The cure proves temporary. They are reunited, refusing to be cured again so that they may maintain their illusions. In *Complete Plays.* Knopf, $5. Royalty: $25.

WERE YOU THERE? by Harold H. Lytle. Interrogator, reader, 6 witnesses, speech choir of 12–50 voices, singing chorus. Plays 50 minutes. In the Court of Universal Conscience, the interrogator examines six witnesses involved closely with the death of Christ, revealing each in turn. One act. Samuel French, Inc., 60¢. Royalty: apply to publisher.

WERE YOU THERE WHEN THEY CRUCIFIED MY LORD?, by Edith H. Willis and Edith Ellsworth. Narrator, 7 men, solo voice or choir. Plays 1 hour. A New Testament interpretation of the Passion Week events, and of those touched by Christ as he went to the cross. Baker's Plays, 60¢ (give author's name when ordering).

WHAT FAITH CAN DO, by Charles J. Ax. Play of the ministry of Christ. In *Bible Plays,* Book I, Christmas. Fortress Press, 75¢.

WHAT IS THE CHURCH? by Esther B. Stricker. Children, large cast (boys and girls). A class studies the Christian church, its beginning and growth, and finds "What is the church?" to be the most difficult of all the questions. Baker's Plays, 60¢.

WHAT IS THIS THING CALLED CHRISTMAS? by Ormal B. Trick. Large cast. Chancel play. Reader and Christmas music accompanying a play on the meaning of Christmas: "God so loved the world that he gave his only begotten son. . . ." Baker's Plays, 60¢.

WHAT MEN LIVE BY, by Leo Tolstoy, adapted by Virginia Church. 7 men, 3 women, 2 children. Plays 45 minutes. Interior set. Christmas play. An angel is entertained by a Russian shoemaker and his wife without their being aware of his identity, and they learn the three things men live by. Baker's Plays, 60¢. Royalty: $10.

WHAT NEVER DIES? by Percival Wilde. 1 man, 3 women. Plays 40 minutes. Interior set. A play of the heights of love and friendship told with sympathy. Baker's Plays, 60¢. Royalty: $10.

WHAT THINK YE OF CHRIST? by Letitia Hollinshead. 6 men, 6 women, extras. Plays 75 minutes. Exterior set. This play affirms that life will not be all green pastures, and the answer to the title question is to be found only through searching the self. Baker's Plays, 60¢.

WHAT'S CHANUKO WITHOUT A PLAY? by Rabbi Norman Goldburg and Mrs. Rose Goldburg. 5 girls, 5 boys, extras. A class does not want a play. Union of American Hebrew Congregations, 25¢.

WHATSOEVER YE SOW, by Mary S. Hitchcock. 6 men, 6 women. Plays 90 minutes. Exterior set. Set in the time of Christ in Jerusalem, the play deals with the tyranny of young Prince Stephen and has a plot free of all dogma of theology. Three acts. T. S. Denison & Co., 85¢ (purchase of 10 copies required).

WHEN LOVE WAS BORN, by Van Denman Thompson. Plays 40–50 minutes. Christmas cantata of varied musical effects. Has the Van Denman Thompson flavor. Eldridge, $1.50. Set of 100 scripts, $3.

WHEN MAYFLOWERS BLOOMED IN PLYMOUTH, by Margaret Leighton. 2 boys, 3 girls. Plays 15 minutes. Concerns faith as seen in New England. In *Junior High School Plays.* Samuel French, Inc., $1.

WHEN THE DEAD AWAKEN AND THREE OTHER PLAYS, by Henrik Ibsen, translated by Michael Meyer. Doubleday, $1.45.

WHEN THE FIRE DIES, by Ramona Maher. 1 man, 4 women. Interior set. An "Americanized" Indian girl returns home on vacation, and is contemptuous of her surroundings until an old woman tells her that those educated as is she are needed to lead the race from ignorance. Baker's Plays, 60¢. Royalty: $5.

WHEN THE LITTLE ANGELS SANG, by Lillian D. George. 2 men, 3 women, offstage chorus. Plays 25 minutes. Interior set. A Nativity play. A pilgrim is robbed of his gift while going to worship the Christchild, but the thief restores the gift when an angel's song changes his heart. T. S. Denison & Co., 50¢ (purchase of 5 copies required).

WHEN THE STAR SHONE, by Lyman C. Bayard. Large adult cast. Plays 2 hours. Christmas pageant. A beautiful presentation of Christ's birth in Bethlehem. Baker's Plays, 60¢.

WHEN THE SUN RISES, by Dorothy C. Allan. 1 man, 2 women. Plays 15 minutes. Interior set. Tom and Louise are evenly balanced between life and death after an auto accident, and before dawn their fate has a unique resolution; a play of both intensity and beauty. Baker's Plays, 60¢.

WHERE LIES THE CHILD, by Dorothy C. Allan. Play, 2 men, 3 women; pageant, 9 men or women. Plays 40 minutes. Interior set. A fusion of holiday spirit of the modern variety and the pageant lore of Christ's birth. Baker's Plays, 60¢.

WHERE LOVE IS, by Leo Tolstoy, adapted by B. Iden Payne. 4 men, 2 women. Plays 30 minutes. Interior set. From Tolstoy's story; a man's vision and the resulting revelation of truth. Baker's Plays, 60¢. Royalty: $5.

WHERE'S YOUR CHRISTMAS SPIRIT? by Mabel Crouch. 7 women. Plays 15 minutes. Interior set. Four girls making money by decorating homes for Christmas convince disagreeable old Susan Drake to celebrate. T. S. Denison & Co., 50¢ (purchase of 7 copies required).

WHEREVER THE STAR SHINES, by Lucille Ahrens Ward. Large cast of older children, choir optional. Plays 1 hour. The star and the message of its foretelling. Eldridge, 60¢.

WHIRLWIND, by Albert Johnson. 2 men, 1 woman. Bare stage, limited properties. A Drama Trio play. A man's search for meaning and God in his suffering, based on the biblical story of Job. Available in manuscript from author, $1. Royalty: first performance, $10; $5 each repeat.

THE WHIRLWIND, by Dorothy Clarke Wilson. 2 men, 2 women. Plays 30 minutes. Interior set. A challenge to a young surgeon in a delicate operation is the center for a strong temperance play. Baker's Plays, 60¢.

THE WHITE CHRISTMAS, by Walter Ben Hare. 8 men, 7 women, extras. Plays 30 minutes. Interior set. Poetic dialogue, Christmas carols, and scripture readings tell the story of Christ's birth. T. S. Denison & Co., 50¢ (purchase of 10 copies required).

WHITE CHRISTMAS, by Dorothy Clarke Wilson. 4 men, 3 women, 2 girls (small). Plays 40 minutes. Interior set. Missionary play about a wealthy family who give money to foreign missions, but do not give of their hearts. One act. Samuel French, Inc., 60¢.

WHITE THORN AT YULE, by Marion Holbrook. 1 man, 1 woman, 1 boy (12 years). Plays 20 minutes. Interior set. A Christmas play. Parents do not understand their son's self-sacrifice and consider him unworthy of the blessing of the blossoming white thorn, yet later find him blessed among men. Baker's Plays, 60¢.

WHO IS THERE TO ASK? by Henzie Raeburn. 4 men, 3 women, 2 nonspeaking parts. Plays 30 minutes. The search for guidance of an adolescent girl with strong instincts for both good and evil. Baker's Plays, $1.25. Royalty: $10.

WHOSOEVER BELIEVETH, by Lloyd Corrigan. 3 men. Interior set. A maimed youth, clearing after the last supper, can change by faith the hatred of his father but is too late to warn Christ of the betrayal. Baker's Plays, 60¢. Royalty: $5.

WHY THE ANGELS SING FOR JOY, by Virginia A. Meyer. Large cast. Church chancel production of Nativity in scenes: "The Star in the East" (Herod and the Magi), "The Vision" (the shepherd's revelation), "The Adoration" (all gathered about the Holy Family). Baker's Plays, 60¢.

WHY THE CHIMES RANG, by E. A. McFadden. 3 men, 1 woman, extras. For Christmas or general church school production. A play of the divinity and beauty of charity. Baker's Plays, 60¢. Royalty: $5.

WHY THE CHIMES RANG, by Martha Race. Christmas pantomime to accompany the story. Baker's Plays, 35¢.

WHY WEEPEST THOU? by William Duncan. 8 men, 4 women, offstage voices. Plays 40 minutes. No scenery. The story of Joseph of Arimathea and a message of hope. One act. Baker's Plays, 60¢.

THE WIDOW'S MITE, by Karin Asbrand. 14 women. A child gives meaning to a rummage sale by being its most-wanted article. Original. A missionary or church play in one act. Eldridge, 60¢ (purchase of 10 copies required).

THE WILD DUCK, by Henrik Ibsen, translated by Una Ellis-Fermor. 9 men, 3 women. Interior sets. A man's attempt at destroying the illusions of another leads to the death of a girl. An examination of illusion, social conscience, and humanity. In *Three Plays by Ibsen*. Penguin Books. Royalty: apply to publisher.

WILD WEST PURIM, by Helen Fine, music by Dr. Moses Eisenberg. 7 boys, 1 girl, male and female extras. Plays 35 minutes. Children's Purim play. American cowboys in Shushan by mistake rescue Queen Esther and give Haman what's coming to him. Fun, songs, and a message. Union of American Hebrew Congregations, 75¢.

THE WILLING SPIRIT, by Nelle A. Holt. Large cast, many small parts for men and women. Plays 1 hour. Interior set. Stewardship play of the responsibilities of church members to maintain the church, told through a family. May be sectioned for rehearsal. Baker's Plays, 60¢.

WINDOWS OF CHRISTMAS, by Ruth W. Kelsey and Margaret Joy. 3 boys, 4 girls, extras. Christmas operetta. Three unhappy children learn from old and new cards come to life the meaning of Christmas. Baker's Plays, $1.50 (purchase of 12 copies required).

WINTERSET, by Maxwell Anderson. 14 men, 4 women, extras. 2 interior sets. Contrast of love, revenge, and guilt in a verse-play set in the New York slums. A young man seeks the real killer for whose crime his father was executed, and finds something more important. Dramatists Play Service, $1.25. Royalty: $25.

THE WISE AND THE FOOLISH VIRGINS, by R. H. Ward. 2 men, 15 women. A modern interpretation of the parable; the seekers are a parson, a publican, a domestic, a postoffice worker, and a factory worker. Worthwhile. Religious Drama Society of Great Britain, 50¢. Royalty: apply to publisher.

THE WISE HAVE NOT SPOKEN, by Paul Vincent Carroll. 12 men, 2 women. A young radical and a priest who stands against violence clash in a play of Irish spiritual life. Dramatists Play Service, $1. Royalty: $25.

THE WISE MEN AT THE WELL, by Esther Willard Bates. The Holy Family, 3 men, 1 girl, 6 children. The little stars, child angels, provide water for the wise men at a dry well while they sleep during their quest. Tableaux optional. Baker's Plays, 60¢. Royalty: $5.

WITCH'S BREW, by Dorothy Macardle. 2 men, 4 women. Plays 30 minutes. Interior set. Set in Ireland in early Christian times. Both the power of God and the pagan powers of a witch girl are invoked to aid a sick woman. Terror, insanity, and hatred rule the hut until the power of God is triumphant over the evil of the witch. Baker's Plays, 60¢. Royalty: $5.

WITH MALICE TOWARD NONE. 4 men, 3 women. Plays 30 minutes. Interior set. For junior and senior high ages. President Lincoln learns that the charitable words of his second Inaugural Address, much denounced by Washington officialdom, have been hailed by many Americans. Plays, Inc., 50¢.

WITH NO RESERVATIONS, by John W. Felton. 5 men, 3 women, 3 kings. Plays 30 minutes. Interior set. Events paralleling Christ's birth, with the arrival of two Cuban refugees, the wife expecting a child, bring the Christmas spirit to a lodge in Florida. Baker's Plays, 60¢. Royalty: $5.

WITHOUT FEAR OR FAVOR. 5 readers. Plays 30 minutes. Immigration and citizenship problems are presented in this volume. Anti-Defamation League of B'nai B'rith, 10¢.

THE WITNESS, by James Brock. 7 men, organist, singer. An allegory of the future which projects the major themes of Advent, the second coming of Christ at the last judgment. In *Modern Chancel Dramas*. Eldridge, $1.25. Royalty: $10.

WITNESS TO THE TRUTH, by five churchmen, edited by the Rev. Henry Sears Sizer, Jr. A Reformation Day service, tracing the pattern of the development of Protestant freedom through the Reformation by focusing on historical characters important to the development. Baker's Plays, 60¢. Royalty: $10.

THE WOMEN AT THE TOMB, by Michel de Ghelderode, translated by George Hauger. 1 man, 11 women. Interior set. The women involved in Christ's life, as well as in the lives of Pilate and Judas, gather in a small house on the evening of the day of Christ's death. In *Ghelderode: Seven Plays.* Samuel French, Inc., $1.95. Royalty: $10.

THE WOMEN AT THE TOMB, by Michel de Ghelderode, translated by Gabriel Smit. 4 women. Plays 20 minutes. An Easter play in verse. In *Ghelderode: Seven Plays.* Netherlands Centre of the Internat'l. Theatre Institute, $1.95. Royalty: $10.

THE WOMEN OF CHRISTMAS, by Claudia Moholy-Nagy. 7 women. The traditional Christmas story set against a background of well-known hymns and carols, with a modern touch in costuming. Baker's Plays, 60¢.

WOMEN OF JESUS' TIME, by Beulah Squires. All-women casts. Contains eleven playlets, including: "Mary, the Mother of Jesus," "One Who Loved Much," "Go . . . Tell," and others. Eldridge, 85¢.

WOMEN OF THE BIBLE, by Walter Ben Hare. Flexible cast. Plays 1 hour. The heroines of the Bible: the Virgin Mary, Rebecca, Sarah, Miriam, the widow of Nain; and Adah, Electra, Ruth, Martha, and Esther—the five points of the eastern star. Appropriate for Eastern Star chapters. Baker's Plays, 60¢.

WONDERFUL WORLD, by Mona Swann. For small children; particularly good in church school. French, Negro, English, Indian, and Rumanian legends. Expression, $1.

THE WOODCARVER, by Morris Brown. 4 men, 4 women. When a man produces a figure of Christ that horrifies those around him, family crisis resolves the conflict. An unusual, yet simple, presentation. Evans Plays, $1.25 plus postage. Royalty: $35–$25.

THE WOODSHED, by L. E. Preston. 3 men, 3 women. Plays 30 minutes. Interior set. Characters imprisoned by guilt and frustration are released from the woodshed only when they repent and face their futures. Baker's Plays, 60¢. Royalty: $5.

THE WORD, by Kaj Munk, translated by R. P. Keigwin. 7 men, 6 women, 2 children, extras. 2 interior sets. In a peasant family the struggle between reason and pure faith comes to its conclusion when a mad son regains his sanity. He alone is able to restore the life of a brother's wife through unmoving faith in God's goodness. In *Five Plays by Kaj Munk.* American-Scandinavian Foundation. Royalty: apply to publisher.

WORD MADE FLESH, by P. W. Turner. Carol service for Christmas, utilizing the entire church assemblage. "This Is the Word" is included. Baker's Plays, $1.25. Royalty: $2.

THE WORKMAN, by George Reynolds. 4 men, 5 women. The sound judgments of a man who reveals himself as being "just a carpenter" settle a threatening strike. Evans Plays, 2*s.* net. Royalty: 25*s.* each performance.

THE WORLD IS IN BETHLEHEM, by Francis Fowler Allen. 3 men, 2 women, 2 children, 2 offstage voices. Plays 30 minutes. A pageant centered on a family living in Bethlehem at the time of Christ's birth. Abingdon Press, 25¢. Package, 25. Set of 12 scripts, $2.50.

THE WORLD IS ROUND, by Armand Salacrou, translated by James H. Clancy. 12 men, 5 women, 4 boys (ages 10–15). Exterior set, interior sets. A play of the man Savonarola, and of the conflict of dedication to the spirit and dedication to the things of the earth. Apply to the translator. Royalty: $35.

WORLD MOTHER, by Gemma D'Auria. 2 men, 1 woman. Bare stage. Women are called upon to save the world through better motherhood. Baker's Plays, 60¢. Royalty: $5.

THE WORLD TOMORROW, by Esther C. Averill. 2 men, 1 woman, 1 boy, 2 girls. Plays 30 minutes. Interior set. A play for high school students. A look at future postwar days when peace will be the subject most talked about. One act. Baker's Plays, 60¢.

THE WORLD WE LIVE IN, by Josef and Karen Capek, adapted and arranged by Owen Davis. 21 men, 9 women (extras). Plays full evening. A man attaches human characteristics to dream insects in this somewhat bitter satire of man and his institutions; the insects come to vie with mankind for supremacy. Samuel French, Inc., $1.25. Royalty: $25–$20.

WORLD WITHOUT END, by Albert Johnson. Plays 2 hours. A choric drama in two acts. The modern quest for faith shown in an interpretation of the theme of the Passion. Baker's Plays, 75¢. Royalty: apply to publisher.

WORLD'S GREAT PLAYS, edited by George Jean Nathan. A collection of seven plays, including: "Faust" by Johann Wolfgang von Goethe; "The Emperor Jones" by Eugene O'Neill; "The Plough and the Stars" by Sean O'Casey; "The Master Builder" by Henrik Ibsen. World, $3.75.

WORSHIP PROGRAMS AND STORIES FOR YOUNG PEOPLE, by Alice A. Bays. A worship book for youth. Themes accompanied by music, hymns, poems, stories, etc. Baker's Plays, $3.50.

WORSHIP PROGRAMS FOR INTERMEDIATES, by Alice A. Bays. Adaptable programs for groups of intermediates, relating religion to life. Baker's Plays, $2.50.

X = O (or A NIGHT OF THE TROJAN WAR), by John Drinkwater. 5 men. Plays 45 minutes. Exterior sets. A poetic treatment of war's futility and tragedy. Samuel French, Inc. Royalty: apply to publisher.

YE SHALL BE MY PEOPLE, by Fred Eastman, music selected by C. Harold Einecke. 2 narrators, 12 nonspeaking parts, choir, extras. A brotherhood pageant designed to be presented with no more furnishings than those of the usual chancel. Baker's Plays, 60¢.

THE YEARS AHEAD, by Elliot Field. 5 men, 4 women, extras. Plays 1 hour. Interior set. A young man chooses between business and missionary work; play portrays the missionary hopes of youth and the question of the parent's influence in a young person's decisions. One act. Baker's Plays, 60¢.

THE YORK CYCLE OF MYSTERY PLAYS, by J. S. Purvis. A collection of forty-nine plays of the medieval cycle, containing a historical reflection of the views of common people, profound religious feeling, and genuine beauty; revived in production for two years by the York Festival Society in Britain. Baker's Plays, $5.50. Royalty: apply to publisher.

THE YORK NATIVITY, by John F. Baird. 15 men, 2 women. Plays 30 minutes. The six plays from the York miracle cycle that form the Nativity story, from the appearance of the angel to Mary through the flight into Egypt. Needs simplicity of production. Samuel French, Inc., 60¢. Royalty: $5.

THE YORK NATIVITY PLAY, arranged by E. Martin Browne. 12 men, 5 women. Dignity, humility, and reality of characterization are distinctive of this play from the fourteenth-century York cycle. Baker's Plays, 85¢. Royalty: $15.

YOU NEVER TOLD ME, by Nora Stirling. What to say and do about sex and venereal disease is the question parents and youth face in this play. Bureau of Public Health Education. (Write publisher for free scripts, in limited supply.)

YOUNG PRINCE OF GLORY, by Joan Brockelsby. Large cast. The Christmas story as seen by the angels, ending at the stable, with a foreshadowing of the Child's life. Baker's Plays, $1. Royalty: $5.

THE YOUNG STRANGER, by Eileen Arthurton. For advanced intermediate and junior age-groups. Religious Drama Society of Great Britain. Royalty: apply to publisher.

YOUR CHURCH AND MINE, by Esther Averill. 4 men, 4 women. Plays 35 minutes. Interior set. A man, through his wife's efforts and a dream, learns the importance of an alliance with the church. Baker's Plays, 60¢.

YOUR TOWN AND MINE, by Robert Ray. 7 men, 7 women. A pastor conflicts with the wealthy minority that controls the finances of his church. Right is triumphant in the end. T. S. Denison & Co., $1. Royalty: $10.

THE YOUTH BOLIVAR. A play for lower and middle grades that tells customs and facts of Venezuela; excellent for world friendship. Plays, Inc., 35¢.

YOUTH PROGRAMS FOR SPECIAL OCCASIONS, by Ruth Schroeder. A collection of thirty-five worship programs for holidays and special church events; includes preludes, prayers, scriptures, etc. Ideal for youth leaders. Eldridge, $3.

YOUTH SERVES THE CHURCH, by Karin Asbrand. 14 girls. Plays 10 minutes. Interior set. A group of young people are convinced by attending church activities that they are not dull, and become church members. In *Easy Church Plays for Women and Girls.* Baker's Plays, $1.25.

THE ZEAL OF THY HOUSE, by Dorothy Sayers. In *Religious Drama 1.* Meridian Books, $1.45.

THE ZOO STORY, by Edward Albee. 2 men. A bitter and ironic play about the inability of man to communicate. With Albee's "The Sandbox." Dramatists Play Service, $1.25. Royalty: $25.

addresses

PUBLISHERS

Abingdon Press
201 Eighth Ave. South
Nashville, Tenn. 37202

Accent
Box 102, University Station
Urbana, Ill. 61801

Allen & Unwin, Ltd.
40 Museum St.
London, W.C.1, England

American Assoc. of Retired Persons
Dupont Building
1346 Connecticut Ave.
Washington, D.C. 20006

American Hospital Assoc.
840 N. Lake Shore Dr.
Chicago, Ill. 60611

American Nat'l. Red Cross
General Supply Office
Washington, D.C. 20006

American Public Welfare Assoc.
1313 E. 60th St.
Chicago, Ill. 60637

American Theatre Wing, Inc.
531 W. 48th St.
New York, N.Y. 10036

American Unity
1123 Broadway
New York, N.Y. 10010

American-Scandinavian Foundation
127 E. 73rd St.
New York, N.Y. 10021

Anchor Books
see Doubleday & Co.

Anti-Defamation League of B'nai B'rith
315 Madison Ave.
New York, N.Y. 10016

Art Craft Play Co.
P.O. Box 1830
Cedar Rapids, Iowa

Association Films
600 Grand Ave.
Ridgefield, N.J. 07657

Association Press
291 Broadway
New York, N.Y. 10007

Augsburg Publishing House
426 S. Fifth St.
Minneapolis, Minn. 55415

Baker's Plays
100 Summer St.
Boston, Mass. 02110

Bank Street College of Education
69 Bank St.
New York, N.Y. 10014

Banner Play Bureau, Inc.
619 Post St.
San Francisco, Calif. 94109

Bantam Books, Inc.
271 Madison Ave.
New York, N.Y. 10016

Barron's Educational Series, Inc.
113 Crossways Park Dr.
Woodbury, N.Y. 11797

The Bethany Press
Box 179, 2640 Pine Blvd.
St. Louis, Mo. 63166

Bison Books
University of Nebraska Press
Lincoln, Neb. 68508

The Board of Parish Education
Lutheran Church-Missouri Synod
3558 S. Jefferson Ave.
St. Louis, Mo. 63118

The Bodley Head, Ltd.
9 Bow St.
London, W.C.2, England

Boosey and Hawkes, Inc.
30 W. 57th St.
New York, N.Y. 10019

Brandt & Brandt
101 Park Ave.
New York, N.Y. 10017

George Braziller, Inc.
1 Park Ave.
New York, N.Y. 10016

Broadman Press
127 Ninth Ave. North
Nashville, Tenn. 37203

Brooklyn Bureau of Social Service and Children's Aid Society
285 Schermerhorn St.
Brooklyn, N.Y. 11217

Bureau of Public Health Education
New York City Dept. of Health
125 Worth St.
New York, N.Y. 10003

The Cambridge Co.
8949 Sunset Strip
Hollywood, Calif. 90069

Chicago Review
Faculty Exchange, University of Chicago
Chicago, Ill. 60637

Child Welfare League of America
44 E. 23rd St.
New York, N.Y. 10010

Children's Theatre Press
Cloverlot
Anchorage, Ky.

Christian Board of Publication
Box 179, 2640 Pine Blvd.
St. Louis, Mo. 63166

Coach House Press
53 W. Jackson Blvd.
Chicago, Ill. 60604

Cokesbury Press
85 McAllister St.
San Francisco, Calif. 94102

College Book Service, Inc.
40-A S. Bayles Ave.
Port Washington, L.I., N.Y. 11050

William Collins, Ltd.
14 St. James Place
London, S.W.1, England

Concordia Publishing House
3558 S. Jefferson Ave.
St. Louis, Mo. 63118

Constable & Co., Ltd.
10–12 Orange St.
London, W.C.2, England

Crown Publishers, Inc.
419 Park Ave., South
New York, N.Y. 10016

Curtis Brown, Ltd.
60 E. 56th St.
New York, N.Y. 10022

Daamen, Ltd.
Koninginnegracht 26 (P. B. Fg)
The Hague, Netherlands

H. F. W. Deane & Sons, Ltd.
31 Museum St.
London, W.C.1, England

Dell Publishing Co., Inc.
750 Third Ave.
New York, N.Y. 10017

T. S. Denison & Co., Inc.
5100 W. 82nd St.
Minneapolis, Minn. 55431

Dent & Sons, Ltd.
Aldine House, 10–13 Bedford St.
London, W.C.2, England

Dodd, Mead & Co.
79 Madison Ave.
New York, N.Y. 10016

Doubleday & Co., Inc.
277 Park Ave.
New York, N.Y. 10017

Dover Publications, Inc.
180 Varick St.
New York, N.Y. 10014

Dramatic Publishing Co.
86 E. Randolph St.
Chicago, Ill. 60601

Dramatists Play Service, Inc.
440 Park Ave. South
New York, N.Y. 10016

Gerald Duckworth & Co., Ltd.
3 Henrietta St.
London, W.C.2, England

E. P. Dutton & Co., Inc.
201 Park Ave. South
New York, N.Y. 10003

Eldridge Publishing Co.
Franklin, Ohio 45005 and Denver Colo. 80203

English-Speaking Union
37 Charles St., Berkley Square
London, W.1, England

English Theatre Guild, Ltd.
52 Dean St.
London, W.1, England

Episcopal Society for Cultural and Racial Unity
5 Forsyth St., N.W.
Atlanta, Ga. 30303

Evans Plays
500 E. 77th St.
New York, N.Y. 10021

Everyman's Theatre
152 W. 42nd St.
New York, N.Y. 10036

Expression Co.
Magnolia, Mass. 01930

Faber & Faber, Ltd.
24 Russell Square
London, W.C.1, England

The Faith Press, Ltd.
7 Tufton St.
London, S.W.1, England

Family Service Assoc. of America
44 E. 23rd St.
New York, N.Y. 10010

Fortress Press
2900 Queen Lane
Philadelphia, Pa. 19129

Samuel French, Inc.
7623 Sunset Blvd.
Hollywood, Calif.
or
25 W. 45th St.
New York, N.Y. 10036

Friends Book and Supply House
101 Quaker Hill Dr.
Richmond, Ind.

Friendship Press
475 Riverside Dr.
New York, N.Y. 10027

Golden Quill Press
Francestown, N.H. 03043

Goodman Memorial Theatre
Michigan Ave. at Adams St.
Chicago, Ill.

H. W. Gray Co.
159 East 48th St.
New York, N.Y. 10017

Grove Press, Inc.
80 University Place
New York, N.Y. 10003

Harcourt, Brace & World, Inc.
757 Third Ave.
New York, N.Y. 10017

Harper & Row
49 East 33rd St.
New York, N.Y. 10016

George G. Harrap & Co., Ltd.
182 High Holborn
London, W.C.1, England

Hawthorn Books, Inc.
70 Fifth Ave.
New York, N.Y. 10011

Health and Welfare Division, Metropolitan Life Insurance Co.
1 Madison Ave.
New York, N.Y. 10010

Health Education Unit, Heart Disease Control Program
Public Health Service, Dept. of Health, Education, and Welfare
Washington, D.C. 20201

Heinemann Educational Books, Ltd.
48 Charles St., Mayfair
London, W.1, England

William Heinemann, Ltd.
15/16 Queen St., Mayfair
London, W.1, England

The Heuer Publishing Co.
Dows Bldg.
Cedar Rapids, Iowa 52401

Abel Heywood & Son, Ltd.
The White House, Lever St.
Manchester 1, England

Hill & Wang, Inc.
141 Fifth Ave.
New York, N.Y. 10010

Holt, Rinehart & Winston, Inc.
383 Madison Ave.
New York, N.Y. 10017

Horn Book, Inc.
585 Boylston St.
Boston, Mass. 02116

Houghton Mifflin Co.
2 Park St.
Boston, Mass. 02107

Independent Press, Ltd.
Livingstone House, 11 Carteret St.
London, S.W.1, England

Kansas Magazine
Kansas State University
Manhattan, Kan. 66502

Alfred A. Knopf, Inc.
501 Madison Ave.
New York, N.Y. 10022

Librarie Gallimard
5 Rue Sebastien-Bottin
Paris VII, France

Little, Brown and Co.
34 Beacon St.
Boston, Mass. 02106

Longmans, Green & Company, Inc.
48 Grosvenor Street
London, W.1, England

Lutheran Student Assoc. of America
327 S. La Salle St.
Chicago, Ill. 60604

The Macmillan Co.
866 Third Ave.
New York, N.Y. 10022

McKay's Plays, David McKay Co., Inc.
750 Third Ave.
New York, N.Y. 10017

Mentor Press
360 W. 23rd St.
New York, N.Y. 10011

Meridian Books, Inc.
see World Publishing Co.

Mermaid Dramabooks
see Hill & Wang, Inc.

Methuen & Co., Ltd.
11 New Fetter Lane
London, E.C.4, England

J. Garnet Miller, Ltd.
13 Tottenham St.
London, W.1, England

Modern Library, Inc.
see Random House

Moody Press
820 N. La Salle St.
Chicago, Ill. 60610

William Morrow & Co. Inc.
425 Park Ave. South
New York, N.Y. 10016

Nat'l. Assoc. for Mental Health, Inc.
10 Columbus Circle
New York, N.Y. 10019

Nat'l. Conference of Christians and Jews
43 W. 57th St.
New York, N.Y. 10019

Nat'l. Council of Churches
Office of Publication and Distribution
120 E. 23rd St.
New York, N.Y. 10010

Nat'l. Council on Crime and Delinquency
44 E. 23rd St.
New York, N.Y. 10010

Nat'l. Council on Homemaker Service
1790 Broadway
New York, N.Y. 10019

Nat'l. Recreation Assoc.
8 W. Eighth St.
New York, N.Y. 10011

Nat'l. Travelers Aid Assoc.
44 E. 23rd St.
New York, N.Y. 10010

Netherlands Centre of the International Theatre Institute
Noordeinde 130
The Hague, Netherlands

New Directions
order from J. B. Lippincott
E. Washington Square
Philadelphia, Pa. 19105

Northwestern Press
see T. S. Denison & Co., Inc.

Odyssey Press, Inc.
55 Fifth Ave.
New York, N.Y. 10003

Oxford University Press, Inc.
200 Madison Ave.
New York, N.Y. 10016

Pageant Publishers
59 Fourth Ave.
New York, N.Y. 10003

Pelican Books
see Penguin Books, Inc.

Penguin Books, Inc.
3300 Clipper Mill Road
Baltimore, Md. 21211

Pilgrim Press
see United Church Press

Pioneer Drama Service
Cody, Wyo. 82414

Plays for Living
see Family Service Assoc. of America

Plays, Inc.
8 Arlington St.
Boston, Mass. 02116

Princeton University Press
Princeton, N.J. 08540

Random House, Inc.
457 Madison Ave.
New York, N.Y. 10022

Register Press
Yarmouth Port, Mass. 02675

Henry Regnery Co.
114 W. Illinois St.
Chicago, Ill. 60610

Religious Drama Society of Great Britain
166 Shaftesbury Ave.
London, W.C.2, England

Religious Education Press, Ltd.
85 Manor Road, Wallington
Surrey, England

Ruskin House
40 Museum St.
London, W.C.1, England

Rutgers University Press
30 College Ave.
New Brunswick, N.J. 08903

St. Anthony Guild Press
508 Marshall St.
Paterson, N.J. 07503

G. Schirmer, Inc.
609 Fifth Ave.
New York, N.Y. 10017

Charles Scribner's Sons
597 Fifth Ave.
New York, N.Y. 10017

The Seabury Press, Inc.
815 Second Ave.
New York, N. Y. 10017

Sheed and Ward, Inc.
64 University Place
New York, N.Y. 10003

The Sheldon Press
Holy Trinity Church
Marylebone Road
London, N.W.1, England

SPCK
Holy Trinity Church
Marylebone Road
London, N.W.1, England

Standard Publishing Co.
8121 Hamilton Ave.
Cincinnati, Ohio 45231

Theatrework, Ltd.
22 Hans Road
London, S.W.3, England

Union of American Hebrew Congregations
Publications Dept.
838 Fifth Ave.
New York, N.Y. 10021

United Church Press
1505 Race St.
Philadelphia, Pa. 19102

United Community Funds and Councils of America
345 E. 46th St.
New York, N.Y. 10017

The United Presbyterian Church in the U.S.A.
475 Riverside Dr.
New York, N.Y. 10027

University of California Press
Berkeley, Calif. 94720

University of Chicago Press
5750 Ellis Ave., Chicago, Ill. 60637

The Viking Press
625 Madison Ave.
New York, N.Y. 10022

Vocational Rehabilitation Administration
U.S. Dept of Health, Education, and Welfare
Washington, D.C. 20525

Washington Square Press, Inc.
630 Fifth Ave.
New York, N.Y. 10020

Welfare Administration
U.S. Dept. of Health, Education and Welfare
Washington, D.C. 20201

Wetmore Declamation Bureau
1631 S. Paxton St.
Sioux City, Iowa 51106

W. A. Wilde Co.
10 Huron Drive
Natick, Mass. 01760

The World Publishing Co.
2231 W. 110th St.
Cleveland, Ohio 44102

Yale University Press
149 York St.
New Haven, Conn. 06511

AUTHORS AND AGENTS

Walt Anderson
115 W. 86th St.
New York, N.Y. 10024

Elizabeth Berryhill
2938 Magnolia St.
Berkeley, Calif. 94705

Mrs. W. A. Bradley
18 Quai de Bethune
Paris 4, France

James H. Clancy
Dept. of English, Dartmouth University
Hanover, N.H. 03755

Kurt Hellmer
52 Vanderbilt Ave.
New York, N.Y. 10017

Miriam Howell
c/o Ashley Famous Agency, Inc.
1301 Ave. of the Americas
New York, N.Y. 10019

Andrew Imbrie
Music Dept., University of California
Berkeley, Calif. 94704

Albert Johnson
Drama Dept., University of Redlands
Redlands, Calif. 92373

Margot Johnson Agency
405 E. 54th St.
New York, N.Y. 10022

Lucy Kroll
119 W. 57th St.
New York, N.Y. 10019

Maxim Lieber
489 Fifth St.
New York, N.Y. 10009

Edward Longstreth
P.O. Box 736
La Jolla, Calif.

Amy Goodhue Loomis
Vincennes University
Vincennes, Ind. 47591

Margaret Mayoraga
16 Berwick Road
Newton Centre, Mass. 02159

Edna Means Dramatic Service
610 Harmon St.
Tama, Iowa 52339

Mercury Theatre, Ltd.
2 Ladbroke Road
London, W.1, England

Margaret Ramsay
14 Goodwin Court
London, W.C.2, England

Peters & Ramsay
14 Goodwin Court
London, W.C.2, England

Janet Roberts
Ashley Famous Agency, Inc.
1301 Ave. of the Americas
New York, N.Y. 10019

James Schevill
Poetry Center
San Francisco, Calif. 94127

Miss R. J. L. Spalding
see English-Speaking Union

Madame Ninon Tallon-Karlweis
57 W. 58th St.
New York, N.Y. 10019

Margery Vosper, Ltd.
53a Shaftesbury Ave.
London, W.1, England

Ann Watkins, Inc.
77 Park Ave.
New York, N.Y. 10016

Annie Laurie Williams, Inc.
18 E. 41st St.
New York, N.Y. 10017

subject index

BIBLICAL PLAYS

Abraham and Isaac 1
Abraham, Friend of God 1
And He Came to His Father 4
Apple Tree, The 6
At the Well of Bethlehem 7
Athaliah 7

Beautiful Queen, The 9
Before the Flood 9
Bible Character Impersonations 12
Bible Characters in Action 12
Bible Comes Alive, The 12
Bible Plays 12
Bible Plays for Children 12
Bible Plays for Juniors 12
Bible Plays for Small Children 12
Bible Women Come Alive 12
Book of Job, The 14
Book of Job as a Greek Tragedy, The 14
Boy David, The 15
Boy Who Carved Birds, The 15
Business of Good Government, The 17

Cain 18
Captivity 19
Certain Man Had Two Sons, A 21
Children Hear About Easter, The 22
Children of the Bible 23
Coat of Many Colors, The 32

Daniel and the Tempter 36
David 37
David, a Trilogy 37
David and Jonathan 37
Day of Hope, The 37
Deborah 38
Discovery Bible Plays, The 40
Dream of Queen Esther, A 41

Easy Bible Pantomimes 43
Easy Bible Story Dramatizations for Children 43
Elijah, the Firebrand of the Almighty 45
Endor 45
Esther 46

Far Country, The 49
Father, The 49
Finger Plays and How to Use Them 50
First Christmas, The 50
First Corinthians 50
First Miracle, The 51
Firstborn, The 51
Fishers of Men 51
Five Plays 51
Five Virgins, The 51
Flowering Peach, The 52
Flowering Staff, The 52
Follow Thou Me 52
For He Had Great Possessions 52
Fulfillment of the Law, The 54

Gallant Queen 54
Garden, The 54
Giant Killer 55
Gift, The 55
Go Down Moses 56
Good Little Servant 57
Good Soldier, A 57
Great Refusal, The 58
Greater Than Gold 58
Green Pastures, The 59

He Came Seeing 60
He Lives 61
Holy City, The 63

Isaiah, the Statesman Prophet 69
It Came to Pass 69
It Should Happen to a Dog 69

Jericho Road 70
Jericho Road and Other Miracle Plays 70
Jochabed's Sacrifice 70
John 71
Jonah 71
Joseph and His Brothers 71
Journey to Jerusalem 71

King Saul and the Witch of Endor 73
King Shall Reign!, A 73

Let Justice Be Done 75
Light, The 76
Lonely Road 79
Lost Book, The 79
Lost Crown, The 80
Lost People, The 80
Love of Ruth, The 80

Man Born to Be King, The 82
Martha and Mary 83
Mary Magdalene 83
Mary of Magdala 83
Match for the Devil, A 84
Metamorphosis 85
Mighty Hunter, The 86
Moses, the Lawgiver 88
Mother of All Living 88

Never Too Late 90
New Testament Mimes 90
Noah 92
Noah's Flood 92
Noye's Fludde 93

Oaks of Mamre 93
Old Testament Plays 94
Onesimus 96

Pageant of Our Lady 98
Past and Present, Three Short Plays 99
Paul at Corinth 99
Paul at Damascus 99
Paul Before King Agrippa 99
Paul in the Areopagus at Athens 99
Peter at Pentecost 101
Philip, the Desert Evangelist 101
Pilgrims of the Way 102
Plays from the Bible 104
Potter's Field, The 105
Prodigal Son, The 106
Prodigal Son Comes Home, The 106
Promised Ones, The 106
Puppets and Bible Plays 107

Return of the Prophets, The 109
Rock, The 111
Runaway Slave, The 112
Ruth 112

Sacrifice of Isaac, The 112
Sanctuary 113
Shadow of a Cross 117
Simon the Leper 119
Slave Maid of Israel, The 120
Sleep of Prisoners, A 120
So the Blind May See 121
Son of Stephen 122
Stephen, the First Martyr 124
Steward's Daughter, The 124
Story of Jeremiah, The 125
Stumbling Block, The 126

They That Sit in Darkness 129
This Is the Word 130
This Rock 130
To You a Saviour 134
Tobias and Sara 134
Tragedy of Job, The 135
Trial of St. Paul, The 136
Triumph of Job, The 137
Twenty-minute Bible Plays 138

Voice of Moses, The 141

Way to the Kingdom, The 142
Well of Dothan, The 142
What Faith Can Do 143

CHRISTMAS PLAYS

Abingdon Christmas Programs 1
Adeste Fideles 2
Adoration, The 2
Adoration of the Kings and Shepherds, The 2
Alias Santa Claus 2
All Aboard for Christmas 2
American Christmas, An 3
Among Those Presents 3
And a Song Was Born 4
And Lo, the Star 4
And Myrrh 4
And So They Came to Bethlehem 4
And Such a King 4
And There They Found Christ 4
And There Were Shepherds 4
And Usher in the Morning 4
Angel Child 5
Angel in Repair 5
Angel in the Looking Glass 5
Another Easy Christmas Book 5
Answer Is Christmas, The 6
Arise, Thy Light Is Come 7
Artaban, the Story of the Other Wise Man 7
At the Inn 7
Aunt Sabriny's Christmas 8

Back to Bethlehem 8

Bang! Goes Christmas 8
Because We Believe 9
Bed of Hay 9
Before the Sun Arose 9
Beggars' Charity 9
Beginning of the Way 10
Beside the Manger 10
Best Christmas Pantomimes 10
Best Part of Christmas, The 11
Best Selections for Christmas 11
Bethlehem 11
Bethlehem Road, The 11
Bethlehem's Field 11
"Better Yet" Christmas Book, The 11
Big Book of Christmas, The 12
Big Christmas Book, The 13
Birds' Christmas Carol, The 13
Birth of the Song "Silent Night," The 13
Birthday of a King, The 13
Birthday Through the Centuries, A 13
Blessed Nativity 14
Blue Overalls Angel, The 14
Boarding House Christmas, A 14
Born in a Manger 15
Bundle-o'-Cheer Christmas Book, The 17

Calling All Christmases 18
Cancelled Debt, The 18
Candle in the Window, The 18
Candlelighting Service for Christmas and New Year Season, A 19
Canticle of the Nativity, A 19
Carol of the World, The 19
Case of the Silent Caroler, The 20
Catching Up with Christmas 20
Celebrating Christmas 20
Certain Star, A 21
Child for a King, A 22
Child Is Born, A 22
Child of Peace, The 22
Children of the Inn, The 23
Children's Program Book, The 23
Children's Vision, The 23
Chimes on the Hilltop 23
Christ-Child, The 24
Christmas and the Four Freedoms 24
Christmas Angel, The 24
Christmas Angels, The 24
Christmas Apple, The 24
Christmas at Casey's 24
Christmas at Checkpoint Charlie 24
Christmas at 400 Green St. 24
Christmas at Greccio 24
Christmas at Home 24
Christmas at Mother's 25
Christmas at the Crossroads 25
Christmas at the Gables 25
Christmas at the Surprise Tree 25
Christmas Awakening, A 25
Christmas Barricade 25
Christmas Bazaar, The 25
Christmas Bells 25
Christmas Book, The 25
Christmas Book for the Grades, The 25
Christmas Cake 25
Christmas Carol, A 25–26
Christmas Carol, The 26
Christmas Comes to Old Grouch 26
Christmas Crusade, A 26
Christmas Drama Book, The 26
Christmas Dramatic Prelude 26
Christmas Eve Letter 26
Christmas Eve News 26
Christmas Eve Visitor, The 26
Christmas Everywhere 26
Christmas Faith 26
Christmas Festival Book, The 26
Christmas for the Middle Grades 27
Christmas Frolics 27
Christmas Fun in '91 27
Christmas Gift for Nancy 27
Christmas Gift from Heaven, A 27
Christmas Gifts, The 27
Christmas Guest, The 27
Christmas Homecoming 27
Christmas in Art 27
Christmas in Coventry 27
Christmas in Review 27
Christmas in the Heart 27
Christmas in the Market Place 27
Christmas Incorporated 28
Christmas Inside 28

Christmas Is a Miracle 28
Christmas Is a Racket 28
Christmas Is Coming 28
Christmas Is Now 28
Christmas Jewels 28
Christmas Joy Book, The 28
Christmas Lamb, The 28
Christmas Legend, A 28
Christmas Lives 28
Christmas Memories 28
Christmas Novelties 29
Christmas on Cloud 25 29
Christmas on Main Street 29
Christmas on the Village Square 29
Christmas Party, The 29
Christmas Plays 29
Christmas Plays and Programs 29
Christmas Plays for Women and Girls 29
Christmas Plays for Young Actors 29
Christmas Present 29
Christmas Programs for the Church 29
Christmas Recaptured 30
Christmas Revels 30
Christmas Star, The 30
Christmas Star for Olga, A 30
Christmas Story 30
Christmas Story, The 30
Christmas Stranger, The 30
Christmas Tree, The 30
Christmas Tree Forest 30
Christmas Unusual 30
Christmas Visitor, The 30
Christmas Voice, The 31
Christmas Windows 31
Christmasing of Jasper, The 31
Clouded Star, The 31
Cokesbury Christmas Programs 32
Columbine Madonna 32
Come and Adore Him 32
Come to the Manger 32
Come Ye to Bethlehem 32
Coming of Christ, The 33
Coming of the King, The 33
Coming of the Prince of Peace, The 33
Contrite Spirit, The 33
Coventry Nativity Play 34
Cradle, The 34
Cradle of Willow, A 34
Cratchits' Christmas Dinner, The 34
Crib at Greccio, The 34
Cricket on the Hearth, The 34
Curate's Play, The 36
Cymbals in the Marketplace 36

Dancing Doll Decides, The 36
Davy's Star 37
Day of Hope, The 37
Desert Shall Rejoice, The 38
Different Kind of Christmas, A 39
Do It Yourself Christmas Programs 40
Dream Toward Bethlehem 41
Dust of the Road 41
Dust on the Christmas Star 41

Easy Christmas Book, The 43
Easy Christmas Grab Bag, The 43
Easy Church Plays for Children 43
Easy Church Plays for Women and Girls 43
Easy Grade School Plays 44
Easy Programs for Christmas 44
Effect of Caroling, The 44
Emmanuel 45
Empty Room, The 45
Enchanted Christmas Tree, The 45
Enterprising Oswald 46
Eternal Magi, The 46
Eve of Christmas, The 46
Ever on Christmas Eve 46
Everlasting Dream, The 47
Everlasting Light, The 47
Everybody's Christmas Programs 47
Everybody's Rehearsalless Christmas Book 47
Everywhere Christmas 48
Extra Angel, The 48

Father Christmas and the Duchess 49
Festival of the Carols 50
Fiat Lux 50
52 Short Devotional Programs for Youth and Adult 50

First Christmas, The 50
Flight into Egypt, The 51
Follow the Star 52
For the Time Being 53
Forgotten Gift, The 53
Four Christmas Plays from the Horn Book 53
Fourth Wise Man, The 53
From Heaven Above 54
Frozen Heart, The 54
Fulfillment of the Law, The 54
Funny Fidgets 54

Gay Christmas Book, The 55
Geraldine and the White Robe 55
Giant Christmas Book, The 55
Gift of Music 55
Gift of Tenyin, The 55
Gift of the Lamb 55
Gifts, The 55
Gifts for the Christ-child 56
Gifts of Myrrh 56
Glad Time Christmas Book, The 56
Gloria 56
Go Ye to Bethlehem 56
God Created Christmas 56
Good Shepherd, A 57
Good Times Christmas Book 57
Good Will Toward Women 57
Grandpa Hangs the Holly 58
Greatest of These, The 58
Greene Christmas, A 59
Guardian, The 59
Guest House, Very Exclusive 59

Handy Christmas Program Book 59
Happy Christmas to All 60
Hark, the Herald Angels Sing 60
Hark, the Little Angels Speak 60
He Is Come! The Messiah! 60
He Who Walks in Love 61
Heavenly Host, The 61
Hidden Gift, The 62
Hidden Manger, The 62
High School Christmas Book, The 62
Holly and the Ivy, The 63
Holy Family 63
Holy Nativity, The 63
Holy Search, The 63
Holy Wood, The 63
Home for Christmas 64
Home the Star Shone On, The 64
Hope of the World, The 64
How Far Is It to Bethlehem? 65
Human 65
Humblest Place, The 65

I Created Santa Claus 66
If Thine Enemy 66
I'll Be Glad When It's Over 66
Image of Christmas, The 66
In Christmas Carol Land 67
"In My Father's House . . ." 67
In the Beginning 67
In the Fullness of Time 67
In the Same Country 67
In the Shepherd's Field 67
Inn at Bethlehem, The 68
Innkeeper, The 68
Innocent, The 68
Invitation, The 68

Joseph and the Nativity 71
Journey of the Star 71
Journey of the Three Kings, The 71
Joy Is Born 72
Joy to the World 72
Joyful and Triumphant 72
Juggler of Our Lady, The 72
Jumbo Christmas Book, The 72
Junior High Christmas Book 72
Junior Plays for All Occasions 72

King Will Come, A 73
Kneel at the Manger 73

Lady of the Marketplace 74
Left-over Reindeer, The 75
Legend of Baboushka, The 75
Legend of the Christmas Rose 75
Legend of the Christmas Rose, The 75
Lesson from Luke, A 75
Let Nothing Ye Dismay 75
Let Us Receive Christmas 75
Letty's Christmas Prodigal 75
Light in the Window, The 76
Light of Men, The 76
Light on Beacon Hill, A 76

Light Shines, The 76
Light Shone Down 77
Light Up the World 77
Lights of Christmas, The 77
Little Blue Angel, The 77
Little Lame Shepherd, The 77
Little People's Christmas Book 78
Little Shepherd, The 78
Little Shepherd Who Was Left Behind, The 78
Little Star Lost 78
Little Town, The 78
Little Women 78
Littlest Angel 78
Littlest Angel, The 78
Littlest Shepherd, The 78
Live Wire Christmas Book 79
Long Ago in Bethlehem 79
Long Christmas Dinner, The 79
Long Road to Bethlehem, The 79
Lost Christmas, The 79–80
Lost Star, The 80
Love Came at Christmas 80
Love's Gift 80

Man Who Found the King, The 83
Masque of Christmas Eve, A 84
Meaning of Christmas Day, The 85
Merry Christmas to the World 85
Message of the Christmas Angels, The 85
Midnight Clear, The 85
Midwinter Journey 86
Mimi Lights the Candle 86
Missile of Redemption 87
Mr. Christmas 87
Mr. Scrooge Finds Christmas 87
Mrs. Santa Claus 87
Modern Christmas Carol, A 87
Modern Treasury of Christmas Plays 88
Monsieur Santa Claus 88
Most Heavenly Hosts, The 88
Mouse Who Was Stirring, The 89
Mystery Play in Honor of the Nativity of Our Lord, A 89

Nativity 90
Nativity, The 90
Nativity in Statuary 90
Nature of a Gift, The 90
New-born King, The 90
Night Before Christmas, The 90–91
Nightingale, The 91
Nights of Noel 91
No More Christmas 91
No Room at the Inn 91
No Room in the Hotel 91
No Room in the Inn 91–92
Nobody's Child 92
Novellis, Novellis 92

O Holy Night 93
O Little Town of Bethlehem 93
Old English Custom, An 94
Old Old Story, The 94
On Christmas Night 94
On the Road to Egypt 95
Once upon a Christmas 95
Once upon a Christmas Time 95
One Night in Bethlehem 95
One Starry Night 96
Other Shepherd, The 96
Other Wise Man, The 96–97
Our Christmas Heritage 97
Our Greatest Gift 97
Outside the Stable 97

Pageant of the Holy Nativity, A 98
Party at Mount Yu, The 99
Peace I Give unto You 100
Peace Is an Olive Color 100
Peace to Earth 100
Perfect Carol, The 100
Perfect Gift, The 101
Pilgrim's Road to Bethlehem, The 102
Plannin' a Christmas Party 103
Plays, Pageants, and Ceremonials for the Christmas Season 104
Prelude 105
Primary Christmas Program Book 105
Prince of Peace 105
Promised One, The 106
Puppy Love 107

Queen Replies, The 107

Red Candles 108
Reindeer on the Roof 108
Report to Herod 109

Retrieved Christmas, A 109
Ring, Castle Bell 110
Road to Bethlehem, The 110
Room for a King 111
Roses for the King 112

Saint, The 112
St. Francis Brings Bethlehem to Greccio 112
Santa's Neurosis 113
Scarlet Ribbon, The 114
Scrooge 114
Search for Christmas, A 114
Search for the Saviour 114
Season's Greetings, The 114
Second Marriage of Santa Claus, The 115
Second Shepherd's Play, The 115
Seed of Adam and Other Plays 115
Seeing the Star 115
Servant at the Inn, The 116
Shepherd of Bethlehem, The 117
Shepherd Who Stayed, The 117
Shepherd Who Stayed Away, The 117
Shepherd's Christmas, The 117
Shepherd's Star, The 117
Shepherds Abiding 117
Shepherds and the Wise Men, The 117
Shepherds Brought a Song, The 118
Shining Star, The 118
Sign of a Star 118
Silent Night 118
Silver Beads 118
Silver Star of Christmas, The 119
Simeon (The Faithful Servant) 119
Sing Christmas 119
Sing the Songs of Christmas 119
So It's Christmas Again 121
Song in the Night, A 121
Song Is Born, A 121
Song of Glory 122
Songs of Christmas, The 122
Sons of Adam 122
Spirit of Christmas, The 123
Spirit of Christmas Giving, The 123
Spirit of Christmas Time 123
Stable Manger, The 123
Star and the Sixth, The 123
Star Gazer, The 123
Star in the East 123
Star in the Window, The 123
Star Light, Star Bright 123
Star of France, The 123
Star of Light 124
Star of Splendor 124
Star of Wonder 124
Star over Bethlehem 124
Star Song 124
Star Song and Other One-Act Plays 124
Star Too Far, A 124
Station Y-U-L-E 124
Still Shines the Star 124
Story of Artaban, the Other Wise Man, The 125
Story of Christmas 125
Story of Christmas in Mime, The 125
Stranger in Bethlehem, A 125
Sunday School Christmas Program, A 126

Table Set for Himself, The 127
Tell It to the Wind 127
Ten Good Christmas Pantomimes 127
There Was One Who Gave a Lamb 128
There's a Song in the Air 129
They Came Bearing Gifts 129
They Found Christmas 129
This Way to Christmas 130
Three Wise Men 132
Three Women of the Nativity, The 132
Thus It Is Written 132
Tidings of Joy 133
Tidings of Peace 133
Time for Love, A 133
Time of Minor Miracles, A 133
Time to Be Born, A 133
Tiniest Christmas Tree, The 133
Tinsel Fairy, The 133
To Bear the Message 134
To Bethlehem 134
To Hear the Angels Sing 134
To Us a Son 134
Touch of Lilac, A 135

Town Is Born, A 135
Town That Couldn't Have Christmas, The 135
Transparent Curtain Pageants for Christmas 135
Travellers, The 136
Treasury of Christmas Plays, A 136
Trouble with Christmas Presents, The 137
Turn to the East 137
'Twas the Fight Before Christmas 137
'Twas the Night Before Christmas 137
Twelve Days of Christmas 137
Twelve Days of Christmas, The 137
Two Religious Dialogues 138
Two Strangers from Nazareth 138

Unto the Least of These 139
Unto Thy Doors 139
Unto Us 139
Unto Us a Child Is Born 139
"Unto Us Is Born—a Saviour" 139
Unveiling, The 139

Vision, The 141

Way for All, A 142
What Is This Thing Called Christmas? 143
What Men Live By 143
When Love Was Born 143
When the Little Angels Sang 144
When the Star Shone 144
Where Lies the Child 144
Where's Your Christmas Spirit? 144
Wherever the Star Shines 144
White Christmas, The 144
White Thorn at Yule 145
Why the Angels Sing for Joy 145
Why the Chimes Rang 145
Windows of Christmas 146
Wise Men at the Well, The 146
With No Reservations 146
Women of Christmas, The 147
Word Made Flesh 147
World Is in Bethlehem, The 148

York Nativity, The 149
York Nativity Play, The 149
Young Prince of Glory 149

COLLECTIONS

Abingdon Children's Day Programs 1
Abingdon Christmas Programs 1
Abingdon Easter Programs 1
Anthology of English Drama Before Shakespeare 6
Anthology of Greek Drama 6

Banner Anthology of One Act Plays by American Authors 8
Best Christmas Pantomimes 10
Best Plays of the Modern American Theater 11
Best Selections for Christmas 11
Best Selections for Easter 11
Better Plays for Today's Churches 11
"Better Yet" Christmas Book, The 11
Bible Character Impersonations 12
Bible Characters in Action 12
Bible Comes Alive, The 12
Bible Plays 12
Bible Plays for Children 12
Bible Plays for Juniors 12
Bible Plays for Small Children 12
Bible Women Come Alive 12
Big Book of Christmas, The 12
Big Christmas Book, The 13
Bright Ideas for Easter, Mother's Day, and Children's Day 16
Bundle-o'-Cheer Christmas Book, The 17

Candlelight 19
Candlelighting Service, A 19
Candlelighting Service for Christmas and New Year Season, A 19
Career Plays for Young People 19
Chester Miracle Plays, The 22
Chester Mystery Plays, The 22
Children's Program Book, The 23
Choral Speaking Arrangements for the Junior High 23
Choral Speaking Arrangements for the Lower Grades 23

Choral Speaking Arrangements for the Upper Grades 23
Choral Verse Speaking 23
Christmas Book, The 25
Christmas Book for the Grades, The 25
Christmas Drama Book, The 26
Christmas Festival Book, The 26
Christmas for the Middle Grades 27
Christmas Frolics 27
Christmas Joy Book, The 28
Christmas Novelties 29
Christmas Plays 29
Christmas Plays and Programs 29
Christmas Plays for Women and Girls 29
Christmas Plays for Young Actors 29
Christmas Programs for the Church 29
Cokesbury Christmas Programs 32
Cokesbury Easter Programs 32
Collected Plays of Yeats 32
Contemporary Drama 33
Coventry Porch Plays 34
Critics' Choice 34

Discovery Bible Plays, The 40
Do It Yourself Christmas Programs 40
Dramatic Preludes and Services of Worship 41
Dreambook, The 41

Earlier English Drama 42
Easter and the Spring 42
Easter Programs for the Church 42
Easter Suggestion Book 43
Easy Arena Plays 43
Easy Bible Pantomimes 43
Easy Bible Story Dramatizations for Children 43
Easy Christmas Book, The 43
Easy Christmas Grab Bag, The 43
Easy Church Plays for Children 43
Easy Church Plays for Women and Girls 43
Easy Easterettes 43
Easy Grade School Plays 44
Easy Grange Programs 44
Easy Programs for Christmas 44
Easy Programs for Church Holidays 44
Easy Programs for Mother's Day 44
Easy Sunday School Entertainments 44
English Miracle Plays, Moralities and Interludes 46
Eureka Children's Day Recitations 46
Eureka Easter Recitations 46
Everybody's Christmas Programs 47
Everybody's Rehearsalless Christmas Book 47

Favorite Mother's Day Program, The 49
52 Short Devotional Programs for Youth and Adult 50
Finger Plays and How to Use Them 50
Five More Christian Plays 51
Five One-Act Plays 51
Five Plays 51
Four Christmas Plays from the Horn Book 53
Four Easy Skits for Church 53
Four Modern Plays 53
From Story to Stage 54

Gabriel's Ave and Other Religious Plays 54
Gay Christmas Book, The 55
Giant Christmas Book, The 55
Glad Time Christmas Book, The 56
Glad Time Thanksgiving Book, The 56
Golden Book of Church Plays 57
Good Times Christmas Book 57
Great Christian Plays 58

Halloween and Thankgsiving 59
Handy Book for Church Special Days 59
Handy Christmas Program Book 59
High School Christmas Book, The 62
Holiday Book for Verse Choirs 63

Holiday Plays 63
Holiday Plays for Little Players 63
Holiday Plays for Teenagers 63
Holiday Plays for Young Actors 63
Holiday Programs for Boys and Girls 63

Jericho Road and Other Miracle Plays 70
Jewish Holiday on Parade, The 70
Joyous Programs for Springtime Celebrations 72
Jumbo Christmas Book, The 72
Junior High Christmas Book 72
Junior High School Plays 72
Junior Plays for All Occasions 72

Little People's Christmas Book 78
Little Plays of St. Francis 78
Live Wire Christmas Book 79

Master Cat and Other Plays, The 84
Medieval Mysteries, Moralities, and Interludes 85
Meigs Best World Friendship Selections 85
Miracle of Saint Anthony, A 86
Missionary Programs for the Church 87
Modern Chancel Dramas 87
Modern Plays for Special Days 87
Modern Theatre, The 87
Modern Treasury of Christmas Plays 88
More Plays and Pageants for Many Occasions 88
More Religious Plays for Women 88
More Stunt Plays 88
Mothers 88
Mothers and Home 89

New Testament Mimes 90
Nine New Plays for Children 91

Old Testament Plays 94
On Stage for Teen-agers 94
100 Plays for Children 95
One-act Plays for All-girl Casts 96
One Act Plays of Spiritual Power 96

Pageants and Programs for School, Church, and Playground 98
Paramount Children's Day Book 98
Paramount Easter Book 98
Paramount Mother's Day Book, The 99
Past and Present, Three Short Plays 99
Playbook 103
Playette Quartet 103
Plays and Playlets 103
Plays As Experience 103
Plays for Great Occasions 103
Plays for Happier Homes 103
Plays for the Church 104
Plays for the Schoolroom 104
Plays from the Bible 104
Plays of Eugene O'Neill, The 104
Plays of Perplexity 104
Plays, Pageants, and Ceremonials for the Christmas Season 104
Poetic Dramas 104
Primary Christmas Program Book 105
Programs for Women's Groups 106
Puppets and Bible Plays 107

Rally Day and Promotion Day Treasury 108
Readings and Recitations for Sunday School and Church 108
"Real" Christmas Book, A 108
Rehearsal-less Easter Collection 108
Rehearsal-less Fun 108
Religious Drama 108
Religious Drama 2 109
Religious Plays for Women 109
Return of the Prodigal, The 109

St. Anne and the Gouty Rector and Other Plays 112
Sample Set of More Than 40 Plays 113
Seed of Adam and Other Plays 115
Select Dramas for Children's Day 116
Seven Plays 116

Seven Plays for Children 116
Shadow of the Mine and Other Plays of the Coal Fields 117
Simple Chancel Dramas 119
Six Plays of Strindberg 120
Six Short Religious Plays 120
Social Helps for Church Workers 121
'Specially Good Christmas Book, The 122
Spirit of Christmas, The 123
Spirit of Christmas Giving, The 123
Star Song and Other One-Act Plays 124
Strictly Feminine 126
Sunday School Christmas Program, A 126

Tell It with Trumpets 127
Ten Good Christmas Pantomimes 127
Ten Pantomimed Hymns 127
Ten Stirring Bible Plays 128
Thanksgiving Plays and Ways 128
Thanksgiving Program Book 128
Third Windmill Book of One-act Plays 130
Thirty Famous One-act Plays 130
Three Church Dramas 131
Three Medieval Plays 132
Three Plays 132
Three Towneley Plays 132
"To Meet the King" and Three Other Plays 134
Tolerance in Action 134
Transparent Curtain Pageants for Christmas 135
Transparent Curtain Pageants for Easter 136
Treasury of Christmas Plays, A 136
Trial of Jeanne D'Arc and Other Plays, The 136
Twelve Months of Drama for the Average Church 137
Twenty-minute Bible Plays 138
Two Ceremonial Programs for Thanksgiving 138
Two Mother's Day Programs 138
Two Religious Dialogues 138
Two Saints Plays 138
Two-in-One Halloween-Thanksgiving Book, The 138

United Nations Plays and Programs 139

Wakefield Mystery Plays 141
Wedding Anniversary Celebrations 142
World's Great Plays 148
Worship Programs and Stories for Young People 148
Worship Programs for Intermediates 148

York Cycle of Mystery Plays, The 149
Youth Programs for Special Occasions 149
Youth Serves the Church 149

Zeal of Thy House, The 149

EASTER PLAYS

Abingdon Easter Programs 1
Alabaster Box, The 2
All Hail the Risen Lord 2
Alleluia 3
And So He Doth Redeem Us 4
Appointment in Galilee 6
Artaban, the Story of the Other Wise Man 7
As Easter Dawns 7

Barabbas 8
Barter 8
Behold His Glory 10
Behold the Crucified 10
Behold Your King 10
Best Selections for Easter 11
Betrayal, The 11
Boy Who Discovered Easter, The 15
Builders 17
By Christ Alone 18
By Thy Cross and Passion 18
By Thy Faith 18
By Thy Glorious Resurrection 18

Calvary 18
Captains and the Kings, The 19
Casey 20
Cathedral, The 20
Challenge of the Cross, The 21

Chancel Lily, The 21
Children Hear About Easter, The 22
Children of the Good Shepherd 23
Christ Crucified 23
Christ in the Concrete City 23
Christ Is Risen 23
Christ the Lord Is Risen Today 24
Christus Rex 31
Cloth of Sendony, The 31
Cloud of Witnesses, A 31
Cokesbury Easter Programs 32
"Come, See the Place . . ." 32
Come Ye to Calvary 32
Cross of Challenge, The 34
Cross on the Hill, The 35
Crosses on the Hill 35
Crown of Thorns, The 35
Curse and the Crown, The 36

Dark Days, The 36
Darkness Before Dawn 37
Dawn, The 37
Dawning, The 37
Day's Beginning, The 37
Desert Tent, The 38

Easter 42
Easter and the Spring 42
Easter at Galilee 42
Easter Hope, The 42
Easter Programs for the Church 42
Easter Shoes 42
Easter Story, The 42
Easter Strike, An 43
Easter Suggestion Book 43
Easter Tidings 43
Easter Trail, The 43
Easter Wings 43
Easter's Festival 43
Easy Arena Plays 43
Easy Bible Pantomimes 43
Easy Bible Story Dramatizations for Children 43
Easy Easterettes 43
Eureka Easter Recitations 46
Eyes of Faith 48
Eyes upon the Cross 48

Faithless, The 48
Figure on the Cross, The 50
From the Palms to the Lilies 54

Golgotha 57
Good Friday 57
Good Shepherd, A 57

He Is Not Here! He Is Risen! 61
He Is Risen Indeed 61
He Passed This Way 61
Holy Family 63
Holy Wood, The 63
House of Mary, The 65
Housetop, The 65

I Lay in Zion 66
I Made Christ's Cross 66
I Saw Him 66
I Saw the Cross 66
In Joseph's Garden 67
In the Beginning 67
In the Shadow of the Cross 67
In This Sign Conquer 68
Into Thy Kingdom 68
Is It I, Lord? 69
It Is I 69
It's Easter, Dr. Jordan 69

Joseph of Arimathea 71
Joy Fills My Heart 71
Joyous Programs for Springtime Celebrations 72

Kindled Flame, The 73

Last Days, The 74
Light Eternal, The 76
Light of Christ, The 76
Light of the World 76
Light of the World, The 76
Living Lord, The 79
Love Never Dies 80
Lowly King, The 81

Magdalene, The 82
Man Dies, A 82
Mary's Quest 84
Mary's Son 84
Meaning of Easter, The 85
Midnight in the Dungeon 86
Mirage 87
Mourning Before Morning 89
My Father's Business 89

On the Eve of Holy Week 94
On the Hill 95
On the Third Day 95

Other Cross, The 96
Out of Despair 97
Out of the Darkness 97

Pageant of Easter, A 98
Pageant of Jerusalem, A 98
Paramount Easter Book 98
Passion Play at Oberammergau, 1900, The 99
Peace of Bethany 100
People vs. Christ, The 100
Pilate and the Cross 102
Pilate, the Roman Governor 102
Plough and the Stars, The 104
Prince of Peace, The 105
Promise of the Angels 106

Quem Quaeritis 107

Radiant Morning 107
Redeemer's Robe, The 108
Rehearsal-less Easter Collection 108
Release 108
Resurrection, The 109
Risen Christ, The 110
Road to Emmaus, The 110–111
Robe, The 111
Robe and the Thorn, The 111

Seamless Robe, The 114
Shadow of the Cross 117
Silvered Rope, The 119
Simon, Called Peter 119
Simon Peter 119
Simon, the Cross Bearer 119
Soldiers of the Cross 121
Soliloquy on the Sounds of Easter 121
Spark in Judea 122
Spirit and the Truth 122
Spring's Miracle 123
Story of Easter, The 125
Symphony of Easter 127

Terrible Meek, The 128
They Wanted a Leader 129
Third Day, The 129–130
Three Faces of Easter, The 131
Three Marys, The 131
Thy Kingdom Come 132
Thy Will Be Done 132
Touch of a Shadow 135
Transparent Curtain Pageants for Easter 136
Trial of Jesus, The 136
Two Religious Dialogues 138

Unwashed Hands 139
Uplifted Cross, The 139
Upper Room, The 139

Verba Crucis 140
Vigil, The 140

Wake to Thunder 141
Warning, The 142
Way of the Cross 142
Way of the Cross, The 142
We Have Seen the Lord 142
Were You There? 143
Were You There When They Crucified My Lord? 143
Whosoever Believeth 145
Women at the Tomb, The 147
World Without End 148

HISTORICAL PLAYS

Admiral Penn and Son William 2
Altar-piece 3
American Portrait 3
American Saint of Democracy 3

Becket 9
Boy Abe, The 15
Brother Ass and Brother Lion 17

Caine Mutiny Court Martial, The 18
Cyprian 36

Death of a Traitor 38
Deputy, The 38
Design for a Stained Glass Window 38
Devil and Daniel Webster, The 39

Except for John Leland 48

Faith of Our Fathers 48
First Freedom 50
Five Days 51
For Country and Mankind 52
"For Freedom's Sake!" 52

Gallows Glorious 54
Gospel Witch, The 57

Harriet 60

Hollow Crown, The 63
Husband of Poverty, The 66

I Will Give Thanks 66

Jeanne D'Arc 70
Joan of Arc 70
Joan of Lorraine 70
Journey to Judgment 71

La Madre 74
Lady with a Lamp, The 74
Lamp at Midnight 74
Lark, The 74
Last Victory, The 74
Let Man Live 75
Little Poor Man, The 78
Luther 81

Maid of Domremy, The 82
Man for All Seasons, A 83
Man in Leather Breeches, The 83
Marvelous History of St. Bernard, The 83
Mary of Scotland 84
Mary Stuart 84
Murder in the Cathedral 89

Not Martyrs 92

One with the Flame 96
Only Way, The 96

Pageant of Pilgrims, A 98
Parable 98
Pictures in the Fire 102
Prelude to Darkness, The 105
Princess Poverty, The 105
Princess Who Could Not Be Merry, The 106
Prologue to Glory 106

Roger Williams and Mary 111

St. Francis of Assisi 113
Saint Joan 113
Sanctuary 113
Seducer, The 115
Sound from Heaven, A 122

They Made a Path 129
This Union Under God 130

Valley Forge 140

JEWISH PLAYS

Alice in Chanukoland 2

Bespoke Overcoat, The 10
Boys from Modin, The 16

Chanuko Parade, The 21
Chanuko Play, The 21

Dream of Purim, A 41
Dreambook, The 41
Dybbuk, The 42

Eternal Light, The 46
Everything Is for the Best 48

Festival of Lights, The 50
Fiddler's Purim, The 50
Formula, The 53
Freedom Hall 53

G'dee Celebrates the Holidays 55

Holiday Plays 63
How John Learned About Hanukkah 65

In Pesach Land 67

Jewish Holiday on Parade, The 70

King Solomon and the Bee 73
Kings or Better 73

Light unto All the House 76
Loyal Queen Esther, or Never Belittle the Power of a Lady 81

Madison Avenue Purim, The 81
Maybe Even Higher 84
Megillahah Musical, The 85
Miracle for Chanuko, A 86

Pinafore Gone Purimdig 102
Postscript to Purim 105
Purim Merry-go-round 107
Purimnet 107

Ring of Solomon, The 110

Sample Set of More Than 40 Plays 113
Secret Chanukah, The 115
Sefer Mobile, The 116
Shushan Heart, The 118
Sounds Prolong, The 122
Story Book Purim 125
Story of Hanukkah, The 125
Supersonic Purim 127

Table, The 127

"There Was a Man . . ." 128
Tongues in Trees 135
Tree Alone, A 136
Tree in Your Life, A 136
Tree They Want!, A 136
What's Chanuko Without a Play? 143
Wild West Purim 145

MISSIONARY PLAYS

Ba Thane 8
Doctor Decides, The 40
Empty Hands 45
Eternal Magi, The 46
Finger Plays and How to Use Them 50
Go and Tell 56
Make His Name Glorious 82
Missionary Programs for the Church 87
Playette Quartet 103
That Heaven of Freedom 128
"To Thine Own Self . . ." 134
White Christmas 145
Widow's Mite, The 145

THANKSGIVING PLAYS

Cause for Gratitude 20
Crusader for the Day 35
Easy Grade School Plays 44
Faith of Our Fathers 48
Halloween and Thanksgiving 59
Many Thanks 83
Psalm of Thanksgiving, A 107
Return of the Pilgrims, The 109
Second Thanksgiving, The 115
Thankful for What? 128
Thanksgiving Plays and Ways 128
Thanksgiving Program Book 128
Two Ceremonial Programs for Thanksgiving 138

WORLD-FRIENDSHIP PLAYS

American Christmas, An 3
Children of Other Lands 22
Don Pedro of Brazil 40
Food for Freedom 52
Fountain of Peace, A 53
Honoring Friendship 64
Juarez the Just 72
Magic Shoes, The 82
Man in Leather Breeches, The 83
Mary Fisher and the Sultan of Turkey 83
Mary Smith Meets Mr. People 84
Master John 84
Meigs Best World Friendship Selections 85
Mighty Dream, The 86
Mission Accomplished 87
Odd Man, The 93
Playette Quartet 103
Rizal of the Philippines 110
Small Shoes and Small Tulips 121
Tijl Founds Utopia 133
Youth Bolivar, The 149

MISCELLANEOUS PLAYS

According to the Scriptures and And Ye Are Witnesses 1
Acting Out the Truth 1
Acts of St. Peter, The 1
Adam 1
Adam and Eve Meet the Atom 1
Adam the Creator 1
After the Fog Lifts 2
Ajax 2
All My Sons 2
All That Fall 3
American Dream, The 3
American Way, The 3
Among Thieves 3
Anchor, The 3
And Lose His Own Soul 4
And the Fullness Thereof 4
And You Never Know 4
Androcles and the Lion 5
Angel in the Clearing, The 5

Angel in the Window 5
Angel on a Stepladder 5
Answer, The 5
Answered Prayer 6
Answers, The 6
Ante Room 6
Antigone 6
Apples for Teacher 6
Aria Da Capo 7
Armour of Light 7
Asmodée 7
At the Feet of the Madonna 7
At the Junction 7
August Heat 8
Automobile Graveyard, The 8

Ballista 8
Be a Good Neighbor 9
Beacon of Strength 9
Beautiful Dreamers 9
Beautiful People, The 9
Beginning at Jerusalem 10
Bell for Adano, A 10
Bell of St. Hildegarde, The 10
Belvedere 10
Beneath This Spire 10
Between Two Thieves 11
Bewitched 11
Beyond Human Power 11
Bible Salesman, The 12
Big Middle, The 13
Billy Budd 13
Birth by Drowning 13
Bishop's Mantle, The 14
Bitter Bread 14
"Blessed Are They" 14
Blind Men, The 14
Blue-ribbon Plays for Girls 14
Borak 14
Boston O'Tooles, The 15
Both Your Houses 15
Boy Who Knew Jesus, The 15
Boy with a Cart, The 15
Boys at Large 15
Brand 16
Brass Butterfly, The 16
Brass Ring, The 16
Bread 16
Break of Noon 16
Breakfast with Paul 16
Breakthrough 16
Bride in Samaria, A 16
Brides of Begerin, The 16
Brighten Every Corner 17
Broken Circle, The 17
Brother, The 17
Brother Orchid 17
Brother Petroc's Return 17
Brown Bird, The 17
Builders, The 17
Burning Pews 17

Cake-maker, The 18
Call Me Mac 18
Carpenter, The 19
Case Against Eve, The 19
Case of the Missing Handshake, The 20
Castle of Perseverance, The 20
Caught Between 20
Cavalcade of Human Rights 20
Cave Dwellers, The 20
Caves of the Earth 20
Celestial Error 21
Cell, The 21
Centurion's Servant, The 21
Certain Just Man, A 21
Chalk Circle, The 21
Chalk Garden, The 21
Cherry Orchard, The 22
Children, The 22
Children Are Listening, The 22
Children from Galilee, The 22
Children of God 22
Chinese Wall, The 23
Choice to Make, A 23
Choirs of God 23
Christian Family Brown 24
Church Bells 31
Church Clinic, The 31
Church for Sale 31
Circle Beyond Fear, The 31
Circus, Parable, and Construction 31
Clerambard 31
Cocktail Party, The 32
Comedian, The 32
Commandments Today, The 33
Common Treasure, The 33
Complaining Angel, The 33
Conquest in Burma 33
Construction 33

Counted As Mine 33
Coventry 33
Cradle Song, The 34
Crier Calls, The 34
Crime by Persuasion 34
Crucible, The 35
Cry Dawn in Dark Babylon 35
Cry Havoc 35
Cry, the Beloved Country 35
Cup of Kindness, A 35
Cup of Strength, The 35
Cup of Trembling, The 35–36

Dark Eyes 36
Dark Interlude 36
Dark Is Light Enough, The 36
Dark Night, The 36
Darkness At Noon 36
Date for Joanne, A 37
Dawn Will Come 37
Day the Sky Went to School, The 37
Dead End 37
Dear Wormwood 37
Death of a Salesman 38
Debt to Pay, A 38
Decision, The 38
Deep Are the Roots 38
Delinquent, the Hipster, and the Square, The 38
Demon Preacher, The 38
Devil a Saint Would Be, The 39
Devil and the Dream, The 39
Devil Comes to Claim His Own, The 39
Devil to Pay, The 39
Devil's Advocate, The 39
Devil's Disciple, The 39
Dialogues of the Carmelites 39
Dino 39
Displaced Persons 40
Distant Thunder 40
Divine Miracle, The 40
Divorce Granted 40
Doll's House, A 40
Door Is Open, The 40
Door Opens: Everybody Welcome!, The 40
Dope! 40
Down Our Street 41
Drag Race 41
Dragon and the Dove, The 41
Drama of Prayer 41
Dustman, The 41

Easy to Assemble 44
Echo of Wings, An 44
Edge of Gehenna 44
Edwardian Plays 44
Egor Bulychov and the Others 44
Eh? 44
El Cristo 45
Electra 45
Elizabeth the Queen 45
Enemies 45
Enemy of the People, An 46
Eternal Hills, The 46
Even the Hater 46
Ever Since April 47
Every Woman 47
Everybody Likes Pretty Things 47
Everyman 47–48
Everyman and Medieval Miracle Plays 48
Excuse for Living 48
Eye of the Hurricane 48

Family Nobody Wanted, The 48
Family Portrait 49
Family Reunion, The 49
Faust, Part I 49
Fear Is a Murderer 49
Fear Not 49
Fearless Heart, The 49
Feast of the Star, The 49
Fellow Needs a Friend, A 50
Fences 50
Festival of Freedom, A 50
Finger of God, The 50
First Good Joy, The 51
First Legion, The 51
Fisherman's Son, The 51
Flower for Mother's Day, A 52
Flowers for Mother 52
Fog 52
Food of Love, The 52
Football Hero 52
For Heaven's Sake! 52
Forgive Us Our Chicken Coops 53
Fresh Variable Winds 53
Friendly Church, The 53
Friends of Jesus 54

From the Nursery of Heaven 54
Frontier, The 54

Gardener Who Was Afraid of Death, The 54
Gentle One, The 55
Gifts of St. Patrick, The 56
Glass Menagerie, The 56
Glorious Odyssey 56
God So Loved the World 56
Gold, Frankincense and Myrrh 57
Golden Land, The 57
Good King Wenceslas 57
Good Morning, Parson 57
Good Neighbors 57
Good Things for Mother's Day 57
Grab and Grace or The Second Step 58
Great Choice, The 58
Great Theatre of the World, The 58
Greater Than Any Man 58
Green Blackboard, The 58
Green Bough, The 58
Green Wood, The 59
Guidance Through Drama 59
Guiding Hand, The 59

Hamlet, Prince of Denmark 59
Hamp 59
Hannah 60
Hannele 60
Hans Brinker or The Silver Skates 60
Happy Life, The 60
Hasty Heart, The 60
He 60
He Knew the Master 61
He Who Gets Slapped 61
He Who Says Yes, He Who Says No 61
Healing in Its Wings 61
Heart of the House 61
Heart-Sound of a Stranger 61
Heathen Pioneer 61
Hedge, The 62
Hello and Goodbye 62
Henry Hereafter 62
Here Come the Clowns 62
Hernani 62
High Ground (Bona Venture) 62
High Pressure Area 62
High Tor 62
Highway and the Way, The 63
Holy Smoke 63
Home of the Brave 64
Honour Thy Mother 64
Hopeful Travellers, The 64
Hotel Universe 64
Hour Glass, The 64
Hour of Fate, The 64
Hour of Truth, The 64
House Beautiful, The 64
House by the Stable, The 65
House on the Sand, The 65
House That Jack Built, The 65
How Much Is Enough 65
How the Great Guest Came 65
Human Condition, The 65

I Have Spoken to My Children 66
If the Light Be Darkness 66
I'm Talking About Jerusalem 66
In the Presence of Death 67
In White America 68
Infanta 68
Inherit the Wind 68
Ins and Outs, The 68
Invasion from the Stratosphere 68
Invisible One, The 68
Iphigenia at Aulis 69
Irish Miracle 69
It All Adds Up 69
"It Is More Blessed—" 69
It *Is* So! (If You Think So) 69

J.B. 70
Jew of Malta, The 70
Joanna and the Candles 70
John Doe 71
John, Whose Surname Was Mark 71
Journey of Promise 71
Joyful Mystery 72
Joyous Season, The 72
Judith 72
Just Vengeance, The 72

Khanum and Her Treasures, The 73
King Lear 73
Kingdom of God and Other Plays, The 73

Kings in Nomania 73
King's Standards, The 73
Known But to God 73

Ladies of Soissons, The 74
Lamb in the Window, The 74
Last Word, The 74
Least of These, The 74
Legend 75
Life's Crossroads 75
Lift Thine Eyes 76
Light Eternal, The 76
Light of the World 76
Light Within, The 77
Lilies for the King 77
Liliom 77
Little Bell for San Marco, A 77
Little Friend 77
Little Red Apostles, The 78
Living Hymns 79
Loaves and Fishes 79
Lonesome Bibles, The 79
Long View—on Social Work, The 79
Look at Christian Education, A 79
Lost Church, The 80
Lost in the Stars 80
Lourdes 80
Lower Than Angels 81
Lucifer at Large 81
Lute Song 81

Macadam and Eve 81
Macbeth 81
Madman and the Wrecking Crew, The 81
Madwoman of Chaillot, The 82
Magda 82
Magi's Gift, The 82
Major Barbara 82
Man Called Peter, A 82
Man Is Omega 83
Man Without a Soul, The 83
Mannequins' Demise 83
Mariot and Mariette 83
Master Builder, The 84
Master of Santiago, The 84
Member of the Wedding, The 85
Merchant of Venice, The 85
Message of a Song 85
Minor Miracle 86
Miracle At Nain, The 86
Miracle for Mary, A 86
Miracle of the Madonna 86
Miracle Worker, The 86
Mirage 87
Misunderstanding, The 87
Monsignor's Hour 88
Moonset 88
More Blessed to Give 88
Mother in the Shadow 88
Mother's Apron Strings 89
Mother's Gift to Ann 89
Museum Piece 89
Music in the Valley 89
My Heart's in the Highlands 89

Nathan the Wise 89
Native Son 90
Neighbors, The 90
New Brooms 90
New Tax, The 90
Night Comes to the City 91
Night Falls on Spain 91
Night of Reckoning 91
No Exit 91
Noah Gives Thanks 92
Nobody Knows 92
Not by Might 92
Not Without Honor 92
Nothing Is Impossible 92
Nursery Maid of Heaven, The 93
Nutcracker Suite 93

O Distant Land 93
O, Valiant Heart 93
O Worship the King! 93
Oedipus at Colonus 93
Oedipus the King 93
Offending Hand, The 94
Old Man of the Mountains, The 94
Old Pine Tree and Other Noh Plays 94
Old Rugged Cross, The 94
Omar 94
On Borrowed Time 94
On Earth Peace 94
One Family Sings 95
One Foot in Heaven 95
One Red Rose 95
Open Secret 96

Open Windows, The 96
Othello, the Moor of Venice 96
Other One, The 96
Our Lady's Tumbler 97
Our Lean Years 97
Our Town 97
Out of the Bible 97
Outside the Door 97
Outsider, The 98
Outward Bound 98

Packing of the Home Missionary Barrel, The 98
Pageant of the Singing Stars 98
Papa Was a Preacher 98
Parade at the Devil's Bridge 98
Passing of the Third Floor Back, The 99
Passion Flower, The 99
Pastor's Guiding Hand, The 99
Patsy Becomes a Pilgrim Maid 99
Paul Thompson Forever 99
Peace Be to This House 99
Peace on Mars 100
Peer Gynt 100
People vs. the Pharisee, The 100
People Were in Expectation, The 100
Persians, The 101
Person to Person Call 101
Petition, The 101
Petrified Forest, The 101
Philoctetes 101
Piccola 101
Picnic Basket, The 101
Piece of Silver, A 102
Pilgrim Parting 102
Pilgrim's Progress, The 102
Pillars of Society, The 102
Pilot Lights of Apocalypse 102
Ping-Pong 102
Pink Telephone, The 103
Pinnacle 103
Pioneers 103
Play on Covenant, A 103
Point of Beginning 104
Polyeucte 104
Poor Man Who Died Because He Wore Gloves, The 104
Potting Shed, The 105
Power and the Glory, The 105
Powers That Be, The 105
Present Pleasure 105
Prisoner Released, The 106
Prodigal Mother, The 106
Prophecy to the Wind 106
Publican and Sinner 107
Pull Devil, Pull Baker 107
Pullman Car Hiawatha 107
Purlie Victorious 107
Putting First Things First 107

Quem Quaeritis 107

R. U. R. 107
Radio Jerusalem, the Story of Jesus 108
Raveled Sleeve, The 108
Real St. George, The 108
Requiem for a Nun 109
Reticent One, The 109
Return of Chandra, The 109
Return of the Prophets, The 109
Reverie 109
Rhinoceros 110
Richard III 110
Ring Out Wild Bells 110
Romeo and Juliet 111
Room for One More 111
Roomful of Roses, A 111
Rosary, The 111
Rose and Crown, The 112

Sabotage 112
Sacred Romance 112
St. Felix and His Potatoes 112
St. Michael Comes to Shepherd's Bush 113
Saints' Return, The 113
Sandbox, The 113
Santa Claus 113
Sausage Maker's Interlude, The 113
Scapegoat 114
Scarecrow, The 114
Scattered Showers 114
Searching Wind, The 114
Second Spring 115
Secret, The 115
Seeking Years, The 115
Send Out Thy Light 116
Sensation on Budlegh Beacon 116
Separatist, The 116

Sergeant Smith Returns 116
Serjeant Musgrave's Dance 116
Servant in the House, The 116
Seven Mirrors 116
Shadow and Substance 117
Shepherd's Pie 117
Shepherd's Play of the Prodigal Son, The 117
Shirt a Size Too Small, A 118
Shoe on the Other Foot, The 118
Sight to See 118
Sign of Jonah, The 118
Silver Cord, The 118
Silver Tassie, The 119
Silver Trumpet, The 119
Simple Little Affair, A 119
Sir Tommy's Pilgrimage 120
Sister Beatrice 120
Sister Craven 120
Site, The 120
Six Characters in Search of an Author 120
Six Steps Slowly 120
Skin of Our Teeth, The 120
Smallest of All 120
Smell of Cinnamon, A 121
Snakes and Eggs 121
Soldier City, The 121
So She Made a Novena 121
So This Is Bliss 121
Song at the Scaffold 121
Soul in Fine Array, A 122
Soup, Sand, and Sagebrush 122
Spreading the News 123
Stable Boy, The 123
State of Siege 124
State of the Union 124
Stephen D. 124
Storm Is Breaking, A 125
Strange Victory 125
Stranger, The 125
Stranger of Vallenska, The 125
Stranger Passes, A 126
Strong Are Lonely, The 126
Study in Color 126
Summoning of Everyman, The 126
Sunken Bell, The 126
Susan and God 127
Sweet Potato Vine, The 127
Sword and the Scroll, The 127
Take This Man 127
Tardy April 127
Terrible Miss Dove, The 128
Thank You, God, for Everything 128
That Fell Arrest 128
That Home in Nazareth 128
Then Will She Return 128
There Shall Be No Night 128
These Are Not Children 129
They Move On 129
They That Walk in Darkness 129
Thief and the Hangman, The 129
Thine Shall Be the Glory 129
This Freedom 130
This Is My Church 130
This Is the End 130
This Night Shall Pass 130
This Thine House 130
This Way to the Tomb 131
Thistle in Donkey Field, The 131
Thor with Angels 131
Thou Art Peter 131
"Thou Fool!" 131
Thou Shalt Not Lie 131
Three Sisters, The 132
Through a Glass, Darkly 132
Thunder Rock 132
Ticket to Tomorrow 132
Tidings Brought to Mary, The 133
Tiger at the Gates 133
Tinker, The 133
To Temper the Wind 134
Tobias and the Angel 134
Tomorrow Is a Day 134
Touch of the Poet, A 135
Tragical History of Doctor Faustus, The 135
Traveller, The 136
Travelling Man, The 136
Trial, The 136
Triumph of the Defeated, The 137
Twelfth Night at Moulderby Hall 137
Twelve Angry Men 137
Twentieth Century Lullaby 137

Uncle Tom's Cabin 138
Under Milk Wood 138
Under One Roof 138
Undertaking, The 138

Unerring Instinct 138
Unlighted Cross, The 139
Unseen Host, The 139
Unto the End 139
Unto Us the Living 139
Uprooted, The 140

Vagabond, The 140
Valiant, The 140
Velvet Glove, The 140
Verdict of One 140
Very Cold Night, A 140
View from the Bridge, A 140
Vision of Sir Launfal, The 141
Visit, The 141
Voice That Failed, The 141
Voices 141
Voices of Mass and Capital A 141

Wait, The 141
Waiting for Godot 141
Wanderer, The 142
Weavers, The 142
Well of the Saints, The 142
What Is the Church? 143
What Never Dies? 143
What Think Ye of Christ? 143
Whatsoever Ye Sow 143
When Mayflowers Bloomed in Plymouth 143
When the Dead Awaken and Three Other Plays 144
When the Fire Dies 144
When the Sun Rises 144
Where Love Is 144
Whirlwind 144
Whirlwind, The 144
Who Is There to Ask? 145
Why Weepest Thou? 145
Wild Duck, The 145
Willing Spirit, The 145
Winterset 146
Wise and the Foolish Virgins, The 146
Wise Have Not Spoken, The 146
Witch's Brew 146
With Malice Toward None 146
Without Fear or Favor 146
Witness, The 146
Witness to the Truth 146
Women of Jesus' Time 147
Women of the Bible 147
Wonderful World 147
Woodcarver, The 147
Woodshed, The 147
Word, The 147
Workman, The 147
World Is Round, The 148
World Mother 148
World Tomorrow, The 148
World We Live In, The 148

X = O (or A Night of the Trojan War) 148

Ye Shall Be My People 148
Years Ahead, The 148
You Never Told Me 149
Young Stranger, The 149
Your Church and Mine 149
Your Town and Mine 149

Zoo Story, The 149